GREAT
SERMONS
of the WORLD

GREAT SERMONS
of the WORLD

*Sermons from 25 of the world's greatest preachers, including
Augustine, Luther, Calvin, Spurgeon and more.*

CLARENCE E. MACARTNEY, Editor

Great Sermons of the World
Copyright © 1997 by Hendrickson Publishers, Inc.

Published by Hendrickson Publishers, Inc.
P.O. Box 3473
Peabody, Massachusetts 01961–3473

Originally printed in 1926 by The Stratford Company of Boston, Massachusetts.
First reprinted in 1958 by Baker Books, a division of Baker Book House Company.

Printed in the United States of America.

ISBN 1-56563-302-4

Second Hendrickson printing — May 2001

Cover and interior design by Pinpoint Marketing, Kirkland, Wash.
Edited by Agnes Lawless and Sandy Lawliss

Library of Congress Cataloging-in-Publication Data

Great Sermons of the World: trace Christianity through the centuries with the greatest preachers of all time / Clarence E. McCartney, editor
  p.   cm.
Originally published: Boston, MA: Stratford, 1926.
ISBN 1-56563-302-4 (cloth)
1. Sermons.   I. McCartney, Clarence E.
BV4241.G75   1997
252--dc21   97-23007
                                                                  CIP

Introduction

A CELEBRATED PREACHER was once asked by an enthusiastic hearer if he might have the privilege of printing the sermon to which he had just listened. "Yes," answered the preacher, "provided you print the thunder also." Alas, this cannot be done.

We can print the written record of what the preacher said; but the light in his eye, the glow of his cheek, the sweep of his hand, the attitude of his body, the music of his voice, that we cannot print. When we have put down the theme and the divisions and paragraphs and the very words which were spoken, we do not have the preacher. All that we can say of a printed sermon is what Job said of the Creator's majesty, "Lo, these are parts of his ways: but how little a portion is heard of him? but the thunder of his power who can understand?" The greater the preacher, the greater the contrast between the written record and the spoken sermon. One reads of the thronging thousands who listened enthralled to the preaching of Whitefield and then wonders what produced such an impression when he takes up a volume of Whitefield's sermons. The thunder and the lightning are all gone.

Nevertheless, to read a celebrated sermon is like visiting the scene of some great transaction in history. Especially profitable for preachers is the reading of the sermons by the sons of thunder of the pulpit of the past. The noblest passion on earth, preaching is also a great art. All the glory and romance of the Christian pulpit rises before us as we read the utterances of the prophets of God who have reasoned with men of righteousness and temperance and judgment to come.

In compiling this volume of sermons, I have drawn upon every period of Christian preaching, from the days of the apostles down to the present time. I have included also an example of Old Testament eloquence.

The general rule followed has been to select the famous preachers of the different periods. It is true that sometimes the great preachers were not great sermonizers. But however admirable a sermon may be, it can hardly be called one of the world's great sermons unless spoken by one of the great preachers of the day. This has made my task much easier than it would otherwise have been, for none will question the rank of the preachers whose sermons appear in this volume.

In preparing this volume, I have received very helpful suggestions from my friend and former instructor, the Rev. Frederick W. Loetscher, D.D., LL.D., professor of ecclesiastical history in Princeton Theological Seminary.

Contents

The Sermon on the Mount

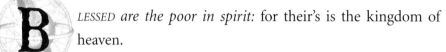**B**LESSED *are the poor in spirit:* for their's is the kingdom of heaven.

Blessed are they that mourn: for they shall be comforted.

Blessed are the meek: for they shall inherit the earth.

Blessed are they which do hunger and thirst after righteousness: for they shall be filled.

Blessed are the merciful: for they shall obtain mercy.

Blessed are the pure in heart: for they shall see God.

Blessed are the peacemakers: for they shall be called the children of God.

Blessed are they which are persecuted for righteousness' sake: for theirs is the kingdom of heaven.

Blessed are ye, when men shall revile you, and persecute you, and shall say all manner of evil against you falsely, for my sake.

Rejoice, and be exceeding glad: for great is your reward in heaven: for so persecuted they the prophets which were before you.

Ye are the salt of the earth: but if the salt have lost his savour, wherewith shall it be salted? it is thenceforth good for nothing, but to be cast out, and to be trodden under foot of men.

Ye are the light of the world. A city that is set on an hill cannot be hid.

Neither do men light a candle, and put it under a bushel, but on a candlestick; and it giveth light unto all that are in the house.

Let your light so shine before men, that they may see your good works, and glorify your Father which is in heaven.

Think not that I am come to destroy the law, or the prophets: I am not come to destroy, but to fulfill.

For verily I say unto you, Till heaven and earth pass, one jot or one tittle shall in no wise pass from the law, till all be fulfilled.

Whosoever therefore shall break one of these least commandments, and shall teach men so, he shall be called the least in the kingdom of heaven: but whosoever shall do and teach them, the same shall be called great in the kingdom of heaven.

For I say unto you, That except your righteousness shall exceed the righteousness of the scribes and Pharisees, ye shall in no case enter into the kingdom of heaven.

Ye have heard that it was said by them of old time, Thou shalt not kill; and whosoever shall kill shall be in danger of the judgment:

But I say unto you, That whosoever is angry with his brother without a cause shall be in danger of the judgment: and whosoever shall say to his brother, Raca, shall be in danger of the council: but whosoever shall say, Thou fool, shall be in danger of hell fire.

Therefore if thou bring thy gift to the altar, and there rememberest that thy brother hath ought against thee;

Leave there thy gift before the altar, and go thy way; first be reconciled to thy brother, and then come and offer thy gift.

Agree with thine adversary quickly, whiles thou art in the way with him; lest at any time the adversary deliver thee to the judge, and the judge deliver thee to the officer, and thou be cast into prison.

Verily I say unto thee, Thou shalt by no means come out thence, till thou hast paid the uttermost farthing.

Ye have heard that it was said by them of old time, Thou shalt not commit adultery:

But I say unto you, That whosoever looketh on a woman to lust after her hath committed adultery with her already in his heart.

And if thy right eye offend thee, pluck it out, and cast it from thee: for it is profitable for thee that one of thy members should perish, and not that thy whole body should be cast into hell.

And if thy right hand offend thee, cut it off, and cast it from thee: for it is profitable for thee that one of thy members should perish, and not that thy whole body should be cast into hell.

It hath been said, Whosoever shall put away his wife, let him give her a writing of divorcement:

But I say unto you, That whosoever shall put away his wife, saving for the cause of fornication, causeth her to commit adultery: and whosoever shall marry her that is divorced committeth adultery.

Again, ye have heard that it hath been said by them of old time, Thou shalt not forswear thyself, but shalt perform unto the Lord thine oaths:

But I say unto you, Swear not at all; neither by heaven; for it is God's throne:

Nor by the earth; for it is his footstool: neither by Jerusalem; for it is the city of the great King.

Neither shalt thou swear by thy head, because thou canst not make one hair white or black.

But let your communication be, Yea, yea; Nay, nay: for whatsoever is more than these cometh of evil.

Ye have heard that it hath been said, An eye for an eye, and a tooth for a tooth:

But I say unto you, That ye resist not evil: but whosoever shall smite thee on thy right cheek, turn to him the other also.

And if any man will sue thee at the law, and take away thy coat, let him have thy cloke also.

And whosoever shall compel thee to go a mile, go with him twain.

Give to him that asketh thee, and from him that would borrow of thee turn not thou away.

Ye have heard that it hath been said, Thou shalt love thy neighbor, and hate thine enemy.

But I say unto you, Love your enemies, bless them that curse you, do good to them that hate you, and pray for them which despitefully use you, and persecute you;

That ye may be the children of your Father which is in heaven: for he maketh his sun to rise on the evil and on the good, and sendeth rain on the just and on the unjust.

For if ye love them which love you, what reward have ye? do not even the publicans the same?

And if ye salute your brethren only, what do ye more than others? do not even the publicans so?

Be ye therefore perfect, even as your Father which is in heaven is perfect.

Take heed that ye do not your alms before men, to be seen of them: otherwise ye have no reward of your Father which is in heaven.

Therefore when thou doest thine alms, do not sound a trumpet before thee, as the hypocrites do in the synagogues and in the streets, that they may have glory of men. Verily I say unto you, They have their reward.

But when thou doest alms, let not thy left hand know what thy right hand doeth:

That thine alms may be in secret: and thy Father which seeth in secret himself shall reward thee openly.

And when thou prayest, thou shalt not be as the hypocrites are: for they love to pray standing in the synagogues and in the corners of the streets, that they may be seen of men. Verily I say unto you, They have their reward.

But thou, when thou prayest, enter into thy closet, and when thou hast shut thy door, pray to thy Father which is in secret; and thy Father which seeth in secret shall reward thee openly.

But when ye pray, use not vain repetitions, as the heathen do: for they think that they shall be heard for their much speaking.

Be not ye therefore like unto them: for your Father knoweth what things ye have need of, before ye ask him.

After this manner therefore pray ye: Our Father which art in heaven, Hallowed be thy name.

Thy kingdom come. Thy will be done in earth, as it is in heaven.

Give us this day our daily bread.

And forgive us our debts, as we forgive our debtors.

And lead us not into temptation, but deliver us from evil: For thine is the kingdom, and the power, and the glory, for ever. Amen.

For if ye forgive men their trespasses, your heavenly Father will also forgive you:

But if ye forgive not men their trespasses, neither will your Father forgive your trespasses.

Moreover when ye fast, be not, as the hypocrites, of a sad countenance: for they disfigure their faces, that they may appear unto men to fast. Verily I say unto you, They have their reward.

But thou, when thou fastest, anoint thine head, and wash thy face;

That thou appear not unto men to fast, but unto thy Father which is in secret: and thy Father, which seeth in secret, shall reward thee openly.

Lay not up for yourselves treasures upon earth, where moth and rust doth corrupt, and where thieves break through and steal:

But lay up for yourselves treasures in heaven, where neither moth nor rust doth corrupt, and where thieves do not break through nor steal:

For where your treasure is, there will you heart be also.

The light of the body is the eye: if therefore thine eye be single, thy whole body shall be full of light.

But if thine eye be evil, thy whole body shall be full of darkness. If therefore the light that is in thee be darkness, how great is that darkness!

No man can serve two masters: for either he will hate the one, and love the other; or else he will hold to the one, and despise the other. Ye cannot serve God and mammon.

Therefore I say unto you, Take no thought for your life, what ye shall eat, or what ye shall drink; nor yet for your body, what ye shall put on. Is not the life more than meat, and the body than raiment?

Behold the fowls of the air: for they sow not, neither do they reap, nor gather into barns; yet your heavenly Father feedeth them. Are ye not much better than they?

Which of you by taking thought can add one cubit unto his stature?

And why take ye thought for raiment? Consider the lilies of the field, how they grow; they toil not, neither do they spin:

And yet I say unto you, That even Solomon in all his glory was not arrayed like one of these.

Wherefore, if God so clothe the grass of the field, which to day is, and to morrow is cast into the oven, shall he not much more clothe you, O ye of little faith?

Therefore take no thought, saying, what shall we eat? or, What shall we drink? or, Wherewithal shall we be clothed?

(For after all these things do the Gentiles seek:) for your heavenly Father knoweth that ye have need of all these things.

But seek ye first the kingdom of God, and his righteousness; and all these things shall be added unto you.

Take therefore no thought for the morrow: for the morrow shall take thought for the things of itself. Sufficient unto the day is the evil thereof.

Judge not, that ye be not judged.

For with what judgment ye judge, ye shall be judged: and with what measure ye mete, it shall be measured to you again.

And why beholdest thou the mote that is in thy brother's eye, but considerest not the beam that is in thine own eye?

Or how wilt thou say to thy brother, Let me pull out the mote out of thine eye; and, behold, a beam is in thine own eye?

Thou hypocrite, first cast out the beam out of thine own eye; and then shalt thou see clearly to cast out the mote out of thy brother's eye.

Give not that which is holy unto the dogs, neither cast ye your pearls before swine, lest they trample them under their feet, and turn again and rend you.

Ask, and it shall be given you; seek, and ye shall find; knock, and it shall be opened unto you:

For every one that asketh receiveth; and he that seeketh findeth; and to him that knocketh it shall be opened.

Or what man is there of you, whom if his son ask bread, will he give him a stone?

Or if he ask a fish, will he give him a serpent?

If ye then, being evil, know how to give good gifts unto your children, how much more shall your Father which is in heaven give good things to them that ask him?

Therefore all things whatsoever ye would that men should do to you, do ye even so to them: for this is the law and the prophets.

Enter ye in at the strait gate: for wide is the gate, and broad is the way, that leadeth to destruction, and many there be which go in thereat:

Because strait is the gate, and narrow is the way, which leadeth unto life, and few there be that find it.

Beware of false prophets, which come to you in sheep's clothing, but inwardly they are ravening wolves.

Ye shall know them by their fruits. Do men gather grapes of thorns, or figs of thistles?

Even so every good tree bringeth forth good fruit; but a corrupt tree bringeth forth evil fruit.

A good tree cannot bring forth evil fruit, neither can a corrupt tree bring forth good fruit.

Every tree that bringeth not forth good fruit is hewn down, and cast into the fire.

Wherefore by their fruits ye shall know them.

Not every one that saith unto me, Lord, Lord, shall enter into the kingdom of heaven; but he that doeth the will of my Father which is in heaven.

Many will say to me in that day, Lord, Lord, have we not prophesied in thy name? and in thy name have cast out devils? and in thy name done many wonderful works?

And then will I profess unto them, I never knew you: depart from me, ye that work iniquity.

Therefore whosoever heareth these sayings of mine, and doeth them, I will liken him unto a wise man, which built his house upon a rock:

And the rain descended, and the floods came, and the winds blew, and beat upon that house; and it fell not: for it was founded upon a rock.

And every one that heareth these sayings of mine, and doeth them not, shall be likened unto a foolish man, which built his house upon the sand:

And the rain descended, and the floods came, and the winds blew, and beat upon that house; and it fell: and great was the fall of it.

The Book of Isaiah, Chapters 63–64

WHO *is this that cometh* from Edom, with dyed garments from Bozrah? this that is glorious in his apparel, travelling in the greatness of his strength? I that speak in righteousness, mighty to save.

Wherefore art thou red in thine apparel, and thy garments like him that treadeth in the winefat?

I have trodden the winepress alone; and of the people there was none with me: for I will tread them in mine anger, and trample them in my fury; and their blood shall be sprinkled upon my garments, and I will stain all my raiment. For the day of vengeance is in mine heart, and the year of my redeemed is come. And I looked, and there was none to help; and I wondered that there was none to uphold: therefore mine own arm brought salvation unto me; and my fury, it upheld me. And I will tread down the people in mine anger, and make them drunk in my fury, and I will bring down their strength to the earth.

I will mention the lovingkindnesses of the Lord, and the praises of the Lord, according to all that the Lord hath bestowed on us, and the great goodness toward the house of Israel, which he hath bestowed on them according to his mercies, and according to the multitude of his lovingkindnesses. For he said, Surely they are my people, children that will not lie: so he was their Saviour. In all their affliction he was afflicted, and the angel of his presence saved them: in his love and in his pity he redeemed them: and he bare them, and carried them all the days of old.

But they rebelled, and vexed his holy Spirit: therefore he was turned to be their enemy, and he fought against them. Then he remembered the days of old, Moses, and his people,saying, Where is he that brought them up out of the sea with the shepherd of his flock? where is he that put his holy Spirit within him? That led them by the right hand of Moses with his glorious arm, dividing the water before them, to make himself an everlasting name? That led them through the deep, as an horse in the wilderness, that they should not stumble? As a beast goeth down into the valley, the Spirit of the Lord caused him to rest: so didst thou lead thy people, to make thyself a glorious name.

Look down from heaven, and behold from the habitation of thy holiness and of thy glory: where is thy zeal and thy strength, the sounding of thy bowels and of thy mercies toward me? are they restrained? Doubtless thou art our father, though Abraham be ignorant of us, and Israel acknowledge us not: thou, O Lord, art our father, our redeemer; thy name is from everlasting. O Lord, why hast thou made us to err from thy ways, and hardened our heart from thy fear? Return for thy servants' sake, the tribes of thine inheritance. The people of thy holiness have possessed it but a little while: our adversaries have trodden down thy sanctuary. We are thine: thou never barest rule over them; they were not called by thy name.

Oh that thou wouldest rend the heavens, that thou wouldest come down, that the mountains might flow down at thy presence, as when the melting fire burneth, the fire causeth the waters to boil, to make thy name known to thine adversaries, that the nations may tremble at thy presence! When thou didst terrible things which we looked not for, thou camest down, the mountains flowed down at thy presence. For since the beginning of the world men have not heard, nor perceived by the ear, neither hath the eye seen, O God, beside thee, what he hath prepared for him that waiteth for him. Thou meetest him that rejoiceth and worketh righteousness, those that remember thee in thy ways: behold, thou art wroth; for we have sinned: in those is continuance, and we shall be saved. But we are all as an unclean thing, and all our righteousnesses are as filthy rags; and we all do fade as a leaf; and our iniquities, like the wind, have taken us away. And there is none that calleth upon thy name, that stirreth up himself to take hold of thee: for thou hast hid thy face from us, and hast consumed us, because of our iniquities.

But now, O Lord, thou art our father; we are the clay, and thou our potter; and we all are the work of thy hand. Be not wroth very sore, O Lord, neither remember iniquity for ever: behold, see, we beseech thee, we are all thy people. Thy holy cities are a wilderness, Zion is a wilderness, Jerusalem a desolation. Our holy and our beautiful house, where our fathers praised thee, is burned up with fire: and all our pleasant things are laid waste. Wilt thou refrain thyself for these things, O Lord? wilt thou hold thy peace, and afflict us very sore?

The Sermon Which Won Three Thousand Souls:
St. Peter's Sermon at Pentecost—The Acts 2:14–39

Y E *men of Judaea,* and all ye that dwell in Jerusalem, be this known unto you, and hearken to my words: for these are not drunken, as ye suppose, seeing it is but the third hour of the day. But this is that which was spoken by the prophet Joel;

And it shall come to pass in the last days, saith God, I will pour out of my Spirit upon all flesh: and your sons and your daughters shall prophesy, and your young men shall see visions, and your old men shall dream dreams: and on my servants and on my handmaidens I will pour out in those days of my Spirit; and they shall prophesy: And I will shew wonders in heaven above, and signs in the earth beneath; blood, and fire, and vapour of smoke: The sun shall be turned into darkness, and the moon into blood, before that great and notable day of the Lord come: and it shall come to pass, that whosoever shall call on the name of the Lord shall be saved.

Ye men of Israel, hear these words; Jesus of Nazareth, a man approved of God among you by miracles and wonders and signs, which God did by him in the midst of you, as ye yourselves also know: him, being delivered by the determinate counsel and foreknowledge of God, ye have taken, and by wicked hands have crucified and slain: whom God hath raised up, having loosed the pains of death: because it was not possible that he should be holden of it. For David speaketh concerning him,

I foresaw the Lord always before my face, for he is on my right hand, that I should not be moved.

Therefore did my heart rejoice, and my tongue was glad; moreover also my flesh shall rest in hope: because thou wilt not leave my soul in hell, neither wilt thou suffer thine Holy One to see corruption. Thou hast made known to me the ways of life; thou shalt make me full of joy with thy countenance.

Men and brethren, let me freely speak unto you of the patriarch David, that he is both dead and buried, and his sepulchre is with us unto this day. Therefore being a prophet, and knowing that God had sworn with an oath to him, that of the fruit of his loins, according to the flesh, he would raise up Christ to sit on his throne; he, seeing this before, spake of the resurrection of Christ, that his soul was not left in hell, neither his flesh did see corruption. This Jesus hath God raised up, whereof we all are witnesses. Therefore being by the right hand of God exalted, and having received of the Father the promise of the Holy Ghost, he hath shed forth this, which ye now see and hear. For David is not ascended into the heavens: but he saith himself,

The Lord said unto my Lord, Sit thou on my right hand, until I make thy foes thy footstool.

Therefore let all the house of Israel know assuredly, that God hath made that same Jesus, whom ye have crucified, both Lord and Christ.

Repent, and be baptized every one of you in the name of Jesus Christ for the remission of sins, and ye shall receive the gift of the Holy Ghost. For the promise is unto you, and to your children, and to all that are afar off, even as many as the Lord our God shall call.

Clement of Rome: *Christ and the Church*

THE MOST ANCIENT EXAMPLE of Christian preaching, outside the New Testament, is the so-called Second Epistle of Clement, addressed to the Church at Corinth. As the reader will see, this epistle is in reality a sermon addressed to "brothers and sisters." Clement of Rome was one of the great figures of the early church and may have been that Clement to whom Paul refers in the letter to the Philippians as his "faithful fellow laborer." He is accounted one of the Apostolic Fathers and the second or third bishop of Rome. Eusebius makes him bishop of Rome from A.D. 92 to 101. From this Clement, we have an Epistle to the Corinthians which is of very great importance as an early witness to the great Christian doctrines, such as the Trinity, the Atonement and Justification by grace. But the Second Epistle to the Corinthians attributed to Clement of Rome is regarded as a forgery. Some preacher or writer wished to give currency to his production by the weight of Clement's name. Yet the Epistle, in reality, the sermon, is of immense interest to the church today as the oldest known specimen of postapostolic preaching. Its somewhat commonplace utterances throb with life because they are to us the earliest accents of the Christian pulpit. In this sermon, the preacher quotes two sayings of Christ which were evidently current at that time, but of which there is no record in the New Testament.

This first of Christian sermons shows how the preacher's themes—God, Christ, the soul, judgment, heaven and hell—do not change from age to age and how the Christ preached by this unknown preacher in the early morning of Christianity is the same as the Christ preached today—Jesus Christ the same yesterday, today, and forever.

Christy and the Church

W E ought to think highly of Christ. Brethren, it is fitting that you should think of Jesus Christ as of God—as the Judge of the living and the dead. And it does not become us to think lightly of our salvation; for if we think little of him, we shall also hope but to obtain little *from* him. And those of us who hear carelessly of these things, as if they were of small importance, commit sin, not knowing whence we have been called, by whom, and to what place, and how much Jesus Christ submitted to suffer for our sakes. What return, then, shall we make to him, or what fruit that shall be worthy of that which he has given to us? For, indeed, how great are the benefits which we owe to him! He has graciously given us light; as a Father, He has called us sons; he has saved us when we were ready to perish. What praise, then, shall we give to him, or what return shall we make for the things which we have received? We were deficient in understanding, worshipping stones, wood, gold, silver, and brass, the works of men's hands; and our whole lives were nothing else than death. Involved in blindness and with such darkness before our eyes, we have received sight and through his will, have laid aside that cloud by which we were enveloped. For he had compassion on us and mercifully saved us, observing the many errors in which we were entangled, as well as the destruction to which we were exposed and that we had no hope of salvation except it came to us from him. For he called us when we were not and willed that out of nothing we should attain a real existence.

True confession of Christ. Let us, then, not only call him Lord, for that will not save us. For he saith, "Not everyone that saith to Me, Lord, Lord, shall be saved, but he that worketh righteousness."

Wherefore, brethren, let us confess him by our works, by loving one another, by not committing adultery, speaking evil of one another, or cherishing envy, but being continent, compassionate, and good. We ought also to sympathize with one another and not be avaricious. By such works, let us confess him and not by those that are of an opposite kind. And it is not fitting that we should fear men, but rather God. For this reason, if we should do such wicked things, the Lord hath said, "Even though ye were gathered together to me in my very bosom, yet if ye were not to keep my commandments, I would cast you off and say unto you, Depart from me; I know not whence ye are, ye workers of iniquity."

This world should be despised. Wherefore, brethren, leaving willingly our sojourn in this present world, let us do the will of him that called us and not fear to depart out of this world. For the Lord said, "Ye shall be as lambs in the midst of wolves." And Peter answered and said unto him, "What, then, if the wolves shall tear in pieces the lambs?" Jesus said unto Peter, "The lambs have no cause after they are dead to fear the wolves; and in like manner, fear not ye them that kill you and can do nothing more unto you; but fear him who, after you are dead, has power over both soul and body to cast them into hell-fire." And consider, brethren, that the sojourning in the flesh in this world is but brief and transient, but the promise of Christ is great and wonderful, even the rest of the kingdom to come and of life everlasting. By what course of conduct, then, shall we attain these things, but by leading a holy and righteous life, by deeming these worldly things as not belonging to us, and not fixing our desires upon them? For if we desire to possess them, we fall away from the path of righteousness.

The present and future worlds are enemies to each other. Now the Lord declares, "No man can serve two masters." If we desire, then, to serve both God and mammon, it will be unprofitable for us. "For what shall it profit a man if he shall gain the whole world, and lose his own soul?" (Mark 8:36) This world and the next are two enemies. The one urges to adultery and corruption, avarice and deceit; the other bids farewell to these things. We cannot therefore be the friends of both; and it behooves us, by renouncing the one, to make sure of the other. Let us reckon that it is better to hate the things present, since they are trifling, transient, and corruptible, and to love those which are to come as being good and incorruptible. For if we do the will of Christ, we shall find rest; otherwise, nothing shall deliver us from eternal punishment if we disobey his commandments. For thus also saith the Scripture in Ezekiel, "Though Noah, Job, and Daniel were in it, as I live, saith the Lord God, they shall delivernei-ther son nor daughter" (Ezek. 14:20). Now, if men so eminently righteous are not able by their righteousness to deliver their chil-dren, how can we hope to enter into the royal residence of God unless we keep our baptism holy and undefiled? Or who shall be our advocate, unless we be found possessed of works of holiness and righteousness?

We must strive in order to be crowned. Wherefore, then, my breth-ren, let us struggle with all earnestness, knowing that the contest is in our case close at hand and that many undertake long voyages to strive for a corruptible reward; yet all are not crowned, but those only that have labored hard and striven gloriously. Let us therefore so strive, that we may all be crowned. Let us run the straight course, even the race that is incorruptible; and let us in great numbers set out for it and strive that we may be crowned. And should we not all be able to ob-tain the crown, let us at least come near to it. We must remember that he who strives in the corruptible contest, if he be found acting unfair-ly, is taken away and scourged, and cast forth from the lists. What then think ye? For of those who do not preserve the seal unbroken, the Scripture saith, "Their worm shall not die, neither shall their fire be quenched; and they shall be an abhorring unto all flesh" (Isa.66:24).

The necessity of repentance while we are on earth. As long, therefore, as we are upon earth, let us practice repentance, for we are as clay in the hand of the artificer. For the potter, if he make a vessel and it be distorted or broken in his hands, fashions it over again; but if he have before this cast it into the furnace of fire, he can no longer find help for it. So let us also, while we are in this world, repent with our whole hearts of the evil deeds we have done in the flesh that we may be saved by the Lord while we have yet an opportunity of repentance. For after we have gone out of the world, no further power of confessing or repenting will belong to us. Wherefore, brethren, by doing the will of the Father, keeping the flesh holy, and observing the commandments of the Lord, we shall obtain eternal life. For the Lord saith in the Gospel: "If ye have not kept that which was small, who will commit to you the great? For I say unto you, that he that is faithful in that which is least, is faithful also in much." This, then, is what he means: "Keep the flesh holy and the seal undefiled that ye may receive eternal life."

We shall be judged in the flesh. And let none of you say that this very flesh shall not be judged nor rise again. Consider in what state you were saved, in what you received sight, if not while you were in this flesh. We must therefore preserve the flesh as the temple of God. For as you were called in the flesh, you shall also come to be judged in the flesh. As Christ the Lord who saved us, though he was first a Spirit, became flesh, and thus called us, so shall we also receive the reward in this flesh. Let us therefore love one another that we may all attain to the kingdom of God. While we have an opportunity of being healed, let us yield ourselves to God that hears us, and give him a recompense. Of what sort? Repentance out of sincere hearts; for he knows all things beforehand and is acquainted with what is in our hearts. Let us therefore give him praise, not with our mouths only, but also with the heart, that he may accept us as sons. For the Lord has said, "Those are my brethren who do the will of my Father."

Vice is to be forsaken and virtue followed. Wherefore, my brethren, let us do the will of the Father who called us, that we may live. Let us earnestly follow after virtue, but forsake every wicked tendency which would lead us into transgression, and flee from ungodliness, lest evils overtake us. For if we are diligent in doing good, peace will follow us. On this account, such men cannot find peace, who are influenced by human terrors, and prefer present enjoyment to the promise which shall afterwards be fulfilled. They know not what torment present enjoyment incurs or what felicity is involved in the future promise. And if, indeed they themselves only did such things, it would be the more tolerable. But now they persist in imbuing innocent souls with their pernicious doctrines, not knowing that they shall receive a double condemnation, both they and those that hear them.

We ought to serve God, trusting in his promises. Let us therefore serve God with pure hearts, and we shall be righteous; but if we do not serve him, because we do not believe his promises, we shall be miserable. For the prophetic word also declares, "Wretched are those of a double mind and who doubt in their hearts, who say, All these things have we heard even in the times of our fathers; but though we have waited day by day, we have seen none of them accomplished. Ye fools! compare yourselves to a tree; take, for instance, the vine. First of all, it sheds its leaves, then the bud appears; after that the sour grape, and then the fully ripened fruit. So, likewise, my people have borne disturbances and afflictions, but afterwards shall they receive their good things." Wherefore, my brethren, let us not be of a double mind, but let us hope and endure, that we also may obtain the reward. For he is faithful who has promised that he will bestow on every one a reward according to his works. If, therefore, we shall do righteousness in the sight of God, we shall enter into his kingdom, and shall receive the promises, "Eye hath not seen, nor ear heard, neither have entered into the heart of man" (1 Cor. 2:9).

We are constantly to look for the kingdom of God. Let us expect, therefore, hour by hour, the kingdom of God in love and righteousness, since we know not the day of the appearing of God. For the Lord himself, being asked by one when his kingdom would come, replied, "When two shall be one and that which is without as that which is within, and the male with the female, neither male nor female." Now, two are one when we speak the truth one to another, and there is unfeignedly one soul in two bodies. And "that which is without as that which is within" means this: he calls the soul "that which is within" and the body "that which is without." As, then, your body is visible to sight, so also let your soul be manifest by good works. And "the male with the female, neither male nor female"; this means, that a brother seeing a sister should think nothing about her as of a female nor she think anything about him as a male. If you do these things, he says, the kingdom of my Father shall come.

The living church is the body of Christ. Wherefore, brethren, if we do the will of God our Father, we shall be of the first church, that is, spiritual, that was created before the sun and moon; but if we do not the will of the Lord, we shall be of the Scripture that saith, "My house was made a den of robbers." So then let us choose to be of the church of life that we may be saved. I do not, however, suppose you are ignorant that the living church is the body of Christ; for the Scripture saith, "God made man, male and female." The male is Christ, the female is the church. And the Books and the apostles plainly declare that the church is not of the present, but from the beginning. She was spiritual, as our Jesus also was, but was manifested in the last days that he might save us. Now the church, being spiritual, was manifested in the flesh of Christ, thus signifying to us that if any of us keep her in the flesh and do not corrupt her, he shall receive her again in the Holy Spirit: for this flesh is the copy of the spirit. No one then who corrupts the copy shall partake of the original. This then is what he means, "Keep the flesh, that ye may partake of the spirit." But if we say that the flesh is the church and the spirit Christ, then he that has shamefully used the flesh has shamefully used the church. Such a personthen shall not partake of the spirit, which is Christ. Such life and incorruption this flesh can partake of when the Holy Spirit is joined to it. No one can utter or speak "what the Lord hath prepared" for his elect.

Faith and love, the proper return to God. Now I do not think I have given you any light counsel concerning self-control, which if anyone do he will not repent of it, but will save both himself and me who counselled him. For it is no light reward to turn again a wandering and perishing soul that it may be saved. For this is the recompense we have to return to God who created us, if he that speaks and hears both speaks and hears with faith and love. Let us therefore abide in the things which we believed, righteous and holy, that with boldness we may ask of God who saith, "While thou art yet speaking, I will say, Lo, I am here." For this saying is the sign of a great promise; for the Lord says of himself that he is more ready to give than he that asks, to ask. Being therefore partakers of so great kindness, let us not be envious of one another in the obtaining of so many good things. For as great as is the pleasure which these sayings have for them that have done them, so great is the condemnation they have for them that have been disobedient.

The excellence of almsgiving. Wherefore, brethren, having re- ceived no small occasion for repentance, while we have the opportu- nity, let us turn unto God who called us, while we still have him as one that receives us. For if we renounce these enjoyments and con- quer our souls in not doing our evil desires, we shall partake of the mercy of Jesus. But you know that the Day of Judgment even now "cometh as a burning oven" and some "of the heavens shall melt." All the earth shall be as lead melting on the fire, and then the hidden and open works of men shall appear. Giving, therefore, is a good thing, as repentance from sin; fasting is better than prayer, but giving than both; "but love covereth a multitude of sins." Prayer out of a good conscience delivers from death. Blessed is everyone who is full of these, for almsgiving lightens the burden of sin.

The danger of impenitence. Let us therefore repent with our whole hearts, that none of us perish by the way. For if we have commandments that we should draw away men from idols and instruct them, how much more ought a soul already knowing God not to perish! Let us therefore assist one another that we may also help those weak as to what is good in order that all may be saved; and let us convert and admonish one another. And let us not think to give heed and believe now only while we are admonished by the presbyters, but also when we have returned home, remembering the commandments of the Lord. Let us not be dragged away by worldly lusts, but let us attempt to make advances in the commandments of the Lord, that all being of the same mind, we may be gathered together unto life. For the Lord said, "I come to gather together all the nations, tribes, and tongues." He speaks this of the day of his appearing when he shall come and redeem us, each one according to his works. And the unbelievers "shall see his glory" and strength. They shall think it strange when they see the sovereignty of the world in Jesus, saying, "Woe unto us! You were he, and we did not know, did not believe, and we did not obey the presbyters when they declared unto us concerning our salvation." And "their worm dieth not, and their fire is not quenched, and they shall be for a spectacle unto all flesh." He speaks of that Day of Judgment when they shall see those among us that have been ungodly and acted deceitfully with the commandments of Jesus Christ. But when the righteous who have done well, and endured torments, and hated the enjoyments of the soul, shall behold those who have gone astray and denied Jesus through their words or their works, how they are punished with grievous torments in an unquenchable fire, shall give glory to God, saying, "There will be hope for him who has served God with his whole heart."

The Preacher confesses his own sinfulness. Let us also become of the number of them who give thanks, and have served God, not of the ungodly that are judged. For I myself also, being an utter sinner and not yet escaped from temptation, but still being in the midst of the engines of the devil, give diligence to follow after righteousness that I may have strength to come even near it, fearing the judgment to come.

He justifies his exhortation. Wherefore, brethren and sisters, after the God of truth has been heard, I read to you an entreaty that you may give heed to the things that are written in order that you may save both yourselves and him who reads among you. As a reward, I ask you to repent with your whole hearts, thus giving to yourselves salvation and life. For by doing this, we shall set a goal for all the young to strive for piety and the goodness of God. And let us not, unwise ones that we are, be affronted and displeased, whenever someone admonishes and turns us from iniquity to righteousness. Sometimes while we are practicing evil things, we do not perceive it on account of the double-mindedness and unbelief that is in our breasts, and we are "darkened in our understanding" by our vain lusts. Let us then practice righteousness that we may be saved unto the end. Blessed are they that obey these ordinances. Even if for a little time they suffer evil in the world, they shall enjoy the immortal fruit of the resurrection. Let not then the godly man be grieved, if he be wretched in the times that now are; a blessed time waits for him. He, living again above with the fathers, shall be joyful for an eternity without grief.

Concluding word of consolation. Doxology. Neither let it trouble your understanding that we see the unrighteous having riches and the servants of God enduring poverty. Let us therefore, brethren and sisters, be believing. We are striving in the contest of the living God; we are disciplined by the present life in order that we may be crowned by that to come. None of the righteous received fruit speedily, but awaited it. If God gave immediate reward to the righteous, we would be exercising ourselves in business, not in godliness. We would seem to be righteous, while pursuing not what is godly, but what is gainful. And on this account, divine judgment surprised a spirit that was not righteous and loaded it with chains.

To the only God invisible, the Father of truth, who sent forth to us the Savior and Prince of incorruption, through whom also he manifested to us the truth and the heavenly life, to him be the glory forever and ever. Amen.

St. John Chrysostom: *The Greatness of St. Paul*

Saint John Chrysostom (the Golden-mouthed) is, after the apostles, the most famous preacher in the history of Christianity. He was born at Antioch in 347 and died in Pontus in 407. He commenced the study of rhetoric and showed great promise for the future, but through the pious endeavors of his mother, Anthusa, he embraced Christianity and retired to the desert, where he spent ten years in meditation and self-denial. After this, he became a deacon and then a presbyter at Antioch. He soon attracted attention as a preacher, especially through a series of sermons on the Statues, delivered at a time when the Emperor Theodosius was contemplating severe reprisals against the populace of Antioch where his Statues had been destroyed in a riot.

As Archbishop of Constantinople, he preached boldly against the policies of the Empress Eudoxia. His uncompromising attitude towards the court and the licentious and avaricious ecclesiastics made him the victim of an ecclesiastical conspiracy, and he was condemned for contumacy by the synod called by his foes and taken to Bithynia. The popular fury was so great that the Emperor had him recalled. But he was soon sent into exile again and, after being carried about from place to place, expired on his way to the desert of Pityus.

His sermons are for the most part expository, or running comments upon the text of a passage in the Bible. In this way, he covered large portions of the New Testament. He had a wide range and could strike every note in the human breast. One of the noblest specimens of his eloquence is his last homily on the Epistle to the Romans. It is not only one of the finest examples of patristic eloquence, but perhaps the greatest tribute that has ever been paid to St. Paul.

The Greatness of St. Paul

W HO *is there then* to pray over us, since Paul has departed? These who are the imitators of Paul.

Only let us yield ourselves worthy of such intercession that it may not be that we hear Paul's voice here only, but that hereafter, when we are departed, we may be counted worthy to see the wrestler of Christ. Or rather, if we hear him here, we shall certainly see him hereafter, if not as standing near him, yet see him we certainly shall, glistening near the throne of the King. Where the cherubim sing the glory, where the seraphim are flying, there shall we see Paul, with Peter, and as a chief and leader of the choir of the saints, and shall enjoy his generous love. For if when here he loved men so, that when he had the choice of departing and being with Christ he chose to be here, much more will he there display a warmer affection.

I love Rome even for this, although indeed one has other grounds for praising it, both for its greatness, its antiquity, its beauty, its populousness, its power, its wealth, and for its successes in war. But I let all this pass, and esteem it blessed on this account, that both in his lifetime he wrote to them, loved them so, talked with them while he was with us, and brought his life to a close there. Wherefore, the city is more notable upon this ground than upon all others together. And as a body great and strong, it has as two glistening eyes the bodies of these saints. Not so bright is the heaven, when the sun sends forth his rays, as is the city of Rome, sending out these two lights into all parts of the world. From thence will Paul be caught up, from thence Peter. Just bethink you, and shudder at the thought of what a sight Rome will see when Paul arises suddenly from that deposit, together with Peter, and is lifted up to meet the Lord. What a rose will Rome send up to Christ! What two crowns will the city have about it! What golden chains will she be girded with! What foundations possess! Therefore, I admire the city, not for the much gold, not for the columns, not for the other display there, but for these pillars of the church.

Would that it were now given me to throw myself round the body of Paul, be riveted to the tomb, and to see the dust of that body that "filled up that which was lacking" after Christ, that bore "the marks," that sowed the gospel everywhere, yes, the dust of that body through which he ran to and fro everywhere! the dust of that body through which Christ spoke, and the light shone forth more brilliant than any lightning, and the voice started out (more awful than any thunder to the devils!) through which he uttered that blessed voice, saying, "I could wish that myself were accursed, for my brethren," through which he spake "before kings and was not ashamed," through which we come to know Paul, through which also Paul's Master. Not so awful to us is the thunder, as was that voice to the demons! For if they shuddered at his clothes, much more did they at his voice. This led them away captive, this cleansed out the world, this put a stop to diseases, cast out vice, lifted the truth on high, had Christ riding upon it, and everywhere went about with him; and what the cherubim were, this was Paul's voice, for as he was seated upon those powers, so was he upon Paul's tongue. For it had become worthy of receiving Christ by speaking those things only which were acceptable to Christ, and flying as the seraphim to height unspeakable! For what more lofty than that voice which says, "For I am persuaded, that neither death, nor life, nor angels, nor principalities, nor powers, nor things present, nor things to come, nor height, nor depth, nor any other creature, shall be able to separate us from the love of God, which is in Christ Jesus our Lord" (Rom. 8: 38–39)? What pinions does not this discourse seem to you to have? What eyes? It was owing to this that he said "for we are not ignorant of his devices" (2 Cor. 2:11).

Owing to this did the devils flee not only at hearing him speak, but even at seeing his garments.

This is the mouth, the dust whereof I would like to see, through which Christ spoke great and secret things and greater than in his own person (for as he wrought, so he also spoke greater things by the disciples), through which the Spirit gave those wondrous oracles to the world. For what good thing did not that mouth effect? Devils it drove out, sins it loosed, tyrants it muzzled, philosophers' mouths it stopped, the world it brought over to God, savages it persuaded to learn wisdom, all the whole order of the earth it altered. Things in Heaven, too, it disposed what way it wanted, binding whom it would and loosing in the other world "according unto the power given unto it."

Nor is it that mouth only, but the heart too I would like to see the dust of, which a man would not do wrong to call the heart of the world, a fountain of countless blessings, and a beginning and element of our life. For the spirit of life was furnished out of it all, and was distributed through the members of Christ, not as being sent forth by arteries, but by a free choice of good deeds. This heart was so large as to take in entire cities, peoples, and nations. "For my heart," he says, "is enlarged." Yet even a heart thus large, did this charity that enlarged it many a time straiten and oppress. For he says, "Out of much affliction and anguish of heart I wrote unto you" (2 Cor. 2:4). I were desirous to see that heart even after its dissolution, which burned at each one that was lost, which travailed a second time with the children that had proved abortions, which saw God ("for the pure in heart," he says, "shall see God"), which became a sacrifice ("for a sacrifice to God is a contrite heart"), which was loftier than the heavens, which was wider than the world, which was brighter than the sun's beam, which was warmer than fire, which was stronger than adamant, which sent forth rivers ("for rivers," it says, "of living water shall flow out of his belly"), wherein was a fountain springing up and watering, not the face of the earth, but the souls of men, whence not rivers only, but even fountains of tears issued day and night, which lived the new life, not this of ours (for "I live," he says, "yet not I, but Christ liveth in me," so Paul's heart was His heart, a tablet of the Holy Spirit, and a book of grace); which trembled for the sins of others (for "I fear," he says, "lest by any means I have bestowed labor upon you in vain; lest as the serpent beguiled Eve; lest when I come I should find you not such as I would"); which both feared for itself, and was confiding, too (for I fear, he says, "lest that by any means when I have preached to others, I myself should be a castaway" (1 Cor. 9:27). And, "I am persuaded that neither . . . angels, . . . nor powers, . . . shall be able to separate us," Rom. 8:38); which was counted worthy to love Christ as no other man loved him; which despised death and hell, yet was broken down by brothers' tears (for he says, "What mean ye to weep and to break mine heart?" Acts 21:13); which was enduring, yet could not bear to be absent from the Thessalonians by the space of an hour!

I long to see the dust of hands that were in a chain, through the imposition of which the Spirit was furnished, through which the divine writings were written (for "ye see how large a letter I have written unto you with mine own hand" (Gal. 6:11), and again, "The salutation of Paul with mine own hand," 2 Thess. 3:17); of those hands at the sight of which the serpent "fell off into the fire."

I long to see the dust of those eyes which were blinded gloriously, which recovered their sight again for the salvation of the world; which even in the body were counted worthy to see Christ, which saw earthly things, yet saw them not, which saw the things which are not seen, which saw not sleep, which were watchful at midnight, which were not affected as our eyes are.

I would also see the dust of those feet which ran through the world and were not weary, which were bound in the stocks when the prison shook, which went through parts habitable or uninhabited, which walked on so many journeys.

And why need I speak of single parts? I would see the tomb where the armor of righteousness is laid up, the armor of light, the limbs which now live, but which in life were made dead; and in all whereof Christ lived, which were crucified to the world, which were Christ's members, which were clad in Christ, were a temple of the Spirit, an holy building, "bound in the Spirit," riveted to the fear of God, which had the marks of Christ. This body is a wall to that city, which is safer than all towers, and than thousands of battlements. And with it is that of Peter. For he honored him while alive. For he "went up to see Peter" and therefore even when departed grace allowed him to stay with him.

I would see the spiritual lion. For as a lion breathing forth fire upon the herds of foxes, so rushed he upon the clan of demons and philosophers, and as the burst of some thunderbolt was borne down into the host of the devil. For he did not even come to set the battle in array against him, since he feared so and trembled at him, as that if he saw his shadow, and heard his voice, he fled even at a distance. And so did he deliver over to him the fornicator, though at a distance, and again snatched him out of his hands; and so others also, that they might be taught "not to blaspheme." And consider how he sent forth his own followers against him, rousing them, supplying them. And at one time he says to the Ephesians, "We wrestle not against flesh and blood, but against principalities, against powers" (Eph. 6:12). Then, too, he puts our prize in heavenly places. For we struggle not for things of the earth, he says, but for heaven, and the things in the heavens. And to others, he says, "Know ye not that we shall judge angels? How much more things that pertain to this life?" (1 Cor. 6:3).

Let us then, laying all this to heart, stand nobly; for Paul was a man, partaking of the same nature with us, and having everything else in common with us. But because he showed such great love toward Christ, he went up above the heavens and stood with the angels. And so if we, too, would rouse ourselves up some little and kindle in ourselves that fire, we shall be able to emulate that holy man. Were this impossible, he would never have cried aloud and said, "Be ye followers of me, even as I also am of Christ" (1 Cor. 11:1). Let us not then admire him only, or be struck with him only, but imitate him, that we too may, when we depart hence, be counted worthy to see him, and to share the glory unutterable, which God grant that we may all attain to by the grace and love toward man of our Lord Jesus Christ, through whom, and with whom, be glory to the Father, with the Holy Ghost, now and evermore. Amen.

Saint Augustine: *The Ten Virgins*

SAINT AUGUSTINE IS one of the greatest names in the history of the Christian church. He was a brand plucked from the burning, like Paul himself, a mighty trophy of the Holy Spirit. He was born at Tagaste, Africa, on the 13th of November, 354, and died at Hippo, Africa, August 28, 430. His father was a pagan, but his mother, Monica, was a Christian of wonderful beauty of character and depth of faith. As a youth Augustine was trained for the career of a rhetorician. He lived in sin with a girl who bore him a son, to whom he was deeply devoted, and to whom he gave the name, Adeodatus, "Given by God." During these years of licentious living, his faithful mother never ceased to pray and strive for his conversion. It was to her that the bishop of Tagaste made the celebrated remark, which has comforted so many anxious mothers, that "a son of so many tears cannot be lost."

When he was following his profession of a rhetorician at Milan, Augustine came under the influence of Ambrose, bishop of Milan, and was moved towards the Christian life. But he was so enmeshed in sensuality that he shrank from the sacrifice which a confession of faith involved. After intense spiritual struggles, graphically described in his *Confessions,* Augustine at last found Christ and peace. In 396, he was made bishop of the see of Hippo, in North Africa. Henceforth, he becomes one of the great figures of the church of that age, indeed, of all ages. His powerful mind poured out a series of books, the greatest of which is *The City of God*, a vast work in which he attempts to vindicate Christianity and conceives the church as a new and divine order rising out of the ruins of the Roman Empire. He engaged in many controversies, the most important of which was the controversy with Pelagius and the Pelagians. Against Pelagius, who held that Adam's sin was purely personal and affected only himself, Augustine held the doctrine of original sin, that men inherit from Adam a sinful nature, and so are under condemnation. Augustine is claimed by all schools in the Christian church, and both Catholic and Protestant take him as, next to St. Paul, the great teacher concerning the meaning of sin and the state of human nature.

His sermon on "The Ten Virgins" is an interesting treatment of one of the great themes of the pulpit, the second advent of Christ. Especially beautiful are its closing words: "Our lamps flicker amid the winds and temptations of this life; but only let our flame burn strongly, that the wind of temptation may increase the fire, rather than put it out."

The Ten Virgins

"Then shall the kingdom of heaven be likened unto ten virgins" (Matt. 25:1).

YOU *who were present yesterday* remember my promise, which with the Lord's assistance, is to be made good today, not to you only, but to the many others also who have come together. It is no easy question, who the ten virgins are, of whom five are wise, and five foolish. Nevertheless, according to the context of this passage which I have wished should be read again to you today, Beloved, I do not think, as far as the Lord vouchsafes to give me understanding, that this parable or similitude relates to those women only who by a peculiar and more excellent sanctity are called virgins in the church, whom by a more usual term we also call, "the Religious"; but if I mistake not, this parable relates to the whole church. But though we should understand it of those only who are called "the Religious," are they but ten? God forbid that so great a company of virgins should be reduced to so small a number! But perhaps one may say, "But what if though they be so many in outward profession, yet in truth they are so few, that scarce ten can be found!" It is not so. For if he had meant that the good virgins only should be understood by the ten, he would not have represented five foolish ones among them. If this is the number of the virgins which are called, why are the doors of the great house shut against five?

So then let us understand, dearly Beloved, that this parable relates to us all, that is, to the whole church together, not to the clergy only of whom we spoke yesterday; nor to the laity only; but generally to all. Why then are the virgins five and five? These five and five virgins are all Christian souls together. But that I may tell you what by the Lord's inspiration I think, it is not souls of every sort, but such souls as have faith, and seem to have good works in the church of

God; and yet even of them, "five are wise and five are foolish." First
then, let us see why they are called "five," and why "virgins," and then
let us consider the rest. Every soul in the body is therefore denoted by
the number five, because it makes use of five senses. There is nothing
of which we have perception by the body, but by the five folded gate:
the sight, the hearing, the smelling, the tasting, or the touching.
Those who abstain from unlawful seeing, unlawful hearing, unlawful
smelling, unlawful tasting, and unlawful touching, by reason of his
uncorruptness has gotten the name of virgin.

But if it be good to abstain from the unlawful excitements of the
senses, and on that account every Christian soul has gotten the name
of virgin, why are five admitted and five rejected? They are both virgins, and yet are rejected. It is not enough that they are virgins and
that they have lamps. They are virgins by reason of abstinence from
unlawful indulgence of the senses; they have lamps by reason of
good works. Of which good works the Lord saith, "Let your light so
shine before men, that they may see your good works, and glorify
your Father which is in heaven" (Matt. 5:16). Again he says to his disciples, "Let your loins be girded about and your lights burning" (Luke
12:35). In the "girded loins" is virginity; in the "burning lamps"
good works.

The title of virginity is not usually applied to married persons;
yet even in them, there is a virginity of faith which produces wedded
chastity. Know, holy Brethren, that every one who, as touching the
soul, has uncorrupted faith and practices abstinence from things
unlawful, and does good works, is not unsuitably called "a virgin."
The whole church, which consists of virgins, boys, married men, and
married women, is by one name called a virgin. How do we prove
this? Hear the apostle saying, not to the religious women only but to
the whole church together, "I have espoused you to one husband, that
I may present you as a chaste virgin to Christ" (2 Cor. 11:2). And

because the devil, the corrupter of this virginity, is to be guarded against, the Apostle added, "But I fear, lest by any means, as the serpent beguiled Eve through his subtilty, so your minds should be corrupted from the simplicity that is in Christ" (2 Cor. 11:3). Few have virginity in the body; in the heart, all ought to have it. If then abstinence from what is unlawful be good, whereby it has received the name of virginity, and good works are praiseworthy, which are signified by the lamps, why are five admitted and five rejected? If there be a virgin and one who carries a lamp, who yet is not admitted, where shall he see himself, who neither preserves a virginity from things unlawful and who not wishing to have good works walks in darkness?

Of these then, my brethren, yea, of these let us the rather treat. He who will not see what is evil, he who will not hear what is evil, he who turns away his smell from the unlawful fumes, and his taste from the unlawful food of the sacrifices, he who refuses the embrace of another man's wife, breaks his bread to the hungry, brings the stranger into his house, clothes the naked, reconciles the litigious, visits the sick, buries the dead; he surely is a virgin, surely he hath lamps. What more do we seek? Something yet I seek. The Holy Gospel has set me on search. It has said that even of these, virgins and carrying lamps, some are wise and some foolish. By what do we see this? By what make the distinction? By the oil. Some great, some exceedingly great thing does this oil signify. Do you think it is not love? This we say as searching out what it is; we hazard no precipitate judgment. I will tell you why love seems to be signified by the oil. The apostle says, "Yet shew I unto you a more excellent way. Though I speak with the tongues of men and of angels, and have not charity, I am become as sounding brass, or a tinkling cymbal" (1 Cor. 13:1). Charity is that way above the rest, which is with good reason signified by the oil, for oil swims above all liquids. Pour in water, pour in oil upon it, and the oil will swim above. Pour in oil, pour in water upon it, and the oil will swim above. If you keep the usual order, it will be uppermost; if you change the order, it will be uppermost. "Charity never faileth."

Let us treat now of the five wise and the five foolish virgins. They wished to go to meet the Bridegroom. What is the meaning of "to go and meet the Bridegroom"? To go with the heart, to be waiting for his coming. But he tarried. "While he tarries, they all slept." What is "all"? Both the foolish and the wise "all slumbered and slept." Is this sleep good? What is this sleep? Is it that at the tarrying of the Bridegroom, because "iniquity shall abound, the love of many shall wax cold" (Matt. 24:12)? Are we to understand this sleep so? I like it not. I will tell you why. Because among them are the wise virgins; and certainly when the Lord said, "Because iniquity shall abound, the love of many shall wax cold," he went on to say, "But he that shall endure unto the end, the same shall be saved" (v. 13). Where would those wise virgins be? Are they not among those that "shall endure unto the end"? They would not be admitted within at all, Brethren, for any other reason than because they have endured unto the end. No coldness of love then crept over them; in them love did not wax cold, but preserves its glow even unto the end. And because it glows even unto the end, therefore are the gates of the Bridegroom opened to them. They are told to enter in, as that excellent servant, "Enter thou into the joy of thy lord" (Matt. 25:21). What then is the meaning of they "all slept"? There is another sleep which no one escapes. Remember the apostle saying, "But I would not have you to be ignorant, brethren, concerning them which are asleep" (1 Thess. 4:13), that is, concerning them which are dead? For why are they called "they which are asleep," but because they are in their own day? Therefore "they all slept." Do you think that because one is wise, he does not die? Be the virgin foolish, or be she wise, all suffer equally the sleep of death.

But men continually say to themselves, "Lo, the Day of Judgment is coming now. So many evils are happening, so many tribulations thicken; behold, all things which the prophets have spoken are well-nigh fulfilled. The Day of Judgment is already at hand." They who speak thus, in faith, go outwith such thoughts to "meet the Bridegroom." But, lo! war upon war, tribulation upon tribulation, earthquake upon earthquake, famine upon famine, nation against nation, and still the Bridegroom comes not yet. While then he is expected to come, all they who are saying, "Lo, he is coming, and the Day of Judgment will find us here," fall asleep. While they are saying this, they fall asleep. Let each one then have an eye to this his sleep and persevere even unto his sleep in love; let sleep find him so waiting. For suppose that he has fallen asleep. "Will not he who falls asleep afterwards rise again?" Therefore, "they all slept." Both the wise and the foolish virgins in the parable all slept.

"And at midnight there was a cry made." What is "at midnight"? When there is no expectation, no belief at all of it. Night indicates ignorance. A man makes a calculation with himself: "Lo, so many years have passed since Adam, and the six thousand years are being completed, and then immediately according to the computation of certain expositors, the Day of Judgment will come." Yet these calculations come and pass away, and still the coming of the Bridegroom is delayed, and the virgins who had gone to meet him sleep. And, lo, when he is not looked for, when men are saying, "The six thousand years were waited for, and, they are gone by. How then shall we know when he will come?" He will come at midnight. What is, "will come at midnight"? Will come when you are not aware. Why will he come when you are not aware of it? Hear the Lord himself. "It is not for you to know the times or the seasons, which the Father hath put in his own power" (Acts 1:7). "The day of the Lord," says the apostle, "so cometh as a thief in the night" (1 Thess. 5:2). Therefore, watch by night so you will not be surprised by the thief. For the sleep of death—whether you will or not—will come.

"And at midnight there was a cry made" (Matt. 25:6). What cry
was this, but that of which the apostle says, "In the twinkling of an
eye, at the last trump"? "For the trumpet shall sound, and the dead
shall be raised incorruptible, and we shall be changed" (1 Cor. 15:52).
And so when the cry was made at midnight, "Behold, the Bridegroom cometh," what follows? "Then all those virgins arose." What is,
"they" all arose? "The hour is coming," said the Lord himself, "in the
which all that are in the graves shall hear his voice, and shall come
forth" (John 5:28–29). Therefore, at the last trumpet, they all arose.
"They that were foolish took their lamps, and took no oil with them:
but the wise took oil in their vessels with their lamps" (Matt. 25:3–4).
What is the meaning of "took no oil in their vessels"? What is "in their
vessels"? In their hearts. The apostle says, "Our glorying is this, the
testimony of our conscience." There is the oil, the precious oil; this oil
is of the gift of God. Men can put oil into their vessels, but they cannot create the olive. See, I have oil, but did you create the oil? It is of
the gift of God. You have oil. Carry it with you. What is "carry it with
thee"? Have it within, to please God.

Those foolish virgins who brought no oil with them, wish to
please men by that abstinence of theirs whereby they are called virgins, and by their good works, when they seem to carry lamps. And
if they wish to please men, and on that account do all these praiseworthy works, they do not carry oil with them. If you then carry it
with you, carry it within where God sees; there carry the testimony
of your conscience. For he who walks to gain the testimony of another does not carry oil with him. If you abstain from things unlawful
and do good works to be praised of men, there is no oil within. And
so when men begin to leave off their praises, the lamps fail. Observe
then, beloved, before those virgins slept, it is not said that their lamps
were extinguished. The lamps of the wise virgins burned with an
inward oil, with the assurance of a good conscience, with an inner

glory, with an inmost charity. Yet the lamps of the foolish virgins burned also. Why did they burn? Because there was yet no want of the praises of men. But after that they arose, in the resurrection from the dead, they began to trim their lamps, that is, began to prepare to render unto God an account of their works. And because there is then no one to praise, every man is wholly employed in his own cause, there is no one then who is not thinking of himself, therefore were there none to sell them oil; so their lamps began to fail, and the foolish went to the five wise and said, "Give us of your oil; for our lamps are gone out" (v. 8). They looked for what they had been accustomed to seek for, to shine with others' oil, to walk after others' praises.

But the wise said, "Not so; lest there be not enough for us and you: but go ye rather to them that sell, and buy for yourselves" (v. 9). This was not the answer of those who give advice, but of those who mock. Why do they mock? Because they were wise, because wisdom was in them. For they were not wise of their own; but that wisdom was in them, of which it is written in a certain book, she shall say to those that despised her, when they have fallen upon the evils which she threatened them, "I will laugh over your destruction." What wonder then is it, that the wise mock the foolish virgins? And what is this mocking?

"Go ye rather to them that sell, and buy for yourselves," you who never lived well, but because men praised you, who sold you oil. What means this, "sold you oil"? Sold praises. Who sell praises, but flatterers? How much better had it been for you not to have acquiesced in flatterers and to have carried oil within, and for a good conscience's sake to have done all good works. Then might ye say, "The righteous shall correct me in mercy and reprove me, but the oil of the sinner shall not fatten my head." Rather, he says, let the righteous correct me, let the righteous reprove me, let the righteous buffet me, than the oil of the sinner fatten mine head. What is the oil of the sinner but the blandishments of the flatterer?

"Go ye" then "to them that sell;" this have you been accustomed
to do. But we will not give to you. Why? "Lest there be not enough
for us and you." What is, "lest there be not enough"? This was not
spoken in any lack of hope, but in a sober and godly humility. For
though the good man have a good conscience, how does he know
how God may judge who is deceived by no one? He has a good conscience, no sins conceived in the heart solicit him, yet, though his
conscience be good, because of the daily sins of human life, he saith
to God, "Forgive us our debts"; seeing he has done what comes next,
"as we also forgive our debtors." He has broken his bread to the hungry from the heart, from the heart has clothed the naked; out of that
inward oil he has done good works, and yet in that judgment even
his good conscience trembles.

See then what this, "Give us oil," is. They were told, "Go ye rather
to them that sell." Since you have been used to live upon the praises
of men, you do not carry oil with you; but we can give you none "lest
there be not enough for us and you." For scarcely do we judge of ourselves, how much less can we judge of you? What is "scarcely do we
judge of ourselves"? Because "when the righteous King sitteth on the
throne, who will glory that his heart is pure?" It may be you do not
discover anything in your own conscience. But he who sees better,
whose divine glance penetrates into deeper things, discovers something, he sees it may be something, he discovers something. How
much better for you to say to him, "Enter not into judgment with thy
servant?' Yea, how much better, "Forgive us our debts?" Because it
shall be also said to thee because of those torches, because of those
lamps, "I was hungry, and ye gave me meat." What then? Did not the
foolish virgins do so, too? Yes, but they did it not before him. How
then did they do it? As the Lord forbids, who said, "Take heed that ye
do not your alms before men to be seen of them: otherwise ye have
no reward of your Father which is in heaven. . . . And when thou

prayest, thou shalt not be as the hypocrites are: for they love to pray standing in the synagogues and in the corners of the streets, that they may be seen of men. Verily I say unto you, They have their reward" (Matt. 6:1,5). They have bought oil, they have given the price, they have not been defrauded of men's praises, they have sought men's praises and have had them. These praises of men aid them not in the Judgment Day. But the other virgins, how have they done? "Let your light shine before men, that they may see your good works, and glorify your Father which is in heaven" (Matt. 5:16). He did not say, "may glorify you." For you have no oil of your own self. Boast and say, I have it; but from him, "for what hast thou that thou hast not received?" So then in this way acted the one, and in that the other.

Now it is no wonder that "while they went to buy," while they are seeking for persons by whom to be praised and find none; while they are seeking for persons by whom to be comforted, and find none; that the door is opened, and "the Bridegroom comes." The bride, the church, is glorified then with Christ, that the several members may be gathered together into their whole. "And they that were ready went in with him into the marriage: and the door was shut" (v. 10). Then the foolish virgins came afterwards; but had they bought any oil, or found any from whom they might buy it? Therefore, they found the doors shut; they began to knock, but too late.

It is said, and it is true, and no deceiving saying, "Knock, and it shall be opened unto you;" but now when it is the time of mercy, not when it is the time of judgment. For these times cannot be confounded, since the church sings to her Lord of "mercy and judgment." It is the time of mercy; repent. Can you repent in the time of judgment? You will be then as those virgins against whom the door was shut. "Lord, Lord, open to us." What! Did they not repent that they had brought no oil with them? Yes, but of what profit was their late repentance, when the true wisdom mocked them? Therefore, "the door was shut."

And what was said to them? "I know you not." Did not he know them, who knoweth all things? What did he mean, "I know you not?" I refuse, I reject you. In my art, I do not acknowledge you; my art knows no vice. Now this is a marvelous thing, it does not know vice, and it judges vice. It does not know it in the practice of it; it judges by reproving it. Thus then, "I know you not."

The five wise virgins came and "went in." How many are you, my Brethren, in the profession of Christ's name! Let there be among you the five wise, but be not five such persons only. Let there be among you the five wise belonging to this wisdom of the number five. For the hour will come, and come when we know not. It will come at midnight; Watch ye. Thus did the gospel close; "Watch, therefore, for ye know neither the day nor the hour" (v. 13). But if we are all to sleep, how shall we watch? Watch with the heart, watch with faith, watch with hope, watch with love, watch with good works; and then, when you shalt sleep in your body, the time will come that you shall rise. And when you shall have risen, make ready the lamps. Then shall they go out no more, then shall they be renewed with the inner oil of conscience; then shall that Bridegroom fold you in his spiritual embrace, then shall he bring you into his house where you shall never sleep, where your lamp can never be extinguished. But at present we are in labor, and our lamps flicker amid the winds and temptations of this life. But only let our flame burn strongly, that the wind of temptation may increase the fire, rather than put it out.

The Venerable Bede: *The Meeting of Mercy and Justice*

THE VENERABLE BEDE was born in 672 and died in 735. Most of his life was spent in the monastery at Jarrow-on-Tyne. His most noted work was his *Ecclesiastical History of the English Nation.* His last hours were spent in finishing his translation into the vernacular of the Gospel of St. John. Unfortunately, this work has not survived.

There is an immense mass of sermons from the Middle Ages, but few of them are available in English. The medieval preachers had no doubts about heaven, hell, the soul, and the redeeming work of Jesus Christ. After the vagueness of many of our modern sermons, it is refreshing to take up a sermon from the Middle Ages.

As will be seen in the sermon by Bede, there was much of the storyteller's art in the sermons of these ancient preachers.

The Meeting of Mercy and Justice

Mercy and truth are met together (Ps. 85:10).

*T*HERE *was a certain father* of a family, a powerful King, who had four daughters, of whom one was called Mercy; the second, Truth; the third, Justice; the fourth, Peace; of whom it is said, "Mercy and Truth are met together; Justice and Peace have kissed each other." He had also a certain most wise Son, to whom no one could be compared in wisdom. He had, also, a certain servant, whom he had exalted and enriched with great honor; for he had made him after his own likeness and similitude, and that without any preceding merit on the servant's part. But the lord, as is the custom with such wise masters, wished prudently to explore and to become acquainted wit, the character and the faith of his servant, whether he were trustworthy towards himself or not. So he gave him an easy commandment, and said, "If you do what I tell you, I will exalt you to further honors; if not, you shall perish miserably."

The servant heard the commandment, and without any delay, went and broke it. Why need I say more? Why need I delay you by my words and by my tears? This proud servant, stiff-necked, haughty, and puffed up with conceit, sought an excuse for his transgression, and retorted the whole fault on his Lord. For when he said, "The woman whom thou gavest to be with me, she deceived me," he threw all the fault on his Maker. His Lord, more angry for such contumptuous conduct than for the transgression of his command, called four most cruel executioners, and commanded one of them to cast him into prison, another to behead him, the third to strangle him, and the fourth to afflict him with grievous torments. By and by, when occasion offers, I will give you the right name of these tormentors.

These torturers, then, studying how they might carry out their own cruelty, took the wretched man and began to afflict him with all manner of punishments. But one of the daughters of the King, by name Mercy, when she had heard of this punishment of the servant, ran hastily to the prison. Looking in and seeing the man given over to the tormentors, she could not help having compassion upon him, for it is the property of Mercy to have mercy. She tore her garments and struck her hands together, and let her hair fall loose about her neck. Crying and shrieking, she ran to her father, and kneeling before his feet, began to say with an earnest and sorrowful voice: "My beloved father, am not I thy daughter Mercy? and art not thou called merciful? If thou art merciful, have mercy upon thy servant. If thou wilt not have mercy upon him, thou canst not be called merciful; and if thou art not merciful, thou canst not have me, Mercy, for thy daughter." While she was thus arguing with her father, her sister Truth came up and demanded why Mercy was weeping. "Your sister Mercy," replied the father, "wishes me to have pity upon that proud transgressor whose punishment I have appointed." Truth, when she heard this, was excessively angr, and looked sternly at her father. "Am not I," said she, "thy daughter Truth? Art not thou called true? Is it not true that thou fixed a punishment for him, and threatened him with death by torments? If thou art true, thou wilt follow that which is true; if thou dost not follow it, thou canst not be true; if thou art not true, thou canst not have me, Truth, for thy daughter." Here, you see, "Mercy and Truth are met together." The third sister, namely, Justice, hearing this strife, contention, quarreling, and pleading, and summoned by the outcry, began to inquire the cause from Truth. And Truth, who could only speak that which was true, said, "This sister of ours, Mercy, if she ought to be called a sister who does not agree with us, desires that our father should have pity on that proud transgressor." Then Justice, with an angry countenance and meditating on a grief which she had not expected, said to her father, "Am not I thy daughter Justice? Art thou not called just? If thou art just, thou wilt exercise justice on the transgressor; if thou dost not exercise that justice, thou canst not be just; if thou art not just, thou canst not have me, Justice, for thy daughter." So here were Truth and Justice on the one side, and Mercy on the other. Peace fled into a far distant country. For where there is strife and contention, there is no peace; and by how much greater the contention, by so much further Peace is driven away.

Peace, therefore, being lost, and his three daughters in warm discussion, the King found it an extremely difficult manner to determine what he should do, or to which side he should lean. For if he gave ear to Mercy, he would offend Truth and Justice; if he gave ear to Truth and Justice, he could not have Mercy for his daughter; and yet it was necessary that he should be both merciful and just, peaceful and true. There was great need then of good advice. The Father, therefore, called his wise Son, and consulted him about the affair. Said the Son, "Give me, my Father, this present business to manage, and I will both punish the transgressor for thee, and will bring back to thee in peace thy four daughters." "These are great promises," replied the Father, "if the deed only agrees with the word. If thou canst do that which thou sayest, I will act as thou shalt exhort me."

Having therefore received the royal mandate, the Son took his sister Mercy along with him. "Leaping upon the mountains, passing over the hills," they came to the prison, and "looking through the windows, looking through the lattice," he beheld the imprisoned servant, shut out from the present life, devoured of affliction, and "from the sole of the foot even to the crown there was no soundness in him." He saw him in the power of death, because through him death entered into the world. He saw him devoured because, when a man is once dead, he is eaten of worms. And because I now have an opportunity of telling you, you shall hear the names of the four tormentors. The first, who put him in prison, is the Prison of the present life, of which it is said, "Woe is me that I am constrained to dwell in Mesech." The second, who tormented him, is the Misery of the World, which besets us with all kinds of pain and wretchedness. The third, who was putting him to death, is Death, which destroys and slays all; the fourth, who was devouring him, is the Worm. . . . Therefore the Son, beholding his servant given over to these four tormentors, could not but have mercy upon him, because Mercy was his companion, and bursting into the prison of death, "conquered death, bound the strong man, took his goods," and distributed the spoils. And "ascending up on high, led captivity captive and gave gifts for men." He brought back the servant into his country, crowned with double honor, and endued with a garment of immortality. When Mercy beheld this, she had no grounds for complaint. Truth found no cause of discontent, because her Father was found true. The servant had paid all his penalties. Justice in like manner complained not because justice had been executed on the transgressor; and thus "he who had been lost was found." Peace, therefore, when she saw her sisters at concord, came back and united them. And now, behold "Mercy and Truth are met together, Justice and Peace have kissed each other." Thus, therefore, by the Mediator of men and angels, man was purified and reconciled, and the hundredth sheep was brought back to the fold of God. To which fold Jesus Christ bring us, to whom is honor and power everlasting. Amen.

Thomas á Kempis: *Taking Up the Cross*

THOMAS Á KEMPIS WAS BORN in 1381 at Kampen, on the shore of the Zuiderzee, Netherlands, and died at the Monastery of Mount St. Agnes, in Zwolle, in 1471. Seventy years of his long life were spent at the Augustinian convent of Mount St. Agnes. It was there he produced that immortal classic of the devotional life, *The Imitation of Christ*, which, as Dr. Charles Hodge once wrote, "has diffused itself like incense through the aisles and the alcoves of the universal church."

His sermon, "Taking Up the Cross," is a beautiful and eloquent tribute to Christ and the Cross.

Taking Up the Cross

But God forbid that I should glory, save in the cross of of our Lord
Jesus Christ (Gal. 6:14).

BELOVED *brethren,* blessed Paul, the excellent beholder
of heavenly secrets, sets forth to us in the aforesaid
words, that the Cross is the right way of living well, is
the best teaching how to suffer adversity, is the firmest ladder whereby we may ascend to heaven by its most unconquered sign. It is this
which leads its lovers into the country of eternal light, of eternal
peace, of eternal blessedness, which the world cannot give, nor the
devil take away. Human frailty abhors the suffering of poverty, contempt, vileness, hunger, labor, pain, necessity, derision, which all are
so often its lot, and which weigh down and disturb men. But all these
things joined together form by their manifold sufferings a salutary
Cross, God so ordering this dispensation for us. To the true bearers
of the Cross, they open the gate of the celestial kingdom. To them
that fight, they prepare the palm of life; to them that conquer, they
give the diadem of eternal glory. O truly blessed Cross of Christ,
which bore the King of Heaven, and which didst bring to the whole
world the joy of salvation! By thee the devils art put to flight; the
weak are cured; the timid are strengthened; the sinful are cleansed;
the idle are excited; the proud are humbled; the hard-hearted are
touched; and the devout are bedewed with tears. Blessed are they
who daily call to mind the Passion of Christ, and desire to carry their
own cross after Christ. Good and religious brethren, who are
enrolled under obedience, have, in the daily affliction of their bodies,
and in the resignation of their own wills, a cross which in its outward
aspect is heavy and bitter. But it is internally full of sweetness because
of the hope of eternal salvation, and the affluence of divine comfort

which is promised to those that are broken in heart. If they do not feel it at once, or perceive it bestowed upon them by slow degrees, nevertheless they ought to expect it with patience, and to resign themselves to the divine will. For he himself best knows the time of showing mercy and the method of assisting the afflicted, as the physician is best acquainted with the art of curing, and the master of the ship with the craft of steering. Those who have taken up the Cross in their hearts have great confidence and cause of glorying, in the Cross of Jesus Christ. They confide not nor trust that they shall be saved in their own merits and works, but through the mercy of God, and the merits of Christ Jesus, crucified for our sins, in whom they believe faithfully; whom with their hearts they love, with their mouths they confess, praise, preach, honor, and extol. God proves his familiar friends by the holy Cross, whether they love him truly or in presence, and whether they can perfectly observe his commandments.

Principally, however, they are proved by tolerance of injuries and the removal of internal consolations; by the death of friends, and by the loss of property; by pains in the head, and injuries in the limbs; by abstinence from food, and roughness of garments; by the hardness of their bed, and the coldness of their feet; by the long watches of the night, and the labors of the day; by the silence of the mouth, and the reproofs of superiors; by worms that gnaw, and tongues that detract. In their sufferings, however, they are consoled by the devout meditation of the Lord's Passion, as many devout persons know very well in their own hearts. It is theirs to taste the hidden honey from the rock, and the oil of mercy that drops from the blessed wood of the holy Cross; whose taste is most delicious; whose odor is most sweet; whose touch is most healthy; whose fruit is most happy. O most truly worthy and precious tree of life, planted in the midst of the church for the medicine of the soul! O Jesus of Nazareth! Thou that wast crucified for us! Thou loosenest the bands of sinners; freest the souls of saints; humblest the necks of the haughty; breakest down the power of the wicked; comfortest the faithful; puttest to flight the unbelievers; deliverest the pious; punishest the hardened; overthrowest the adversaries. Thou raisest up those who are fallen; Thou settest at liberty those who are oppressed; Thou smitest those who do hurt; Thou defendest those who are innocent; Thou lovest those who are true; Thou hatest those who are false; Thou despisest the carnal; Thou hast regard to the spiritual; Thou receivest those who come to Thee; Thou hidest those who take refuge in Thee. Those who call upon Thee, Thou hearest; those who visit Thee, Thou rejoicest; those who seek Thee, Thou helpest; those who cry to Thee, Thou strengthenest. Thou honorest those who honor Thee; Thou praisest those who praise Thee; Thou lovest those who love Thee; Thou glorifiest those who adore Thee; Thou blessest those who bless Thee; Thou exaltest those who exalt Thee. On those who look to Thee Thou lookest; those who kiss Thee, Thou kissest; those who embrace Thee, Thou embracest; those who follow Thee, Thou leadest to heaven.

O religious brother, why art thou sorrowful, and why dost thou complain of the weight of thy cross, in long vigils; in many fasts; in labor and silence; in obedience and strict discipline? which things were instituted at the inspiration of God, by holy fathers for thy profit, and the salvation of thy soul; in order that by them thou mightest walk securely and prudently, who canst not govern thyself well and virtuously. Dost thou think that without the Cross and without grief thou canst enter into the kingdom of heaven, when Christ neither could nor would, nor did any of his most beloved friends and saints gain from him such a privilege? For he himself said, "Ought not Christ to suffer, and so enter into his glory?" Thou art altogether mistaken in thy thought: thou attendest not to the footsteps of Christ shown to thee; for he, by the Cross, passed from this world to his Heavenly Father. Ask whom thou wilt of the victors and citizens of the celestial kingdom how he came to possess forever this glory of God. Was it not by the Cross and by suffering? Well, then, brethren, take up the sweet and light yoke of the Lord. Embrace with all affection the holy Cross—it flowers with all virtues; it is full of celestial unction—to the end that it may lead you without mistake, with the hope of glory, to life eternal.

What more shall I say? This is the way, and there is none other; the right way, the holy way, the perfect way, the way of Christ, the way of the just, the way of the elect that shall be saved. Walk in it, persevere in it, endure in it, live in it, die in it, breathe forth your spirits in it. The Cross of Christ conquers all the machinations of the devil; the Cross draws to itself the hearts of all the faithful; it destroys all things evil and confers on us all things good through Jesus Christ, who hung and died upon it. There is no armor so strong, no arrow so sharp and so terrible against the power and cruelty of the devil, none which he so fears as the sign of the Cross, in which he brought to pass that the Son of God should be suspended and slain, who was innocent and pure from all spot. O truly blessed Cross of Christ, most worthy of all honor, to be embraced with all love; that causes those who love thee to bear their burdens with ease, that consoles the sorrowful in enduring reproaches; that teaches the penitent how to obtain pardon for every offense. This is honorable to the holy angels; most lovely to men, most terrible to devils; despised by the proud, acceptable to the humble; rough to the carnal, sweet to the spiritual; insipid to the foolish, delicious to the devout; affable to the poor, companionable to the stranger; friendly to the afflicted, consoling to the sick, comfort to the dying. Lay up, therefore, the sacred wounds of Jesus in the recesses of your heart; they have a savor beyond all spices to the devout soul that is in affliction and that seeks not consolation from men.

Follow Christ, who leads by his Passion and his Cross to eternal rest and light, because if ye are now his companions in tribulation, ye will shortly sit down with him at the heavenly table in perpetual exultation. Plant in the garden of your memory the tree of the holy Cross; it produces a very efficacious medicine against all the suggestions of the devil. Of this most noble and fertile tree, the root is humility and poverty; the bark, labor and penitence; the branches, mercy and justice; the leaves, true honor and modesty; the scent, sobriety and abstinence; the beauty, chastity and obedience; the splendor, right faith and firm hope; the strength, magnanimity and patience; the length, long-suffering and perseverance; the breadth, benignity and concord; the height, love and wisdom; the sweetness, love and joy; the fruit, salvation and life eternal. Well, then, and worthily, sings the church of the Holy Cross,

> Faithful Cross, above all other
> One and only noble tree;
> None in foliage, none in blossom
> None in fruit thy peers may be!

There was no such plant to be found in the gardens of Solomon, no herb so salutary for the curing of all diseases, as the tree of the holy Cross, which bears its spices of divine virtue, for the obtaining of human salvation. This is that most fruitful tree, blessed above all the trees of paradise; stretching forth its lovely branches, adorned with green leaves, extended with rich fruit through the world; by its altitude, touching heaven; by its profundity, penetrating hell; by its extent, surrounding mountains and hills; by its magnitude, filling the round world; by its fortitude, conquering wicked kings and the persecutors of the faith; by its mercy, attracting the weak; by its suavity, healing sinners. This is the glorious palm that is rightly called Christiferous, carried on the shoulders of Jesus, set up on the mountain of Calvary; condemned by the Jews, set at naught by the Gentiles, reviled by the wicked, lamented by the faithful, implored by the pious.

Blessed is the man, faithful is that servant, who perpetually carries the sacred wounds of Jesus in his heart; and, if adversity meets him, receives it as from the hand of God and piously endures it, that he may at least in some degree become conformed to the crucified. He is worthy to be visited and consoled by Christ, who studies fully to conform himself in life and in death to His Passion. This is the way of the holy Cross, this is the doctrine of the Savior, this is the wisdom of saints, this is the rule of monks, this the life of the good, this the lection of clerks, this the meditation of the devout; to imitate Christ humbly, to suffer evil for Christ, to choose the bitter instead of the sweet; to despise honors, to bear contempt with equanimity, to abstain from evil delights; to fly the occasions of vice, to avoid dissipation; to lament for our own sins and for those of others, to pray for the troubled and the tempted, to render thanks for benefactors, to make supplication for adversaries that they may be converted; to rejoice with them that are in prosperity, to grieve with them that suffer injury, to succor the indigent; not to seek high things, to choose that which is humble, to love that which is simple; to cut off superfluities, to be contented with a little, to labor for virtues, to struggle every day against vices; to subdue the flesh by fasting, to strengthen the spirit by prayer and by reading, to refuse human praise; to seek solitude, to love silence, to be at leisure for God; to sigh for things celestial, to despise from the heart all that is earthly, to think that nothing save God can bring comfort. He that does this, may say with blessed Paul the Apostle, "To me to live is Christ, and to die is gain." And again: "God forbid that I should glory, save in the cross of our Lord Jesus Christ, by whom the world is crucified unto me, and I unto the world" (Gal. 6:14). O religious monk and follower of the stricter life, depart not from the Cross which thou hast taken up; but bear it and carry it with thee even to death; and thou shalt find eternal rest and celestial glory and honor. When any tribulation meets thee, it is Christ who lays his Cross upon thee, and shows thee the way by which thou must go to the heavenly kingdom. But if any one boasts himself and hopes in the glories and in the honors of this world, he is truly deceived, and he will carry with him nothing at all of that which he has been accustomed to love in the world. But he who boasts himself in Christ, and despises all things for the sake of Christ, shall be consoled by Christ in the present life. In the life to come he shall be filled with celestial blessings and shall felicitously rejoice with Christ and with all saints, world without end. May Jesus Christ grant it to us, who for us suffered and died upon the cross, to whom be praise and glory, to ages of ages. Amen.

Martin Luther: *St. Stephen*

MARTIN LUTHER WAS BORN on November 10th, 1483, at Eisleben, Germany, and died there on February 18, 1546. After a high-school training at Eisenach and a college training at Erfurt, where he took his bachelor's degree, Luther went as a teacher to the new University of Wittenberg. On All Saints' Day, 1517, he nailed his "Ninety-five Theses" to the doors of the cathedral at Wittenberg and thus inaugurated the mighty protest of the Reformation. On October 16, 1521, before the Diet of Worms, he took his stand for the great Protestant principle, the supremacy of the Scriptures. Luther was preeminently a man of genius, and all his work—teaching, preaching, debating, pamphleteering, translating and hymn-writing—shows the mark of genius. If in the Protestant church the pulpit is the throne of the preacher and pastor, Luther did much to make it so. He himself was an indefatigable and popular preacher, a Boanerges in every sense of the word. Much of the power of great speakers and preachers is due to the unusual occasion. Luther preached in a time of tremendous excitement, and his violent denunciations and burning conviction reflect the spirit of the times. For readers today, his sermons are somewhat marred by their invective and denunciation. But in the midst of these violent philippics, one comes upon exquisite passages of Christian teaching. His homiletical plan he summed up in three rules: "Get up freshly, open your mouth widely, be done quickly."

In his moving sermon on Stephen, Luther makes effective use of the beautiful idea, borrowed from St. Augustine, that the prayer of the dying martyr for those who stoned him was the means of the conversion of St. Paul.

St. Stephen

THE *epistle text* seems to be not at all difficult; it is plain. It presents in Stephen an example of the faith of Christ. Little comment is necessary. We shall examine it briefly. The first principle it teaches is, we cannot secure the favor of God by erecting churches and other institutions. Stephen makes this fact plain in his citation from Isaiah.

We must not, however, be led to conclude it is wrong to build and endow churches. But it is wrong to go to the extreme of forfeiting faith and love in the effort, presuming thereby to do good works meriting God's favor. It results in abuses precluding all moderation. Every nook and corner is filled with churches and cloisters, regardless of the object of church-building.

There is no other reason for building churches than to afford a place where Christians may assemble to pray, to hear the gospel, and to receive the sacraments, if indeed there is a reason. When churches cease to be used for these purposes, they should be pulled down, as other buildings are when no longer of use. As it is now, the desire of every individual in the world is to establish his own chapel or altar, even his own mass, with a view of securing salvation, of purchasing heaven.

Is it not a miserable, deplorable error and delusion to teach innocent people to depend on their works to the great disparagement of their Christian faith? Better to destroy all the churches and cathedrals in the world, to burn them to ashes—it is less sinful even when done through malice—than to allow one soul to be misled and lost by such error. God has given no special command in regard to the building of churches, but he has issued his commands in reference to our souls—his real and peculiar churches. Paul says concerning them: "Ye are the temple of God. . . . If any man defile the temple of God, him shall God destroy" (1 Cor. 3:16–17).

I continue to assert that for the sake of exterminating the error mentioned, it would be well to overthrow at once all the churches in the world and to utilize ordinary dwellings or the open air for preaching, praying, and baptizing, and for all Christian requirements.

Especially is there justification for so doing because of the worthless reason the Papists assign for building churches. Christ preached for over three years, but only three days in the temple at Jerusalem. The remainder of the time, he spoke in the schools of the Jews, in the wilderness, on the mountains, in ships, at the feasts, and otherwise in private dwellings. John the Baptist never entered the temple; he preached by the Jordan River and in all places. The apostles preached in the marketplace and streets of Jerusalem on the day of Pentecost. Philip preached in a chariot to the eunuch. Paul preached to the people by the riverside, in the Philippian jail, and in various private dwellings. In fact, Christ commanded the apostles to preach in private houses. I presume the preachers mentioned were equally good with those of today.

You see now some reason why lightning strikes the costly Papist churches more frequently than it does other buildings. Apparently, the wrath of God especially rests upon them because there greater sins are committed, more blasphemies uttered, and greater destruction of souls and of churches wrought than take place in brothels and in thieves' dens. The keeper of a public brothel is less a sinner than the preacher who does not deliver the true gospel, and the brothel is not so bad as the false preacher's church. Even were the proprietor of the brothel daily to prostitute virgins, godly wives, and nuns, awful and abominable as such action would be, he would not be any worse nor would he work more harm than those papistical preachers.

Does this astonish you? Remember, the false preacher's doctrine effects nothing but daily to lead astray and to violate souls newly born in baptism—young Christians, tender souls, the pure, consecrated virgin brides of Christ. Since the evil is wrought spiritually, not bodily, no one observes it; but God is beyond measure displeased. In his wrath he cries through the prophets in unmistakable terms, "Thou harlot who invitest every passerby!" So little can God tolerate false preaching, Jeremiah in his prayer makes this complaint: "They ravished the women in Zion, and the maids in the cities of Judah" (Lam. 5:11). Now, spiritual virginity, the Christian faith, is immeasurably superior to bodily purity; for it alone can obtain heaven.

Let us, therefore, beloved friends, be wise; wisdom is essential. Let us truly learn we are saved through faith in Christ and that alone. This fact has been made sufficiently manifest. Then let no one rely upon his own works. Let us in our lifetimes engage only in such works as shall profit our neighbors, being indifferent to testament and institution, and direct our efforts to bettering the full course of our neighbors' lives.

It is related of a pious woman, St. Elizabeth, that once upon entering a cloister and seeing on the wall a fine painting portraying the sufferings of our Lord, she exclaimed: "The cost of this painting should have been saved for the sustenance of the body; the sufferings of Christ are to be painted on your hearts." How forcibly this godly utterance is directed against the things generally regarded precious ! Were St. Elizabeth so to speak today, the Papists assuredly would burn her for blaspheming against the sufferings of Christ and for condemning good works. She would be denounced as a heretic, though her merits were to surpass the combined merits of ten saints.

Stephen not only rejects the conceptions of the Jews in regard to churches and their erection, but also denounces all their works, saying they have received the Law by the disposition of angels and have not kept it. So the Jews, in return, reprove Stephen as if he had spoken against the temple and, further, blasphemed the law of Moses and would teach strange works. True, Stephen could not rightly have charged them with failure to observe the Law so far as external works are considered. For they were circumcised, and observed the rules in regard to meats, apparel, festivals, and all Moses' commands. It was their consciousness of having observed the Law that led them to stone him.

But Stephen's words were prompted by the same spirit that moved Paul when he said that by the deeds of the Law, no one is justified in the sight of God, faith alone being the justifier. Where the Holy Spirit is not present to grant grace, man's heart cannot favor the Law of God; it would prefer the Law did not exist. Every individual is conscious of his own apathy and disinclination toward what is good, and of his readiness to do evil. As Moses says, "The imagination of man's heart is evil from his youth" (Gen. 8:21).

When Stephen declares the Jews always resist the Holy Spirit, he means to imply that through their works they become presumptuous, are not inclined to accept the Spirit's aid, and are unwilling their works be rejected as ineffectual. Ever working and working to satisfy the demands of the Law, but without fulfilling its least requirement, they remain hypocrites to the end. Unwilling to embrace the faith whereby they would be able to accomplish good works, and the grace of the Spirit that would create a love for the Law, they make impossible the free, spontaneous observance of it. But the voluntary observer of the Law, and no other, God accepts.

Stephen calls the Jews "stiffnecked, uncircumcised in heart and ears" because they refuse to listen and understand. They continually cry, "Good works, good works! Law, Law!" though not effecting the least thing themselves. Just so do our Papists. As their forefathers did, so do the descendants, the mass of this generation; they persecute the righteous and boast it is done for the sake of God and his Law. Now we have the substance of this lesson. But let us examine it a little further.

First, we see in Stephen's conduct love toward God and man. He manifests his love to God by earnestly and severely censuring the Jews, calling them betrayers, murderers, and transgressors of the whole Law, yes, stiffnecked and saying they resist the fulfillment of the Law and resist also the Holy Spirit himself. More than that, he calls them "uncircumcised in heart and ears." How could he have censured them any more severely? So completely does he strip them of every creditable thing, it would seem as if he were moved by impatience and wrath.

But whom today would the world tolerate were he to attempt such censure of the Papists? Stephen's love for God constrained him to his act. No one who possesses the same degree of love can be silent and calmly permit the rejection of God's commandments. He cannot dissemble. He must censure and rebuke every opposer of God. Such conduct he cannot permit even if he risks his life to rebuke it.

We must infer from Stephen's example that he who silently ignores the transgression of God's commands or any sin has no love for him. Then how is it with the hypocrites who applaud transgression, with calumniators and those who laugh and eagerly listen to and speak about the faults of others?

We have just had occasion to state that Stephen was a layman, an ordinary Christian, not a priest. But the Papists sing his praises as a Levite, who read the epistle or the Gospel lesson at the altar. The Papists, however, pervert the truth entirely. It is necessary for us, therefore, to know what Luke says. He tells how the Christians in the inception of the church at Jerusalem made all their possessions common property and the apostles distributed to each member of the congregation as he needed. But, as it happened, the widows of the

Grecian Jews were not provided for as were the Hebrew widows; hence, arose complaint. The apostles, seeing how the duty of providing for these things would be so burdensome as to interfere in a measure with their duties of praying and preaching, assembled the multitude of the disciples and said: "It is not reason that we should leave the word of God, and serve tables. Wherefore, brethren, look ye out from among you seven men of honest report, full of the Holy Ghost and wisdom, whom we may appoint over this business. But we will give ourselves continually to prayer, and to the ministry of the word" (Acts 6:2–3).

So Stephen, in connection with six others, was chosen to distribute the goods. Thence comes the word "deacon," servant or minister. These men served the congregation, ministering to their temporal wants.

Plainly, then, Stephen was a steward, or an administrator and guardian of the temporal goods of the Christians; his duty was to administer them to those in need. In course of time, his office was perverted into that of a priest who reads the epistle and Gospel lessons. The only trace left of Stephen's office is the slight resemblance found in the duty of the nuns' provosts, and in that of the administrators of hospitals and of the guardians of the poor. The readers of the epistle and Gospel selections should be, not the consecrated, the shorn, the bearers of dalmatics, and brushers of flies at the altar, but ordinary, godly laymen who keep a record of the needy and have charge of the common fund for distribution as necessity requires. Such was the actual office of Stephen. He never dreamed of reading epistles and Gospels, of bald pates, and dalmatics. Those are all human devices.

As to the question that may arise whether an ordinary layman may be allowed to preach: Though Stephen was not appointed to preach— the apostles, as stated, reserved that office for themselves—but to perform the duties of a steward, yet when he went to the market-place and mingled among the people, he immediately created a stir by performing signs and wonders, as the epistle says, and he even censured the rulers. Had the Pope and his followers been present, they certainly would have inquired as to his credentials—his church passport and his ecclesiastical character. Had he been lacking a bald pate and a prayer book, undoubtedly he would have been committed to the flames as a heretic, since he was not a priest nor a clergyman. These titles, which the Scriptures accord all Christians, the Papists have appropriated to themselves alone, terming all other men "the laity," and themselves "the church," as if the laity were not a part of the church. At the same time, these people of boasted refinement and nobility do not in a single instance fill the office or do the work of a priest, of a clergyman, or of the church. They but dupe the world with their human devices.

The precedent of Stephen holds good. His example gives all men authority to preach wherever they can find hearers, whether it be in a building or at the market place. He does not confine the preaching of God's Word to bald pates and long gowns. At the same time he does not interfere with the preaching of the apostles. He attends to the duties of his own office and is readily silent where it is the place of the apostles to preach.

In the second place, Stephen's conduct is a beautiful example of love for fellowmen in that he entertains no ill will toward even his murderers. However severely he rebukes them in his zeal for the honor of God, such is the kindly feeling he has for them that in the very agonies of death, having made provision for himself by com-mending his spirit to God, he has no further thought about himself but is all concern for them. Under the influence of that love, he yields up his spirit. Not undesignedly does Luke place Stephen's prayer for his murderers at the close of the narrative. Note also, when praying for himself and commending his spirit to God, he stood, but he knelt to pray for his murderers. Further, he cried with a loud voice as he prayed for them, which he did not do for himself.

How much more fervently he prayed for his enemies than for himself! How his heart must have burned, his eyes have overflowed, and his entire body been agitated and moved with compassion as he beheld the wretchedness of his enemies! It is St. Augustine's opinion that Paul was saved by this prayer. And it is not unreasonable to believe that God truly heard it and that from eternity he foresaw a great result from this dispensation. The person of Paul is evidence of God's answer to Stephen's prayer. It could not be denied, though all may not have been saved.

Stephen aptly chooses his words, saying, "Lay not this sin to their charge" (Acts 7:60), that is, make not their sin unremovable, like a pillar or a foundation. By these words Stephen makes confession, repents and renders satisfaction for sin, in behalf of his murderers. His words imply: "Beloved Lord, truly they commit a sin, a wrong. This cannot be denied." Just as it is customary in repentance and confession simply to deplore and confess the guilt. Stephen then prays, offering himself up, that abundant satisfaction may surely be made for sin.

Note how great an enemy and at the same time how great a friend true love can be; how severe its censures and how sweet its aid. It is like a nut with a hard shell and a sweet kernel. Bitter to our old Adam nature, it is exceedingly sweet to the new man in us.

This epistle lesson, by the example given, inculcates the forcible doctrine of faith and love; and more, it affords comfort and encouragement. It not only teaches; it incites and impels. Death, the terror of the world, it styles a sleep; Luke says, "He fell asleep," that is, Stephen's death was quiet and painless; he departed as one goes to sleep, unknowing how, and unconsciously falls asleep.

The theory that the Christian's death is a sleep, a peaceful passing, has safe foundations in the declaration of the Spirit. The Spirit will not deceive us. Christ's grace and power make death peaceful. Its bitterness is far removed by Christ's death when we believe in him. He says, "If a man keep my saying, he shall never see death" (John 8:51). Why shall he not see it? Because the soul, embraced in his living word and filled with that life, cannot be sensible of death. The word lives and knows no death; so the soul which believes in that word and lives in it likewise does not taste death. This is why Christ's words are called words of life. They are the words of life; he who hangs upon them, who believes in them, must live.

Comfort and encouragement are further increased by Stephen's assertion, "I see the heavens opened, and the Son of man standing on the right hand of God" (Acts 7:56). Here we see how faithfully and lovingly Christ watches over us and how ready he is to aid us if we but believe in him and will cheerfully risk our lives for his sake. The vision was not given solely on Stephen's account; it was not recorded for his profit. It was for our consolation, to remove all doubt of our privilege to enjoy the same happy results, provided we conduct ourselves as Stephen did.

The fact that the heavens are open affords us the greatest comfort and removes all terror of death. What should not stand open and ready for us when the heavens, the supreme work of creation, are waiting wide for us and rejoicing at our approach? It may be your desire to see them visibly open to you. But were everyone to behold, where would faith be? That the vision was once given to man is enough for the comfort of all Christians, for the comfort and strengthening of their faith and for the removal of all death's terrors. For as we believe, so shall we experience, even though we see not physically.

Would not the angels, yes, all creatures, lend willing assistance when the Lord himself stands ready to help? Remarkably, Stephen saw not an angel, not God himself, but the man Christ, he who most delights humanity and who affords man the strongest comfort. Man, especially when in distress, welcomes the sight of another man in preference to that of angels or other creatures.

Our artful teachers who would measure the works of God by their own reason or the seas with a spoon, ask: "How could Stephen look into the heavens when our vision cannot discern a bird when it soars a little high? How could he see Christ distinctly enough to recognize him for a certainty? A man upon a high steeple appears to us a child, and we cannot recognize his person." They attempt to settle the question by declaring Stephen's vision must have been supernaturally quickened, permitting him to see clearly into infinite space. But suppose Stephen had been under a roof or within a vault? Away with such human nonsense! Paul when near Damascus certainly heard the voice of Christ from heaven, and his hearing was not quickened for the occasion. The apostles on Mount Tabor, John the Baptist, and again the people—these all heard the voice of the Father with their ordinary hearing. Is it not more difficult to hear a voice from a great distance above than to see an object in the same place? The range of our vision is immeasurably wider than the scope of our hearing.

When God desires to reveal himself, heaven and everything else requisite are near. It matters not whether Stephen were beneath a roof or in the open air; heaven was near to him. Abnormal vision was not necessary. God is everywhere; there is no need that he come down from heaven. A vision at close range of God actually in heaven is easily possible without the quickening or perverting of the senses.

It matters not whether or not we fully comprehend how such a vision is effected. It is not intended that the wonders of God be brought within our grasp; they are manifested to induce in us belief and confidence. Explain to me, ye of boasted wisdom, how the comparatively large apple or pear or cherry can be grown through the tiny stem; or even explain less mysterious things. But permit God to work; believe in his wonders, and do not presume to bring him within your comprehension.

Who can number the virtues illustrated in Stephen's example? There loom up all the fruits of the Spirit. We find love, faith, patience, benevolence, peace, meekness, wisdom, truth, simplicity, strength, consolation, philanthropy. We see there also hatred and censure for all forms of evil. We note a disposition not to value worldly advantage nor to dread the terrors of death. Liberty, tranquillity, and all the noble virtues and graces are in evidence. There is no virtue but is illustrated in this example; no vice it does not rebuke. Well may the evangelist say Stephen was full of faith and power. Power here implies activity. Luke would say, "His faith was great; hence his many and mighty works." For when faith truly exists, its fruits must follow. The greater the faith, the more abundant its fruits.

True faith is a strong, active, and efficacious principle. Nothing is impossible to it. It rests not nor hesitates. Stephen, because of the superior activity of his faith, performed not merely ordinary works, but wrought wonders and signs publicly—great wonders and signs, as Luke says. This is written for a sign that the inactive individual lacks in faith, and has no right to boast of having it. Not undesignedly is the word "faith" placed before the word "power." The intention was to show that works are evidences of faith and that without faith, nothing good can be accomplished. Faith must be primary in every act. To this end may God assist us. Amen.

John Calvin: *Enduring Persecution*

JOHN CALVIN WAS BORN at Noyon, France, in 1509, and died at
Geneva, in 1564. After Martin Luther, Calvin is the greatest figure in
the history of Protestantism. At the age of twenty-seven he published his celebrated *Institutes,* a profound theological treatise. In
1536, Calvin visited Geneva and was persuaded by Farrel, the Swiss
reformer, to join with the Protestants of that city. There Calvin made
Geneva the bright and shining light of the Protestant world. Geneva
became the house of refuge for persecuted Protestants from all parts
of Europe and Calvin the spiritual father and adviser of the churches
in France, Holland, and Great Britain. His was the organizing mind
of the Protestant churches; in education, civil government, theology, and ecclesiastical organization, his influence was felt throughout
the world. A system of theology, Calvinism, takes its name from him
and still dominates large portions of the Protestant world. Bancroft
pays Calvin this well-merited tribute: "So he continued year after
year, solitary and feeble, yet toiling for humanity, till, after a life of
glory, he bequeathed to his personal heirs a fortune in books and
furniture, stocks and money, not exceeding two hundred dollars,
and to the world a purer reformation, a republican spirit in religion,
with the kindred principles of republican liberty."

Most of the sermons of Calvin were preached in the Church of
St. Peter at Geneva. We associate Calvin with the great and difficult
themes of God's sovereign decrees and predestination. But in the
sermon which follows, "Enduring Persecution," we see him as pastor
and preacher. The sermon is comprehensible by all, yet shows the
smooth working of that wonderful intellect. Persecution for Christ's
sake was not then an abstract theme, for those to whom Calvin
preached stood daily in jeopardy for their lives.

Enduring Persecution

Let us go forth out of the tents after Christ, bearing his reproach (Heb. 13:13).

ALL *the exhortations* which can be given us to suffer patiently for the name of Jesus Christ and in defense of the gospel will have no effect if we do not feel assured of the cause for which we fight. When we are called to part with life, it is absolutely necessary to know on what grounds. The firmness necessary we cannot possess, unless it be founded on certainty of faith.

It is true that persons may be found who will foolishly expose themselves to death in maintaining some absurd opinions and reveries conceived by their own brain, but such impetuosity is more to be regarded as frenzy than as Christian zeal; and, in fact, there is neither firmness nor sound sense in those who thus, at a kind of haphazard, cast themselves away. But however this may be, it is in a good cause only that God can acknowledge us as his martyrs. Death is common to all, and the children of God are condemned to ignominy and tortures just as criminals are; but God makes the distinction between them, inasmuch as he cannot deny his truth. On our part, then, it is requisite that we have sure and infallible evidence of the doctrine which we maintain; and hence, as I have said, we cannot be rationally impressed by any exhortations which we receive to suffer persecution for the gospel if no true certainty of faith has been imprinted in our hearts. To hazard our lives upon a peradventure is not natural, and though we were to do it, it would only be rashness, not Christian courage. In a word, nothing that we do will be approved of God if we are not thoroughly persuaded that it is for him and his cause we suffer persecution and the world is our enemy.

Now, when I speak of such persuasion, I mean not merely that we must know how to distinguish between true religion and the abuses or follies of men, but also that we must be thoroughly persuaded of the heavenly life and the crown which is promised us above, after we shall have fought here below. Let us understand, then, that both of these requisites are necessary and cannot be separated from each other.

The points, accordingly, with which we must commence, are these: We must know well what our Christianity is, what the faith which we have to hold and follow—what the rule which God has given us; and we must be so well furnished with such instruction as to be able boldly to condemn all the falsehoods, errors, and superstitions which Satan has introduced to corrupt the pure simplicity of the doctrine of God.

We now see *The True Method of Preparing to Suffer for the Gospel.* First, we must have profited so far in the school of God as to be decided in regard to true religion and the doctrine which we are to hold. We must despise all the wiles and impostures of Satan and all human inventions as things frivolous and carnal, inasmuch as they corrupt Christian purity; therein differing, like true martyrs of Christ, from the fantastic persons who suffer for mere absurdities. Second, feeling assured of the good cause, we must be inflamed, accordingly, to follow God whithersoever he may call us. His word must have such authority with us as it deserves, and, having withdrawn from this world, we must feel enraptured in seeking the heavenly life.

But it is more than strange, that though the light of God is shining more brightly than it ever did before, there is a lamentable want of zeal. In short, it is impossible to deny that it is to our great shame, not to say fearful condemnation, that we have so well known the truth of God and have so little courage to maintain it.

Above all, when we look to the martyrs of past times, well may we detest our own cowardice! The greater part of those were not persons much versed in Holy Scripture, so as to be able to dispute on all subjects. They knew that there was one God, whom they behoved to worship and serve; that they had been redeemed by the blood of Jesus Christ, in order that they might place their confidence of salvation in him and in his grace; and that all the inventions of men, being mere dross and rubbish, they ought to condemn all idolatries and superstitions. In one word, their theology was in substance this: There is one God who created all the world and declared his will to us by Moses and the prophets, and finally by Jesus Christ and his apostles; and we have one sole Redeemer, who purchased us by his blood, and by whose grace we hope to be saved. All the idols of the world are cursed and deserve execration.

With a system embracing no other points than these, they went boldly to the flames, or to any other kind of death. They did not go in twos or threes, but in such band, that the number of those who fell by the hands of tyrants is almost infinite.

What then should be done in order to inspire our breasts with true courage? We have, in the first place, to consider how precious the confession of our faith is in the sight of God. We little know how much God prizes it, if our lives, which are nothing, are valued by us more highly. When it is so, we manifest a marvelous degree of stupidity. We cannot save our lives at the expense of our confession without acknowledging that we hold them in higher estimation than the honor of God and the salvation of our souls.

A heathen could say, "It was a miserable thing to save life by giving up the only things which made life desirable!" And yet he and others like him never knew for what end men are placed in the world, and why they live in it. We know far better what the chief aim of life should be, namely, to glorify God, in order that he may be our glory. When this is not done, woe to us! We cannot continue to live for a single moment upon the earth without heaping additional curses on our heads. Still, we are not ashamed to purchase some few days to languish here below, renouncing the eternal kingdom by separating ourselves from him by whose energy we are sustained in life.

But as persecution is always harsh and bitter, let us consider, *How and By What Means Christians May Be Able to Fortify Themselves with Patience, so as Unflinchingly to Expose Their Lives for the Truth of God.* The text which we have read out, when it is properly understood, is sufficient to induce us to do so. The apostle says, "Let us go forth from the city after the Lord Jesus, bearing his reproach." In the first place, he reminds us, although the swords should not be drawn over us nor the fires kindled to burn us, we cannot be truly united to the Son of God while we are rooted in this world. Wherefore, a Christian, even in repose, must always have one foot lifted to march to battle, and not only so, but he must have his affections withdrawn from the world, although his body is dwelling in it.

Meanwhile, to solace our infirmities and mitigate the vexation and sorrow which persecution might cause us, a good reward is held forth. In suffering for the cause of God, we are walking step-by-step after the Son of God and have him for our guide. Were it simply said that to be Christians we must pass through all the insults of the world boldly, to meet death at all times and in whatever way God may be pleased to appoint, we might apparently have some pretext for replying. It is a strange road to go at a peradventure. But when we are commanded to follow the Lord Jesus, his guidance is too good and honorable to be refused.

Are we so delicate as to be unwilling to endure anything? Then we must renounce the grace of God by which he has called us to the hope of salvation. There are two things which cannot be separated—to be members of Christ and to be tried by many afflictions.

It were easy indeed for God to crown us at once without requiring us to sustain any combats; but as it is his pleasure that until the end of the world Christ shall reign in the midst of his enemies, so it is also his pleasure that we, being placed in the midst of them, shall suffer their oppression and violence till he deliver us. I know, indeed, that the flesh kicks when it is to be brought to this point, but still the will of God must have the mastery.

In ancient times, vast numbers of people, to obtain simple crowns of leaves, refused no toil, no pain, no trouble. It even cost them nothing to die, and yet every one of them gambled in a race, not knowing whether he was to gain or lose the prize. God holds forth to us the immortal crown by which we may become partakers of his glory. He does not mean us to fight at haphazard, but all of us have a promise of the prize for which we strive. Have we any cause then to decline the struggle? Do we think it has been said in vain, "If we die with Jesus Christ, we shall also live with him?" Our triumph is prepared, and yet we do all we can to shun the combat.

To leave no means which may be fitted to stimulate us unemployed, God sets before us *Promises* on the one hand, and *Threatenings* on the other. Do we feel that the promises have not sufficient influence, let us strengthen them by adding the threatenings. It is true we must be perverse in the extreme not to put more faith in the promises of God when the Lord Jesus says that he will own us as his before his Father, provided we confess him before men.

But if God cannot win us to himself by gentle means, must we not be mere blocks if his threatenings also fail? Jesus summons all those ,who from fear of temporal death shall have denied the truth, to appear at the bar of his Father, and says, that then body and soul will be consigned to perdition. In another passage he says he will disclaim all who shall have denied him before men. These words, if we are not altogether impervious to feeling, might well make our hair stand on end!

It is in vain for us to allege that pity should be strewn us, inasmuch as our natures are so frail; for it is said, on the contrary, that

Moses, having looked to God by faith, was fortified so as not to yield under any temptation. Wherefore, when we are thus soft and easy to bend, it is a manifest sign. I do not say that we have no zeal, no firmness, but that we know nothing either of God or his kingdom.

There are two points to be considered. The first is that the whole body of the church in general has always been, and to the end will be, liable to be afflicted by the wicked. Therefore, on seeing how the church of God is trampled upon in the present day by proud worldlings, how one barks and another bites, how they torture, how they plot against her, how she is assailed incessantly by mad dogs and savage beasts, let it remind us that the same thing was done in all the olden times.

Meanwhile, the issue of her afflictions has always been fortunate. At all events, God has caused that though she has been pressed by many calamities, she has never been completely crushed; as it is said, "The wicked with all their efforts have not succeeded in that at which they aimed." St. Paul glories in the fact and shows that this is the course which God in mercy always takes. He says, "We endure tribulations, but we are not in agony; we are impoverished, but not left destitute; we are persecuted, but not forsaken; cast down, but we perish not; bearing everywhere in our body the mortification of the Lord Jesus, in order that his life may be manifested in our mortal bodies" (2 Cor. 4:8–10).

I only touch on this article briefly to come to the second, which is more to our purpose, that *We Ought to Take Advantage of the Particular Examples of the Martyrs Who Have Gone Before Us.* These are not confined to two or three, but are, as the apostle says, "a great and dense cloud." By this expression, he intimates that the number is so great that it ought completely to engross our sight. Not to be tedious, I will only mention the Jews, who were persecuted for the true religion, not only under the tyranny of King Antiochus, but also a little after his death. We cannot allege that the number of sufferers was small, for it formed a large army of martyrs. We cannot say that it consisted of prophets whom God had set apart from common people, for women and young children formed part of the band. We cannot say that they got off at a cheap rate, for they were tortured as cruelly as it was possible to be. Accordingly, we hear what the apostle says, "Some were stretched out like drums, not caring to be delivered, that they might obtain a better resurrection; others were proved by mockery and blows, or bonds and prisons; others were stoned or sawn asunder; others traveled up and down, wandering among mountains and caves" (Heb. 11:35–38).

Let us now compare their case with ours. If they so endured for the truth, which was at that time so obscure, what ought we to do in the clear light which is now shining? God speaks to us with open mouth; the great gate of the kingdom of heaven has been opened, and Jesus Christ calls us to himself, after having come down to us that we might have him present to our eyes. What a reproach would it be to us to have less zeal in suffering for the gospel than those had who only hailed the promises afar off, who had only a little wicket opened whereby to come to the kingdom of God, and who had only some memorial and type of Jesus Christ? These things cannot be expressed in word as they deserve, and therefore I leave each to ponder them for himself.

In the first place, then, the Christian man, wherever he may be, must resolve, notwithstanding dangers or threatenings, to walk in simplicity as God has commanded. Let him guard as much as he can against the ravening of the wolves, but let it not be with carnal craftiness. Above all, let him place his life in the hands of God. Has he done so? Then if he happens to fall into the hands of the enemy, let him think that God, having so arranged, is pleased to have him for one of the witnesses of his Son. Therefore, he has no means of drawing back without breaking faith with him to whom we have promised all duty in life and in death, him whose we are and to whom we belong, even though we should have made no promise.

Let it be held, then, as a fixed point among all Christians that they ought not to hold their lives more precious than the testimony to the truth, inasmuch as God wishes to be glorified thereby. Is it in vain that he gives the name of *witnesses* (for this is the meaning of the word martyr) to all who have to answer before the enemies of the faith? Here every one is not to look for his fellow, for God does not honor all alike with the call. And as we are inclined to look, we must be the more on our guard against it. Peter having heard from the lips of our Lord Jesus that he should be led in his old age where he would not, asked what was to become of his companion John. There is not one of us who would not readily have put the same question, for the thought which instantly rises in our minds is, *Why do I suffer rather than others?* On the contrary, Jesus Christ exhorts all of us in common and each of us in particular to hold ourselves "ready," in order that according as he shall call this one or that one, we may march forth in our turn.

I explained above how little prepared we shall be to suffer martyrdom if we be not armed with the divine *Promises.* It now remains to show somewhat more fully *What the Purport and Aim of These Promises Are*—not to specify them all in detail, but to show the principal things which God wishes us to hope from him to console us in our afflictions. Now these things, taken summarily, are three. The first is, *That Inasmuch as Our Lives and Deaths Are in His Hand, He Will So Preserve Us by His Might That Not a Hair Will be Plucked Out of Our Heads Without His Leave.* Believers, therefore, ought to feel assured into whatever hands they may fall that God is not divested of the guardianship which he exercises over their persons. Were such a persuasion well imprinted on our hearts, we should be delivered from the greater part of the doubts and perplexities which torment us and obstruct us in our duties.

We see tyrants let loose; thereupon, it seems to us that God no longer possesses any means of saving us, and we are tempted to provide for our own affairs as if nothing more were to be expected from him. On the contrary, his providence, as he unfolds it, ought to be regarded by us as an impregnable fortress. Let us labor, then, to learn the full import of the expression that our bodies are in the hands of him who created them. For this reason, he has sometimes delivered his people in a miraculous manner and beyond all human expectation, as Shedrach, Meshach, and Abednego from the fiery furnace; Daniel from the den of lions; Peter from Herod's prison, where he was locked in, chained, and guarded so closely. By these examples, he meant to testify that he holds our enemies in check, although it may not seem so, and has power to withdraw us from the midst of death when he pleases. Not that he always does it, but in reserving authority to himself to dispose of us for life and for death, he would have us to feel fully assured that he has us under his charge. Whatever tyrants attempt and with whatever fury they may rush against us, it belongs to him alone to order our lives.

If he permits tyrants to slay us, it is not because our lives are not dear to him, and in greater honor an hundred times than they deserve. Such being the case, having declared by the mouth of David that the death of the saints is precious in his sight, he says also by the mouth of Isaiah that the earth will discover the blood which seems to be concealed. Let the enemies of the gospel, then, be as prodigal as they will of the blood of the martyrs, they shall have to render a fearful account of it even to its last drop. In the present day, they indulge in proud derision while consigning believers to the flames; and after having bathed in their blood, they are intoxicated by it to such a degree as to count all the murders which they commit mere festive sport. But if we have patience to wait, God will show in the end that it is not in vain he has taxed our lives at so high a value. Meanwhile, let it not offend us that it seems to confirm the gospel, which in worth surpasses heaven and earth.

To be better assured that God does not leave us forsaken in the hands of tyrants, let us remember the declaration of Jesus Christ, when he says that he himself is persecuted in his members. God had indeed said before by Zechariah, "He that toucheth you toucheth the apple of his eye" (Zech. 2:8). But here it is said much more expressly, that if we suffer for the gospel, it is as much as if the Son of God were suffering in person. Let us know, therefore, that Jesus Christ must forget himself before he can cease to think of us when we are in prison or in danger of death for his cause. Let us know that God will take to heart all the outrages which tyrants commit upon us, just as if they were committed on his own Son.

Let us now come to the second point which God declares to us in his promise for our consolation. It is, that *he will so sustain us by the energy of his Spirit that our enemies, do what they may, even with Satan at their head, will gain no advantage over us.* And we see how he displays his gifts in such an emergency; for the invincible constancy which appears in the martyrs abundantly and beautifully demonstrates that God works in them mightily. In persecution there are two things grievous to the flesh, the vituperation and insult of men and the tortures which the body suffers. Now, God promises to hold out his hand to us so effectually, that we shall overcome both by patience. What he thus tells us, he confirms by fact. Let us take this buckler, then, to ward off all fears by which we are assailed, and let us not confine the working of the Holy Spirit within such narrow limits as to suppose that he will not easily surmount all the cruelties of men. Of this we have had, among other examples, one which is particularly memorable. A young man who once lived with us here, having been apprehended in the town of Tournay, was condemned to have his head cut off if he recanted and to be burned alive if he continued steadfast to his purpose! When he was asked what he meant to do, he replied simply, "He who will give me grace to die patiently for his name, will surely give me grace to bear the fire!" We ought to take this expression, not as that of a mortal man, but as that of the Holy Spirit, to assure us that God is not less powerful to strengthen us and render us victorious over tortures, than to make us submit willingly to a milder death. Moreover, we oftentimes see what firmness he gives to unhappy malefactors who suffer for their crimes. I speak not of the hardened, but of those who derive consolation from the grace of Jesus Christ, and by this means, with peaceful hearts, undergo the most grievous punishments which can be inflicted. One beautiful instance is seen in the thief who was converted at the death of our Lord. Will God, who thus powerfully assists poor criminals when enduring the punishment of their misdeeds, be so wanting to his own people while fighting for his cause, as not to give them invincible courage?

The third point for consideration in the promises which God gives his martyrs is, *The fruit which they ought to hope for from their sufferings, and in the end, if need be, from their deaths.* Now, this fruit is that after having glorified his name, after having edified the church by their constancy, they will be gathered together with the Lord Jesus into his immortal glory. But as we have above spoken of this at some length, it is enough here to recall it to remembrance. Let believers, then, learn to lift up their heads toward the crowns of glory and immortality to which God invites them, that thus they may not feel reluctant to quit the present life for such a recompense. To feel well assured of this inestimable blessing, let them have always before their eyes the conformity which they thus have to our Lord Jesus Christ, beholding death in the midst of life, just as he, by the reproach of the Cross, attained to *the glorious Resurrection,* wherein consists all our felicity, joy, and triumph!

John Howe: *The Redeemer's Tears*

JOHN HOWE, THE GREAT PURITAN DIVINE, was born in 1630 and died in 1706. He was educated at Cambridge and was for a time fellow and chaplain at Magdalen College, Oxford. In 1656, he was appointed domestic chaplain to Oliver Cromwell, lord protector of England (1653–58). The reader of Howe's sermons will have some idea of how strongly religion gripped the minds of the Puritans of England when he reflects that it was such a preacher as this whom Cromwell chose for his chaplain. Although a man of great sincerity and courage, Howe was also a man of catholicity of spirit. Of one of his persecutors, he said that he expected to meet him one day in "that place where Luther and Zwingli well agreed." The sermons of the Puritan divines are marred by interminable divisions and subdivisions, and one tries in vain to conceive of the temper of the congregations which gladly tolerated such length, subtle analysis, pedantic allusion, and tiresome classification. Yet these Puritan divines were prophets of God and spoke to the conscience of the nation. Their sermons have strong intellectual fiber, elevation of thought, formidable logic, and true evangelical fervor. One of Howe's hearers, said of him, "He was so long laying the cloth that she always despaired of the dinner." But for those who have patience with his slowness of attack and his baffling and confusing divisions, the perusal of Howe will not be without profit. Because of the limitations of space, I have had to delete large portions from the sermon selected for this volume, "The Redeemer's Tears Over Lost Souls."

In the midst of this great reasoner's discourse, one comes upon not-to-be-forgotten sentences such as this, where he is urging the spiritually dry and barren to wrestle with God: "He hath smitten rocks ere now and made the waters gush out; nor is his hand shortened nor his ear heavy. The danger is not that he will be inexorable, but that thou shouldst." Or this on Christ's tears: "And remember that he who shed tears, did, from the same fountain of love and mercy, shed blood, too."

The Redeemer's Tears

And when he was come near, he beheld the city, and wept over it, saying, If thou hadst known, even thou, at least in this thy day, the things which belong unto thy peace! but now they are hid from thine eyes (Luke 19:41–42).

W E *have here* a compassionate lamentation in the midst of a solemn triumph. He beheld the city, 'tis said, and wept over it. Two things concur to make up the cause of this sorrow: The greatness of the calamity: Jerusalem, once so dear to God, was to suffer, not a scar, but a ruin. "The days shall come upon thee, that thine enemies shall cast a trench about thee, and compass thee round, and keep thee in on every side, and shall lay thee even with the ground, and thy children within thee; and they shall not leave in thee one stone upon another" (Luke 19:43–44). And the lost opportunity of preventing it: "If thou hadst known, even thou, at least in this thy day, the things which belong unto thy peace! but now they are hid from thine eyes." And again, "Thou knewest not the time of thy visitation" (v. 44).

First, the calamity was greater in his eyes than it can be in ours. His large and comprehensive mind could take the compass of this sad case. Our thoughts cannot reach far; yet we can apprehend what may make this case very deplorable. We can consider Jerusalem as the city of the great King, where was the palace and throne of the majesty of heaven, choosing to "dwell with men on earth." Here the divine light and glory had long shone; here was the sacred Shechinah, the dwelling place of the Most High, the symbols of his presence, the seat of worship, the mercy seat, the place of receiving addresses and of dispensing favors, "The house of prayer for all nations." To his own people, this was the city of their solemnities whither the tribes went up, the tribes of the Lord, unto the testimony of Israel, to give thanks unto the name of the Lord; for there were set thrones of judgment, the thrones of the house of David. He that was so great a lover of the souls of men, how grateful and dear to his heart had the place been where through the succession of many bypast ages the great God used (though more obscurely) to unfold his kind propensions towards sinners, to hold solemn treaties with them, to make himself known, to draw and allure souls into his own holy worship and acquaintance. And now the dismal prospect presents itself of desolation and ruin, ready to overwhelm all this glory and lay waste the dwellings of divine lover. His sorrow must be conceived proportionable to the greatness of this desolating change.

Secondly, the opportunity of prevention was lost. There was an opportunity: He was sent to "the lost sheep of the house of Israel." He came to them as his own. Had they received him, oh, how joyful a place had Jerusalem been! How glorious had the triumphs of God been there had they repented, believed, obeyed! These were the things that belonged "to their peace;" this was their opportunity, their "day of visitation." These were the things that might have been done within that day, but it was now too late; their day was over, and the things of their peace hid from their eyes. How fervent his desire that they had done otherwise, that they had taken the wise and safe course.

We may therefore thus sum up the meaning and sense of these words: It is a thing in itself very lamentable, and much lamented by our Lord Jesus, when people live under the gospel, have had a day of grace and an opportunity of knowing the things belonging to their peace, have so outworn that day and lost their opportunity that the things of their peace are quite hid from their eyes. We have these distinct heads of discourse to be considered and insisted on.

I. What are the things necessary to be known by such as live under the gospel, as immediately belonging to their peace? We willmore particularly inquire: what those things themselves are, and what sort of knowledge of them it is that here is meant and made necessary.

What the things are which belong to the peace of a people living under the gospel: The things belonging to a people's peace are not the same with all. Living, or not living, under the gospel makes a considerable difference in the matter. Before the incarnation and public appearance of our Lord, something was not necessary among the Jews that afterwards became necessary. It was sufficient to them before to believe in a Messiah to come, more indefinitely. Afterwards, he plainly tells them, "If ye believe not that I am he, ye shall die in your sins" (John 8:24). Believing in Christ cannot be necessary to pagans that never heard of him, *as a duty*, however necessary it may be *as a means*. Their not believing in him cannot be itself a sin, though by it they should want remedy for their other sins. But it more concerns us who do live under the gospel to apprehend aright what is necessary for ourselves. The gospel finds us in a state of apostasy from God, both as our sovereign Ruler and sovereign good, not apt to obey and glorify him, as the former, nor enjoy him and be satisfied in him, as the latter. Repentance towards God cures and removes this disaffection of our minds and hearts towards him under both these notions. By it the whole soul turns to him, with this sense and resolution: "I have been a rebellious, disloyal wretch against the high authority and most rightful government of him who gave me breath and whose creature I am. I will live no longer thus. Now I come back unto thee, oh Lord, thou art my Lord and God. Thee I now choose to serve and obey, as the Lord of my life. Thee I will fear, unto thee I subject myself to live no longer after my own will, but thine."

II. Such as live under the gospel have a day or a present opportunity for the obtaining the knowledge of these things immediately belonging to their peace and of whatever else is necessary. I say nothing about what opportunities they have who never lived under the gospel, who yet no doubt might generally know more than they do and know better what they do know. It is sufficient for us who enjoy the gospel to understand our own advantages. Nor, as to those who do enjoy it, is every one's day of equal clearness. How few in comparison have ever seen such a day as Jerusalem at this time did, made by the immediate beams of the Sun of righteousness, our Lord himself offering to be their instructor, so speaking as never man did with such authority as far outdid their other teachers and astonished the hearers. In what transports did he use to leave those who heard him, wheresoever he came, for they wondered at the gracious words that came out of his mouth. With what mighty and beneficial works did he recommend his doctrine, shining in the glorious power and savoring of the abundant mercy of heaven, so as every apprehensive mind might see the Deity was incarnate. God was come down to work with men and allure them into the knowledge and love of himself. No such day has been seen this many an age. Yet wherever the same gospel comes, it also makes a day of the same kind and affords always true, though diminished light, whereby, however, the things of our peace might be understood and known. For instance,

1. We have the true and distinct state of the quarrel between God and us. Pagans have understood somewhat of the apostasy of man from God, that he is not in the same state wherein he was at first. But while they have understood that something was amiss, they could scarce tell what. The gospel reveals the universal depravity of the degenerate nature of all men and of every faculty in man. The gospel pleads with men as rebels against their rightful Lord. But of this treason against the Majesty of heaven, men little suspect themselves till they are told. The gospel tells them so plainly and represents the matter in so clear light, that they need only to contemplate themselves in that light, and they may see that so it is. Men may indeed, by resolved,

stiff winking, create themselves a darkness amid the clearest light. But open thine eyes, man, thou who livest under the gospel, set thyself to view thine own soul, thou wilt find it is day with thee. Thou hast a day, by being under the gospel, and light enough to see that this is the posture of thy soul and the state of thy case towards God. And it is a great matter towards understanding the things of thy peace, to know what is the true state of the quarrel between God and thee.

2. The gospel affords light to know what the issue of this quarrel is sure to be, if it go on, and there be no reconciliation. It gives us other, plainer accounts of the punishment of the other world which more fully represent the extremity and perpetuity of the future miseries. These accounts help us understand what accession men's own unaltered, vicious habits will have to their miseries. Their own outrageous lusts and passions, which here they made it their business to satisfy, become their insatiable tormentors. Each will receive "the things done in his body, according to what he hath done" (2 Cor. 5:10). "Whatsoever a man soweth, that shall he also reap" (Gal. 6:7). What their own guilty reflections will contribute, the bitings and gnawings of the worm that dies not, the venomous corrosions of the viper bred in their own bosoms, now become a full-grown serpent; what the society and insultation of devils, with whom they are to partake in woes and torments and by whom they have been seduced and trained into that cursed partnership and communion.

3. It also represents God to you as reconcilable through a Mediator. In that gospel, peace is preached to you by Jesus Christ. That gospel lets you see God in Christ reconciling the world unto himself, that sin may not be imputed to them. That gospel proclaims glory to God in the highest, peace on earth, goodwill towards men. So did the voices of angels sum up the glad tidings of the gospel, when that Prince of Peace was born into the world. It tells you "God desires not the death of sinners, but that they may turn and live;" that

he would "have all men to be saved, and to come unto the knowledge of the truth" (1 Tim. 2:4).

III. This day hath its bounds and limits, so that when it is over and lost with such, the things of their peace are forever hid from their eyes. That this day is not infinite and endless, we see in the present instance. Jerusalem had her day; but that day had its period. We see it comes to this at last, that now the things of her peace are hid from her eyes. We generally see the same thing when sinners are so earnestly pressed to make use of the present time. "To day if ye will hear his voice, harden not your hearts" (Ps. 95:8), and quoted and urged in Hebrews 3:8. They are admonished to seek the Lord while he may be found, to call upon him while he is nigh. It seems sometimes he will not be found and will be afar off. They are told this is the accepted time, this is the day of salvation.

This day, with any place or people, supposes a precedent night when the dayspring from on high had not visited their horizon, and all within it sat in darkness and in the region and shadow of death. Yes, and there was a time, we know, of very general darkness, when the gospel day, "the day of visitation," had not yet dawned upon the world, times of ignorance, wherein God winked upon the nations of the earth; the beams of his eye did overshoot them. But when the eyelids of the morning open upon any people, and light shines to them with direct beams, they are now commanded to repent. They are limited to the present point of time with such peremptoriness as that noble Roman used towards a proud prince, asking time to deliberate upon the proposal made to him of withdrawing his forces that molested some of the allies of that state. He drew a line about him with the end of his rod and required him then, before he stirred out of that circle, to make his choice, whether he would be a friend or enemy to the people of Rome. So are sinners to understand the state of their own case. The God of thy life, sinner, in whose hands thy times are, doth with much higher right limit thee to the present time, and expects thy answer to his just and merciful offers and demands. He circumscribes thy day of grace; it is enclosed on both parts, and hath an evening as well as morning; as it had a foregoing, so hath it a subsequent night, and the latter, if not more dark, yet usually much more stormy than the former. God shuts up this day in much displeasure, which hath terrible effects. If it be not expressly told you what the condition of that night is that follows your gospel day; if the watchman being asked, "What of the night?" does only answer it cometh as well as the morning came, black events are signified by that more awful silence. Or 'tis all one if you call it *a day;* there is enough to distinguish it from the *day of grace.* The Scriptures call such a calamitous season indifferently either by the name of night or day; but the latter name is used with some or other adjunct to signify *day* is not meant in the pleasant or more grateful sense: a day of wrath, an evil day, a day of gloominess and thick darkness, not differing from the most dismal night; and to be told the morning of such a day is coming, is all one as that the evening is coming of a bright and a serene day.

1. That there is a great difference between the ends and limits of the day or season of grace as to particular persons and in reference to the collective body of a people inhabiting a place.

2. As to both there is a difference between the ending of such a day, intermissions or dark intervals that may be in it. The gospel may be withdrawn from such a people and be restored.

3. As to particular persons, there may be much difference between such as, while they lived under the gospel, gained the knowledge of the principal doctrines or of the sum or substance of Christianity, though without any sanctifying effect or impression upon their hearts, and such as, through their own negligence, lived under it in total ignorance hereof. The day of grace may not be over with the former,

though they should never live under the ministry of the gospel again. Whereas, with the other sort, when they no longer enjoy the external means, the day of grace is likely to be over, so that there may be no more hope in their case than in that of pagans in the darkest parts of the world; and perhaps much less, as their guilt hath been much greater by their neglect of so great and important things.

IV. If with any that have lived under the gospel, their day is quite expired, and the things of their peace are now forever hid from their eyes. This is in itself a most deplorable case and is much lamented by our Lord Jesus himself. That the case is in itself most deplorable, who does not see? A soul lost, a creature capable of God, upon its way to him, near to the kingdom of God, shipwrecked in the port! Oh sinner, from how high a hope art thou fallen! Into what depths of misery and woe! And that it was lamented by our Lord is in the text. He beheld the city, and wept over it.

And now let us consider what use is to be made of all this. Though nothing can be useful to the persons themselves, whom the Redeemer thus laments as lost, yet that he does so, may be of great use to others.

Use, which will partly concern those who do justly apprehend this is not their case and partly such as may be in great fear that it is.

For such as have reason to persuade themselves it is not their case: The best ground upon which any can confidently conclude this is that they have in this their present day, through the grace of God, already effectually known the things of their peace, such as have sincerely, with all their hearts and souls, turned to God, taken him to be their God, and devoted themselves to him, to be his; in trusting and subjecting themselves to the saving mercy and governing power of the Redeemer, according to the tenor of the gospel covenant, from which they do not find their hearts to swerve or decline, but resolve, through divine assistance, to persevere herein all their days. Now for such as with whom things are already brought to that comfortable conclusion, I only say to them:

Rejoice and bless God that so it is. Christ your Redeemer rejoices with you, and over you; you may collect it from his contrary resentment of their case who are past hope; if he weep over them, he, no doubt, rejoices over you. There is joy in heaven concerning you. Angels rejoice, your glorious Redeemer presiding in the joyful concert. And should not you rejoice for yourselves?

Demean yourselves with that care, caution, and dutifulness that become a state of reconciliation. Realize that your present peace and friendship with God is not original and continued from thence, but hath been interrupted and broken; that your peace is not that of constantly innocent persons. You stand not in this good and happy state because you never offended, but as being reconciled, and who therefore were once enemies. And when you were brought to know in your day, which you have enjoyed, the things belonging to your peace, you were made to feel the smart and taste the bitterness of your having been alienated and enemies in your minds by wicked works. When the terrors of God surrounded you and his arrows stuck fast in you, did you not then find trouble and sorrow? Were you not in a fearful expectation of wrath and fiery indignation to consume and burn you up as adversaries? Would you not then have given all the world for a peaceful word or look, for any glimmering hope of peace? How wary and afraid should you be of a new breach! How you should study acceptable deportments, and to walk worthy of God unto all well-pleasing! How strictly careful should you be to keep faith with him, and abide steadfast in his covenant! How concerned for his interest and in what agonies of spirit when you behold the eruptions of enmity against him from any others, not from any distrust or fear of final prejudice to his interest, but from the apprehension of the unrighteousness of the thing itself, and a dutiful love to his name, throne, and government. How zealous should you be to draw in others! How fervent in your endeavors within your own sphere, and how large in your desires extended as far as the sphere of the universe that every knee might bow to him, and every tongue confess to him!

Most earnestly cry to God and plead with him for his Spirit, by whom the vital unitive bond must be contracted between God and Christ and your souls. So this will be the covenant of life and peace. Lord! How generally do the Christians of our age deceive themselves with a self-sprung religion! Divine indeed in the institution, but merely human, in respect of the radication and exercise; in which respects also it must be divine or nothing. What, are we yet to learn that a divine power must work and form our religion in us, as well as divine authority direct and enjoin it? Do all such Scriptures go for nothing that tell us it is God who must create new hearts and renew right spirits in us; that he must turn us, if ever we be turned; that we can never come to Christ except the Father draw us? Nor is there any cause of discouragement in this if you consider what hath before been said in this discourse. "Ask and it shall be given you; seek, and ye shall find; knock, and it shall be opened unto you" (Luke 11:9). Your heavenly Father will give his Spirit to them that ask, more readily than parents do bread to their children, and not a stone. But what if you have to ask often and wait long, this but the more endears the gift, and shows the high value of it. You are to remember how often you have grieved, resisted, and vexed this Spirit, and that you have made God wait long upon you. What if the absolute sovereign Lord of all expects your attendance upon him? He waits to be gracious, and blessed are they who wait for him. Renew your applications to him. Lay from time to time that covenant before you, which yourselves must be come to a full, entire closure with. And if it is not done at one time, try yet if it will another, and try again and again. Remember it is for your life, for your soul, for your all. But do not satisfy yourself with only such faint motions within thee, as may only be the effects of thy own spirit, of thy dark, dull, listless, sluggish, dead, hard heart, at least not of the efficacious, regenerating influence of the divine Spirit. Didst thou never hear what mighty workings have been in others when God hath been transforming, renewing them, and drawing them into living union with his Son, and himself through him? What an amazing penetrating light hath struck into their hearts, such as when he was making the world, enlightening the chaos. Such as hath made them see things that concerned them as they truly were, and with their own proper face, God, Christ, and themselves, sin and duty, heaven and hell, in their own true appearances. How effectually they have been awakened! How the terrors of the Almighty have beset and seized their souls! What agonies and pangs they have felt in themselves when the voice of God hath said to them, "Awake thou that sleepest, and arise from the dead, and Christ shall give thee light" (Eph. 5:14). How he hath brought them down at his feet, thrown them into the dust, broken them, melted them, made them abase themselves, loathe and abhor themselves, filled them with sorrow, shame, confusion, and with indignation towards their own guilty souls, habituated them to a severity against themselves, unto the most sharp, and yet most unforced self-accusations, self-judging, and self-condemnation. He has even made them lay claim to hell and confess the portion of devils belonged to them as their own most deserved portion. And if now their eyes have been directed towards a Redeemer, and any glimmering of hope hath appeared to them; if now they are taught to understand God saying to them, "Sinner, art thou yet willing to be reconciled and accept a Savior?" Oh the transport into which it puts them! This is life from the dead! What, is there hope for such a lost wretch as I? How tasteful now is that melting invitation! How pleasant an intimation doth it carry with it, "Come unto me, all ye that labour and are heavy laden, and I will give you rest" (Matt. 11:28). If the Lord of heaven and earth looks down from the throne of glory and says, "What! sinner, wilt thou despise my favor and pardon, my Son, thy mighty, merciful Redeemer, my grace and Spirit still?"—What can be the return of the poor abashed wretch, overawed by the glory of the divine majesty, stung with compunction, overcome with the intimation of kindness and love? "I have heard of thee by the hearing of the ear; but now mine eye seeth thee. Wherefore I abhor myself, and repent in dust and ashes" (Job 42:5–6). So inwardly is the truth of that word now felt, "That thou mayest remember and be confounded, and never open thy mouth any more because of thy shame, when I am pacified towards thee, for all that thou hast done, saith the Lord God." But sinner, wilt thou make a covenant with me and my Christ? Wilt thou take me for thy God, and him for thy Redeemer and Lord? And may I, Lord? Yet, may I? Oh admirable grace, wonderful sparing mercy that I was not thrown into hell at my first refusal. Yes, Lord, with all my heart and soul I renounce the vanities of an empty, cheating world and all the pleasures of sin. In thy favor stands my life. Whom have I in heaven but thee? and there is none on earth that I desire beside thee" (Ps. 73:25). And oh, blessed Jesus, Prince of the kings of the earth, who hast loved me, and washed me from my sins in thy blood, and whom the eternal God hath exalted to be a Prince and a Savior, to give repentance and remission of sins, I fall before thee, my Lord and my God; I here willingly tender my homage at the footstool of thy throne. I take thee for the Lord of my life. I absolutely surrender and resign myself to thee. Thy love constrains me henceforth no more to live to myself, but to thee who died for me, and rose again. And I subject and yield myself to thy blessed light and power, Oh Holy Spirit of grace, to be more and more illuminated, sanctified, and prepared for every good word and work in this world, and for an inheritance among them that are sanctified in the other.

Sinner, never give thy soul permission to be at rest till you find it brought to some such transaction with God (the Father, Son, and Spirit) as this; so you can truly say, and feel thy heart is in it. Be not weary or impatient of waiting and striving, till thou canst say, this is now the very sense of thy soul. Such things have been done in the world; (but oh how seldom of latter days!) so God hath worked with men, to save them from going down to the pit, having found a ransom for them. And why may he not yet be expected to do so? He smote rocks before now and made the waters gush out; nor is his hand shortened, nor his ear heavy. The danger is not, sinner, that he will be inexorable, but less thou should. He will be entreated, if thou would be prevailed with to entreat his favor with thy whole heart.

Do not throw away the soul, and so great a hope, through mere sloth and loathness to be at some pains for thy life. Let the text, which hath been thy *directory* about the things that belong to thy peace, be also thy *motive,* so you can behold the Son of God weeping over such as would not know those things. Shall not the Redeemer's tears move thee? Oh hard heart! Consider what these tears import to this purpose:

1. They signify the real depth and greatness of the misery into which thou art falling. They drop from an intellectual and most comprehensive eye that sees far, pierces deeply into things, hath a wide and large prospect, and takes the comfort of that forlorn state into which unreconcilable sinners are hastening, in all the horror of it. The Son of God did not weep vain and causeless tears, or for a light matter; nor did he for himself either spend his own or desire the profusion of others' tears. "Weep not for me, oh daughters of Jerusalem." He knows the value of souls, the weight of guilt, and how low it will press and sink them; the severity of God's justice, the power of his anger, and what the fearful effects of them will be when they finally fall. If thou understandest not these things thyself, believe him that did. At least believe his tears.

2. They signify the sincerity of his love and pity, the truth and tenderness of his compassion. Canst thou think his tears deceitful, his who never knew guile? Was this like the rest of his course? And remember that he who shed tears, did, from the same fountain of love and mercy, shed blood, too. Was that also done to deceive? Thou makest thyself some very considerable thing indeed, if thou thinkest the Son of God counted it worth his while to weep, bleed, and die, to deceive thee into a false esteem of him and his love. But if it be the greatest madness imaginable to entertain any such thought, but that his tears were sincere and inartificial, the natural genuine expressions of undissembled benignity and pity, thou art then to consider what love and compassion thou art now sinning against, what bowels thou spurnest. If thou perish, 'tis under such guilt as the devils themselves are not liable to, who never had a Redeemer bleeding for them, nor, that we ever find, weeping over them.

3. They show the remedilessness of thy case, if thou persist in impenitency and unbelief till the things of thy peace be quite hid from thine eyes. These tears will then be the last issues of (even defeated) love, of love that is frustrated of its kind design. Thou mayst perceive in these tears the steady unalterable laws of heaven, the inflexibleness of the divine justice, that holds thee in unyielding bonds, and hath sealed thee up, if thou prove incurably obstinate and impenitent, unto perdition. So even the Redeemer himself, he that is mighty to save, cannot at length save thee, but only weep over thee, drop tears into thy flame, which assuage it not; but (though they have another design, even to express true compassion) do yet unavoidably heighten and increase the fervor of it, and will do so to all eternity. He even tells thee, sinner, "Thou hast despised my blood; thou shalt yet have my tears." What would have saved thee, now only lament thee lost.

But the tears wept over others, as lost and past hope, why should they not yet melt thee, while as yet there is hope in thy case? If thou be effectually melted in thy very soul, and looking to him whom thou hast pierced, do truly mourn over him, thou mayst assure thyself the prospect his weeping eye had of lost souls did not include thee. His weeping over thee would argue thy case forlorn and hopeless; thy mourning over him will make it safe and happy. That it may be so, consider further, that:

4. They signify how very intent he is to save souls and how gladly he would save thine, if yet thou wilt accept of mercy while it may be had. For if he weep over them that will not be saved, from the same love that is the spring of these tears, would saving mercies proceed to those who are become willing to receive them. And the love that wept over them who were lost, how will it glory in them who are saved! There his love is disappointed and vexed, crossed in its gracious intendment; but here having compassed it, how will he joy over thee with singing, and rest in his love! And thou also, instead of being involved with the unreconciled sinners of the old Jerusalem, shalt be enrolled among the glorious citizens of the new, and triumph together with them in eternal glory.

Robert South: *Man Created in God's Image*

ROBERT SOUTH WAS BORN at Hackney, England, in 1633, and died in 1716. He was as ignoble and contemptible in his public life as he was princely in his pulpit style. His first efforts were in praise of Cromwell and Presbyterianism, but with the Restoration he became the friend of royalty and the ridiculer of Puritanism. Whatever party was in power, South was able to hold his favor and secure promotion. But in spite of this deplorable lack of principle, South was a powerful preacher, or rather, sermonizer, for many of his sermons are destitute of religion. He had a keen, incisive way of putting things, for example, "All creation cracks and bends under the wrath of God." He was a superb handler of the English language, and his sermonic style has been justly admired. It is interesting to know that during the first years of his preaching, the sermons of South were the model for Henry Ward Beecher. In his *Yale Lectures on Preaching*, Beecher says: "I was a great reader of the old sermonizers. I read old Robert South through and through; I saturated myself with South; I formed much of my style and my handling of texts on his methods. I received a vast amount of instruction from others of those old sermonizers, who were as familiar to me as my own name. I preached a great many sermons while reading these old men, and upon their discourses I have founded the framework of my own. After I preached them, I said to myself, 'That will never do; I wouldn't preach that again for all the world.' But I was learning, and nobody ever tripped me up. Whales take in vast quantities of water for the sake of the animalcula it contains, and then blow out the water while keeping in the food. People do pretty much the same. They don't believe half you say. The part that is nutritious they keep, the rest they let alone."

The best known sermon of South is "Man in the Image of God." In this sermon appears the famous sentence, so often quoted: "An Aristotle was but the rubbish of an Adam, and Athens but the rudiments of paradise."

Man Created in God's Image

So God created man in his own image, in the image of God created he him (Gen. 1:27).

OW *hard it is* for natural reason to discover a creation before revealed, or being revealed to believe it. The strange opinions of the old philosophers and the infidelity of modern atheists are too sad a demonstration. To run the world back to its first original and infancy, and to view nature in its cradle, to trace the outgoings of the Ancient of Days in the first instance and specimen of his creative power, is a research too great for any mortal inquiry. And we might continue our scrutiny to the end of the world before natural reason would be able to find out when it began.

In this chapter, we have God surveying the works of the creation and leaving this general impress on character upon them, *that they were exceeding good.* What an omnipotence wrought, we have an omniscience to approve. But as it is reasonable to imagine that there is more of design, and consequently more of perfection, in the last work, we have God here giving his last stroke, and summing up all into man, the whole into a part, the universe into an individual. Whereas in other creatures we have but the trace of his footsteps, in man we have the draught of his hand. In him were united all the scattered perfections of the creature. All the graces and ornaments, all the airs and features of being were abridged into this small, yet full, system of nature and divinity; as we might well imagine that the great artificer would be more than ordinarily exact in drawing his own picture. It is, in short, that universal rectitude of all the faculties of the soul by which they stand apt and disposed to their respective offices and operations, which will be more fully set forth by taking a distinct survey of it, in the several faculties belonging to the soul.

I.   In the understanding.

II. In the will.

III. In the passions or affections.

I. First, for its noblest faculty, the understanding. It was then sublime, clear and aspiring, the soul's upper region, lofty and serene, free from the vapors and disturbances of the inferior affections. It was the leading, controlling faculty; all the passions wore the colors of reason; it did not so much persuade, as command; it was not consul, but dictator. Discourse was then almost as quick as intuition; it was nimble in proposing, firm in concluding; it could sooner determine than now it can dispute.

Now as there are two great functions of the soul, contemplation and practice, according to that general division of objects, some only entertain our speculation, others also employ our actions. So the understanding with relation to these, not because of any distinction in the faculty itself, is accordingly divided into speculative and practical, in both of which the image of God was then apparent.

Now it was Adam's happiness in the state of innocence to have these clear and unsullied. He came into the world a philosopher, which sufficiently appeared by his writing the nature of things upon their names; he could view essences in themselves and read forms without the comment of their respective properties; he could see consequents yet dormant in their principles, effects yet unborn, and in the womb of their causes; his understanding could almost pierce into future contingents, his conjectures improving even to prophecy, or the certainties of prediction; till his fall, he was ignorant of nothing but of sin; or at least he rested in the notion, without the smart of the experiment. Could any difficulty have been proposed, the resolution would

have been as early as the proposal; it could not have had time to settle into doubt. There was then no poring, no struggling with memory, no straining for invention. His faculties were quick and expedite;
they answered without knocking, they were ready upon the first
summons, there were freedom and firmness in all their operations. I
confess, it is difficult for us, who date our ignorance from our first
being, and were still bred up with the same infirmities about us with
which we were born, to raise our thoughts and imagination to those
intellectual perfections that attended our natures in the time of innocence, as it is for a peasant, bred in the obscurities of a cottage, to
fancy in his mind the unseen splendors of a court. But by rating pos-
itives by their privatives and other arts of reason by which discourse
supplies the want of the reports of sense, we may collect the excellency of the understanding then by the glorious remainders of it now, and
guess at the stateliness of the building by the magnificence of its
ruins. All those arts, rarities, and inventions which vulgar minds gaze
at, the ingenious pursue, and all admire, are but the relics of an intellect defaced with sin and time. We admire it now, only as antiquaries
do a piece of old coin, for the stamp it once bore and not for those vanishing lines and disappearing draughts that remain upon it at present. Certainly that must have been very glorious, the decays of which
are so admirable. He that is comely when old and decrepit surely was
very beautiful when he was young. An Aristotle was but the rubbish
of an Adam, and Athens but the rudiments of paradise.

The image of God was no less resplendent in that which we call
man's practical understanding; namely, that storehouse of the soul in
which are treasured up the rules of action and the seeds of morality.
We must observe that many who deny all connate notions in the
speculative intellect do yet admit them in this. Now of this sort are
these maxims: that God is to be worshiped; that parents are to be

honored; that a man's word is to be kept, which being of universal influence as to the regulation of the behavior and converse of mankind, are the ground of all virtue and civility and the foundation of religion.

It was the privilege of Adam innocent to have these notions also firm and untainted, to carry his monitor in his bosom, his law in his heart, and to have such a conscience as might be its own casuist: and certainly those actions must needs be regular where there is an identity between the rule and the faculty. His own mind taught him a due dependence upon God, and chalked out to him the just proportions and measures of behavior to his fellow creatures. He had no catechism but the creation, needed no study but reflection, read no book but the volume of the world, and that too, not for rules to work by, but for objects to work upon. Reason was his tutor and first principles his *magna moralia*. The Decalogue of Moses was but a transcript, not an original. All the laws of nations and wise decrees of states, the statutes of Solomon and the twelve tables, were but a paraphrase upon this standing rectitude of nature, this fruitful principle of justice, that was ready to run out and enlarge itself into suitable determinations upon all emergent objects and occasion. Justice then was neither blind to discern, nor lame to execute. It was not subject to be imposed upon by a deluded fancy, nor yet to be bribed by a glozing appetite, to turn the balance to a false and dishonest sentence. In all its directions of the inferior faculties, it conveyed its suggestions with clearness, and enjoined them with power; it had the passions in perfect subjection; and though its command over them was but suasive and political, yet it had the force of coaction and despotical. It was not then, as it is now, where the conscience has only power to disapprove and to protest against the exorbitances of the passions, and rather to wish, than make, them otherwise. The voice of conscience now is low and weak, chastising the passions, as old Eli did his lustful, domineering sons: *Not so, my sons, not so;* but the voice of conscience then was not, This should, or This ought to be done; but, This *must,* This *shall be* done. It spoke like a legislator; the thing spoken was a law; and the manner of speaking it a new obligation. In short, there was as great a disparity between the practical dictates of the understanding then and now as there is between empire and advice, counsel and command, between a companion and a governor.

And thus much for the image of God, as it shone in man's understanding.

II. Let us in the next place take a view of it, as it was stamped upon the will. The will of man in the state of innocence had an entire freedom, a perfect equipendency and indifference to either part of the contradiction, to stand or not to stand, to accept or not accept the temptation. I will grant the will of man now to be as much of a slave as anyone will have it, and be only free to sin; that is, instead of a liberty, to have only a licentiousness. Yet certainly this is not nature, but chance. We were not born crooked; we learnt these windings and turnings of the serpent; and therefore, it cannot but be a blasphemous piece of ingratitude to ascribe them to God and to make the plague of our nature the condition of our creation.

The will was then ductile and pliant to all the motions of right reason; it met the dictates of a clarified understanding halfway. And the active informations of the intellect, filling the passive reception of the will like form closing with matter, grew actuate into a third and distinct perfection of practice. The understanding and will never disagreed; for the proposals of the one never thwarted the inclinations of the other. Yet neither did the will servilely attend upon the understanding, but as a favorite does upon his prince, where the service is privilege and preferment; or as Solomon's servants waited upon him, it admired its wisdom, and heard its prudent dictates and counsels, both the direction and the reward of its obedience. It is indeed the nature of this faculty to follow a superior guide, to be drawn by the intellect; but then it was drawn as a triumphant chariot, which at the same time both follows and triumphs; while it obeyed this, it commanded the other faculties. It was subordinate, not enslaved to the understanding: not as a servant to a master, but as a queen to her king, who both acknowledges a subjection and yet retains a majesty.

Pass we now downward from man's intellect and will,

III. To the passions, which have their residence and situation chiefly in the sensitive appetite. For we must know that inasmuch as man is a compound and mixture of flesh as well as spirit, the soul, during its abode in the body, does all things by the mediation of these passions and inferior affections.

And first, for the grand leading affection of all, which is love. This is the great instrument and engine of nature, the bond and cement of society, the spring and spirit of the universe. Love is such an affection as cannot so properly be said to be in the soul as the soul to be in that. It is the whole man wrapped up into one desire; all the powers, vigor, and faculties of the soul abridged into one inclination. And it is of that active, restless nature that it must of necessity exert itself. Like fire, to which it is so often compared, it is not a free agent to choose whether it will heat or not, but it streams forth by natural results and unavoidable emanations. So it will fasten upon any inferior, unsuitable object, rather than none at all. The soul may sooner leave off to subsist than to love; like the vine, it withers and dies if it has nothing to embrace. Now this affection in the state of innocence was happily pitched upon its right object: it flamed up in direct fervors of devotion to God and in collateral emissions of charity to its neighbor. It was not then only another and more cleanly name for lust. It had none of those impure heats that both represent and deserve hell. It was a vestal and a virgin fire, and differed as much from that which usually passes by this name nowadays as the vital heat from the burning of a fever.

Then, for the contrary passion of hatred. This, we know, is the passion of defiance, and there is a kind of adversation and hostility included in its very essence and being. But then (if there could have been hatred in the world when there was scarce anything odious) it would have acted within the compass of its proper object, like aloes, bitter indeed, but wholesome. There would have been no rancor, no hatred of our brother; an innocent nature could hate nothing that was innocent. In a word, so great is the commutation that the soul then hated only that which now only it loves, that is, sin.

And if we may bring anger under this head, as being according to some a transient hatred, or at least very like it: this also, as unruly as now it is, yet then it vented itself by the measures of reason. There was no such thing as the transports of malice or the violences of revenge; no rendering evil for evil, when evil was truly a nonentity and nowhere to be found. Anger then was like the sword of justice, keen, but innocent and righteous. It did not act like fury, and then call itself zeal. It always espoused God's honor and never kindled upon anything but in order to a sacrifice. It sparkled like the coal upon the altar with the fervors of piety, the heats of devotion, the sallies and vibrations of an harmless activity. In the next place, for the lightsome passion of joy. It was not that which now often usurps this name—that trivial, vanishing, superficial thing, that only gilds the apprehension and plays upon the surface of the soul. It was not the mere crackling of thorns, a sudden blaze of the spirits, the exultation of a tickled fancy or a pleased appetite. Joy was then a masculine and a severe thing, the recreation of the judgment, the jubilee of reason. It was the result of a real good, suitably applied. It commenced upon the solidifies of truth and the substance of fruition. It did not run out in vice or undecent eruptions, but filled the soul, as God does the universe, silently and without noise. It was refreshing, but composed, like the pleasantness of youth tempered with the gravity of age, or the mirth of a festival managed with the silence of contemplation.

And, on the other side, for sorrow. Had any loss or disaster made but room for grief, it would have moved according to the severe allowances of prudence and the proportions of the provocation. It would not have sallied out into complaint or loudness, nor spread itself upon the face, and write sad stories upon the forehead. No wringing of the hands, knocking the breast, or wishing one's self unborn; all which are but the ceremonies of sorrow, the pomp and ostentation of an effeminate grief, which speak not so much the greatness of the misery as the smallness of the mind. Tears may spoil the eyes, but not wash away the affliction. Sighs may exhaust the man, but not eject the burden. Sorrow then would have been as silent as thoughts, as severe as philosophy. It would have rested in inward senses, tacit dislikes, and the whole scene of it been transacted in sad and silent reflections.

Then again for hope. Though indeed the fullness and affluence of man's enjoyments in the state of innocence might seem to leave no place for hope, in respect of any further addition, but only of the prorogation and future continuance of what already he possessed. Yet, doubtless God, who made no faculty but also provided it with a proper object upon which it might exercise and lay out itself, even in its greatest innocence, did then exercise man's hopes with the expectations of a better paradise, or a more intimate admission to himself. It is not imaginable that Adam could fix upon such poor, thin enjoyments as riches, pleasure, and the gaieties of an animal life. Hope indeed was always the anchor of the soul, yet certainly it was not to catch or fasten upon such mud. And if, as the apostle says, *no man hopes for that which he sees,* much less could Adam then hope for such things as he saw through.

And lastly, for the affection of fear. It was then the instrument of caution, not of anxiety; a guard, and not a torment to the breast that had it. It is now indeed an unhappiness, the disease of the soul; it flies from a shadow and makes more dangers than it avoids; it weakens the judgment and betrays the succors of reason, so hard is it to tremble and not to err, and to hit the mark with a shaking hand. Then it fixed upon him who is only to be feared, God; and yet with a filial fear, which at the same time both fears and loves. It was awe without amazement, dread without distraction. There was then a beauty even in this very paleness. It was the color of devotion, giving a luster to reverence and a gloss to humility.

Thus did the passions then act without any of their present jars, combats, or repugnances, all moving with the beauty of uniformity and the stillness of composure. Like a well-governed army, not for fighting, but for rank and order. I confess the Scriptures do not expressly attribute these several endowments to Adam in his first estate. But all that I have said, and much more, may be drawn out of that short aphorism, *God made man upright.* And since the opposite weaknesses now infest the nature of man fallen, if we will be true to the rule of contraries, we must conclude that those perfections were the lot of man innocent.

Now from this so exact and regular composure of the faculties, all moving in their due place, each striking in its proper time, there arose, by natural consequence, the crowning perfection of all, a good conscience. As in the body when the principal parts, as the heart and liver, do their offices and all the inferior, smaller vessels act orderly and duly, there arises a sweet enjoyment upon the whole, which we call health. So in the soul when the supreme faculties of the will and understanding move regularly, the inferior passions and affections following, there arises a serenity and complacency upon the whole soul, infinitely beyond the greatest bodily pleasures, the highest quintessence and elixir of worldly delights. There is in this case a kind of fragrancy and spiritual perfume upon the conscience, much like what Isaac spoke of his son's garments, *that the scent of them was like the smell of a field which the Lord had blessed.* Such a freshness and flavor is there upon the soul when daily watered with the actions of a virtuous life. Whatsoever is pure is also pleasant.

Having thus surveyed the image of God in the soul of man, we are not to omit now those characters of majesty that God imprinted upon the body. He drew some traces of his image upon this also, as much as a spiritual substance could be pictured upon a corporeal. Adam was then no less glorious in his externals; he had a beautiful body, as well as an immortal soul. The whole compound was like a well-built temple, stately without, sacred within. The elements were at perfect union and agreement in his body; and their contrary qualities served not for the dissolution of the compound, but the variety of the composure. Galen, who had no more divinity than what his physique taught him, barely upon the consideration of this so exact frame of the body, challenges anyone, upon an hundred years study, to find how any least fiber or most minute particle might be more commodiously placed, either for the advantage of use or comeliness. His stature erect and tending upwards to his center; his countenance majestic and comely, with the luster of a native beauty that scorned the poor assistance of art or the attempts of imitation; his body of such quickness and agility that it did not only contain, but also represent, the soul: for we might well suppose, that where God deposited so rich a jewel, he would suitably adorn the case. It was a fit workhouse for sprightly vivid faculties to exercise and exert themselves in. A fit tabernacle for an immortal soul, not only to dwell in, but to contemplate upon, where it might see the world without travel; it being a lesser scheme of the creation, nature contracted a little cosmography or map of the universe. Neither was the body then subject to illness, to die by piecemeal, and languish under coughs, catarrhs, or consumptions. Adam knew no disease, so long as temperance from the forbidden fruit secured him. Nature was his physician; and innocence and abstinence would have kept him healthful to immortality.

Now the use of this point might be various, but at present it shall be only this: to remind us of the irreparable loss that we sustained in our first parents, to show us of how fair a portion Adam disinherited his whole posterity by one single prevarication. Take the picture of a man in the greenness and vivacity of his youth and in the latter date and declensions of his drooping years, and you will scarce know it to belong to the same person; there would be more art to discern than at first to draw it. The same and greater is the difference between man innocent and fallen. He is a new kind or species; the plague of sin has even altered his nature and eaten into his very essentials. The image of God is wiped out, the creatures have shaken off his yoke, renounced his sovereignty, and revolted from his dominion. Disorders and diseases have shattered the excellent frame of his body; and, by a new dispensation, *immortality is swallowed up of mortality*. The same disaster and decay also has invaded his spirituals: the passions rebel, every faculty would usurp and rule, and there are so many governors that there can be no government. The light within us is become darkness, and the understanding that should be eyes to the blind faculty of the will is blind itself, and so brings all the inconveniences that attend a blind follower under the conduct of a blind guide. He that would have a clear, ocular demonstration of this, let him reflect upon that numerous litter of strange, senseless, absurd opinions, that crawl about the world, to the disgrace of reason and the unanswerable reproach of a broken intellect.

The two great perfections that both adorn and exercise man's understanding are philosophy and religion. For the first of these, take it even amongst the professors of it where it most flourished, and we shall find the very first notions of common sense debauched by them. For there have been such as have asserted that there is no such thing in the world as motion; the contradictions may be true. There has not been wanting one that has denied snow to be white. Such stupidity or wantonness had seized upon the most raised wits that it might be doubted whether the philosophers or the owls of Athens were the quicker-sighted. But then for religion; what prodigious, monstrous, misshapen births has the reason of fallen man produced! It is now almost six thousand years that far the greatest part of the world has had no other religion but idolatry: and idolatry certainly is the first—born of folly, the great and leading paradox; in fact, the very abridgment and sum total of all absurdities. Is it not strange that a rational man should worship an ox, no, the image of an ox, that he should fawn upon his dog, bow himself before a cat, adore leeks and garlic, and shed penitential tears at the smell of a deified onion? Yet so did the Egyptians, once the famed masters of all arts and learning. And to go a little further, we have yet a stranger instance in Isaiah: "[A man] heweth him down cedars . . . Then shall it be for a man to burn . . . and the residue thereof he maketh a god" (Isa. 44:14, 16–17). With one part he furnishes his chimney, with the other his chapel. A strange thing, that the fire must consume this part and then burn incense to that. As if there was more divinity in one end of the stick than in the other; or as if it could be graved and painted omnipotent, or the nails and the hammer could give it an apotheosis. So great is the change, so deplorable the degradation of our natures, that whereas before we bore the image of God, we now retain only the image of men.

In the last place, we learn from hence the excellency of Christian religion in that it is the great and only means that God has sanctified and designed to repair the breaches of humanity, to set fallen man upon his legs again, to clarify his reason, to rectify his will, and to compose and regulate his affections. The whole business of our redemption is, in short, only to rub over the defaced copy of the creation, to reprint God's image upon the soul, and to set forth nature in a second and a fairer edition.

The recovery of which lost image, as it is God's pleasure to command, and our duty to endeavor, so it is in his power only to effect.

Jonathan Edwards: *The Blessed Dead*

JONATHAN EDWARDS, THE MOST FAMOUS of American theologians and philosophers, was born at South Windsor, Connecticut, on the fifth of October, 1703, and died at Princeton, New Jersey, in 1758. His father was a minister and a graduate of Harvard College, and his mother a woman of extraordinary mentality and piety. As a child, Edwards gave full promise of his future achievements. At the age of ten, he wrote an essay on the immateriality of the soul, and at the age of twelve wrote what is said to be an excellent treatise on flying spiders. By the time of his graduation from Yale College, in 1720, he had dipped deep into the well of philosophy. After a brief service with a Presbyterian Church in New York and a few years as tutor at Yale College, he became the minister of the Congregational Church at Northampton, Massachusetts. There he married Sarah Pierrepont, a great-granddaughter of the celebrated Thomas Hooker. Very early in his preaching Edwards began to emphasize the high Calvinistic view of the sovereignty of God in the salvation of mankind. Under his preaching a notable revival broke out at Northampton, and from there spread through the colonies and was known as the Great Awakening. Edwards was the leader and defender of this famous revival. In 1749, after a dispute which had arisen over the matter of discipline for those who had been reading improper books, Edwards was deposed from his pulpit and congregation. From Northampton, he went to Stockbridge as village pastor and missionary to the Indians. It was here that, in four months' time, he wrote one of the world's great books and America's chief contribution to philosophy, *The Freedom of the Will*, in which he attempts to refute the doctrine of free will. In 1758, he succeeded his son-in-law, Aaron Burr, as president of

Princeton College, but had been in Princeton for only a few weeks when he died a victim to a scourge of smallpox.

His best known sermon is "Sinners in the Hands of an Angry God," on the text, "Their foot shall slide in due time" (Deut. 32:35). The sermon was preached at Enfield, Connecticut, as a warning and rebuke because of the outbreak of immorality. Edwards preached often on the goodness and the love of God; but whenever his name is mentioned, this is the sermon which men associate with him. There is much in the sermon which offends the religious sensibilities of our day, especially the description of God holding the sinner over hell as one would hold a spider or insect over a fire. No one could preach in those terms today. Yet the pendulum has swung too far in the other direction, and the preaching of today, dwelling exclusively upon the love of God, is hardly of a nature to produce repentance or to let men know that God is of purer eyes than to behold iniquity. Contemporary accounts of the preaching of the sermon tell of the deep impression it made and how the preacher had to stop several times and ask for silence on the part of the conscience-stricken, who were crying aloud in their distress.

For this volume, I have selected the sermon preached by Edwards at the funeral of the celebrated missionary to the Indians, David Brainerd, who died in Edwards' home at Northampton in 1747, and whose diary, now a missionary classic, was published by Edwards. This funeral sermon is a powerful statement of the Christian's hope concerning those who have fallen asleep.

The Blessed Dead

We are confident, I say, and willing rather to be absent from the body, and to be present with the Lord (2 Cor. 5:8).

HE apostle is here giving a reason why he went on with such immovable boldness and steadfastness, through such labors, sufferings, and dangers, in the service of the Lord, for which his enemies, the false teachers among the Corinthians, sometimes reproached him as being beside himself and driven on by a kind of madness. In the latter part of the preceding chapter, he informs the Christian Corinthians that the reason why he did thus was that he firmly believed the promises which Christ had made to his faithful servants of a glorious and eternal reward, and knew that these present afflictions were light and but for a moment in comparison of that far more exceeding and eternal weight of glory. In this chapter, he further insists on the reason of his constancy in suffering and exposing himself to death in the work of the ministry, even the more happy state which he expected after death. This is the subject of the text.

The souls of Christians, when they leave the body, go to be with Christ. They do this in the following respects:

I. They go to live in the same blessed abode with the glorified human nature of Christ.

The human nature of Christ is yet in being. He still continues, and will continue to all eternity, to be both God and man. His whole human nature remains, not only his soul, but also his body. His body rose from the dead; and the same that was raised from the dead is exalted and glorified at God's right hand. That which was dead is now alive and lives forevermore.

There is therefore a certain place, a particular part of the external creation, to which Christ is gone and where he remains. This place is the heaven of heavens, a place beyond all the visible heavens. "Now that he ascended, what is it but that he also descended first into the lower parts of the earth? He that descended is the same also that ascended up far above all heavens" (Eph. 4:10). This is the same which the apostle calls the third heaven: reckoning the aerial heaven as the first, the starry heaven as the second, and the highest heaven as the third. This is the abode of the holy angels; they are called "the angels of heaven," "the angels which are in heaven," "the angels of God in heaven." They are said always to behold the face of the "Father which is in heaven." They are elsewhere often represented as before the throne of God or surrounding his throne in heaven, and sent from there, and descending from there on messages to this world. Thither it is that the souls of departed saints are conducted when they die. They are not reserved in an abode distinct from the highest heaven, a place of rest, which they are kept in till the day of judgment, which some call the Hades of the happy; but they go directly to heaven itself. This is the saints' home, being their Father's house. They are "pilgrims and strangers" on the earth, and this is the "other and better country" to which they are traveling. This is the city to which they belong, "our conversation [citizenship, as the word properly signifies] is in heaven" (Phil. 3:20). Therefore, this undoubtedly is the place to which the apostle refers when he says, "We are willing to forsake our former house, the body, and to dwell in the same house, city or country, wherein Christ dwells," which is the proper import of the words of the original. What can this house, city, or country be but that house which is elsewhere spoken of as their proper home, their Father's house, the city and country to which they properly belong, towards which they are traveling all the while they continue in this world, and the house, city, and country where we know the human nature of Christ is. This is the saints' rest, here their hearts are while they live, and here their treasure is, the "inheritance incorruptible, and undefiled, and that fadeth not away," that is designed for them, is reserved in heaven (1 Pet. 1:4). Therefore, they never can have their proper and full rest till they come there. Undoubtedly, their souls, when absent from the body (the Scriptures represent them as in a state of perfect rest) arrive there. Those two saints who left this world to go to their rest in another world without dying,Enoch and Elijah, went to heaven. Elijah was seen ascending up to heaven, as Christ was; and to the same resting place, is there all reason to think, to which those saints go,who leave the world to go to their rest by death. Moses, when he died in the top of the mount, ascended to the same glorious abode with Elijah, who ascended without dying. They are companions in another world, as they appeared together at Christ's transfiguration. They were together at that time with Christ in the mount when there was a representation of his glory in heaven. Doubtless, also, they were together afterwards with him when he was actually glorified in heaven. There, undoubtedly, it was that the soul of Stephen ascended when he expired. The circumstances of his death demonstrate it, as we have an account of it. "He, being full of the Holy Ghost, looked up steadfastly into heaven, and saw the glory of God, and Jesus standing on the right hand of God, and said, Behold, I see the heavens opened, and the Son of man [i. e., Jesus in his human nature], standing on the right hand of God. Then they cried out with a loud voice, and stopped their ears, and ran upon him with one accord, and cast him out of the city, and stoned him: . . . And they stoned Stephen, calling upon God, and saying, Lord Jesus, receive my spirit" (Acts 7:55–59). Before his death, he had an extra-ordinary view of the glory which his Savior had received in heaven, not only for himself, but for him and all his faithful followers, that he might be encouraged by the hopes of this glory cheerfully to lay down his life for his sake. Accordingly, he dies in the hope of this, say-ing, "Lord Jesus, receive my spirit." By which doubtless he meant,

"Receive my spirit to be with you, in that glory wherein I have now seen you in heaven at the right hand of God." Thither it was that the soul of the penitent thief on the cross ascended. Christ said to him, "Today shalt thou be with me in paradise" (Luke 23:43). Paradise is the same with the third heaven, as appears by 2 Corinthians 12:2–4. There, that which is called the third heaven in the second verse, in the fourth verse is called paradise. The departed souls of the apostles and prophets are in heaven, as is manifest from the words, "Rejoice over her, thou heaven, and ye holy apostles and prophets" (Rev. 18:20). The church of God is distinguished in Scripture from time to time into these two parts: that part of it which is in heaven and that which is in earth—"Jesus Christ, of whom the whole family in heaven and earth is named" (Eph. 3:15). "And, having made peace through the blood of his cross, by him to reconcile all things to himself; by him, I say, whether they be things in earth, or things in heaven" (Col. 1:20). Now what "things in heaven" are they for whom peace has been made by the blood of Christ's cross, and who have by him been reconciled to God, but the saints in heaven? In like manner we read of God's gathering "together in one all things in Christ, both which are in heaven, and which are on earth; even in him" (Eph. 1:10). The "spirits of just men made perfect" are in the same "city of the living God" with the "innumerable company of angels" and "Jesus the mediator of the new covenant," as is manifest. The church of God is often in Scripture called by the name of Jerusalem, and the apostle speaks of the Jerusalem "which is above" or "which is heaven" as the mother of us all; but if no part of the church be in heaven, or none but Enoch and Elias, it is not likely that the church would be called the Jerusalem which is in heaven.

II. They go to dwell in the immediate, full, and constant sight or view of Christ.

When we are absent from our dear friends, they are out of sight, but when we are with them, we have the opportunity and satisfaction of seeing them. While the saints are in the body and are absent from the Lord, he is in several respects out of sight, "whom having not seen, ye love; in whom, though now ye see him not, yet believing" (1 Pet. 1:8). They have indeed in this world a spiritual sight of Christ, but they see "through a glass darkly" and with great interruption; but in heaven they see him "face to face." The pure in heart are blessed; for they shall see God. Their beatifical vision of God is in Christ, who is that brightness or effulgence of God's glory by which his glory shines forth in heaven, to the view of saints and angels there, as well as here on earth. This is the Sun of Righteousness, who is not only the light of this world, but is also the sun which enlightens the heavenly Jerusalem, by whose bright beams the glory of God shines forth, to the enlightening and making happy of all the glorious inhabitants. "The glory of God did lighten it, and the Lamb is the light thereof" (Rev. 21:23). No one sees God the Father immediately. He is the King eternal, immortal, invisible. Christ is the image of that invisible God by which he is seen by all elect creatures. The only begotten Son who is in the bosom of the Father, he has declared him and manifested him. No one has ever immediately seen the Father but the Son; and no one else sees the Father in any other way than by the Son's revealing him. In heaven, the spirits of just men made perfect see him as he is. They behold his glory. They see the glory of his divine nature, consisting in all the glory of the Godhead, the beauty of all his perfections; his great majesty and almighty power; his infinite wisdom, holiness, and grace. They see the beauty of his glorified human nature and the glory which the Father has given him, as God-man and Mediator. For this end Christ desired that his saints might be with him, that they might behold his glory. When the souls of the saints leave their bodies to go to be with Christ, they behold the glory of the work of Redemption, "which the angels desire to look into." They have the clearest view of the unfathomable depth of the wisdom and knowledge of God and the brightest displays of the purity and holiness of God which appears in that work. They see in a far clearer manner than the saints do here "what is the breadth, and length, and depth, and height: and to know the love of Christ," appearing in his redemption (Eph. 3:18–19). As they see the unspeakable riches and glory of God's grace, so they clearly understand Christ's eternal and immeasurable love to them in particular. In short, they see everything in Christ which tends to inflame and gratify love in the most clear and glorious manner, without any darkness or delusion, without any impediment or interruption. Now the saints, while in the body, see somewhat of Christ's glory and love; as we, in the dawn of the morning, see somewhat of the reflected light of the sun mingled with darkness. But when separated from the body, they see their glorious and loving Redeemer as we see the sun when risen above the horizon, by his direct beams in a clear hemisphere and with perfect day.

III. They are brought into a perfect conformity to, and union with, Christ.

Their spiritual conformity is begun while they are in the body. Here, "beholding as in a glass the glory of the Lord, [they] are changed into the same image" (2 Cor. 3:18). But when they come to see him as he is in heaven, then they become like him in another manner. That perfect sight will annihilate all remains of deformity and sinful unlikeness, as all darkness is annihilated before the full blaze of the sun's meridian light. It is impossible that the least degree of obscurity should remain before such light; so it is impossible the least degree of sin and spiritual deformity should remain in such a view of the spiritual beauty and glory of Christ as the saints enjoy in heaven. When they see the Sun of Righteousness without a cloud, they themselves shine forth as the sun and shall be themselves as suns without a spot. Then Christ presents his saints to himself in glorious beauty, "not having spot, or wrinkle, or any such thing" (Eph. 5:27) and having holiness without a blemish. Then their union with Christ is perfected. This also is begun in this world. The relative union is both begun and perfected at once when the soul first closes with Christ by faith. The real union, consisting in the union of heart and affection, is begun in this world and perfected in the next. The union of the heart of a believer to Christ is begun when his heart is drawn to Christ by the first discovery of his divine excellence at conversion. Consequent on this is established a vital union with Christ whereby the believer becomes a living branch of the true vine, living by a communication of the sap and vital juice of the stock and root; a member of Christ's mystical body living by a communication of spiritual and vital influences from the head and by a participation of Christ's own life. But while the saints are in the body, there is much remaining distance between Christ and them. The vital union is very imperfect and so is the communication of spiritual life and vital influence. There is much between Christ and believers to keep them asunder, much indwelling sin; much temptation; a heavy-molded, frail body; and a world of carnal objects to keep the soul from Christ and to hinder a perfect coalescence. But when the soul leaves the body, all these hindrances are removed. Every separating wall is broken down, every impediment is taken out of the way, and all distance ceases; the heart is wholly and perfectly drawn and firmly and forever bound to Christ by a perfect view of his glory. The vital union is then brought to perfection. The soul lives perfectly in and upon Christ, being perfectly filled with his Spirit and animated by his vital influence, living as it were only by Christ's life, without any reminder of spiritual death or carnal life.

IV. They enjoy a glorious and immediate intercourse and conversation with Christ.

While we are present with our friends, we have opportunity for a free and immediate conversation with them, which we cannot have when absent. Therefore, by reason of the far more free, perfect, and immediate intercourse with Christ which the saints enjoy when absent from the body, they are properly represented as present with him.

The most intimate intercourse becomes that relation in which the saints stand to Jesus Christ, and especially becomes that perfect and glorious reunion into which they shall be brought with him in heaven. They are not merely his servants, but his friends, his brethren, and companions, yes, they are the Spouse of Christ. They are espoused or betrothed to Christ while in the body, but when they go to heaven their marriage with him is come, and the King brings them into his palace. Christ conversed in the most friendly manner with his disciples on earth and admitted one of them to lean on his bosom, but they are admitted much more fully and freely to converse with him in heaven. Though Christ be there in a state of glorious exaltation, reigning in the majesty and glory of the sovereign Lord and God of heaven and earth, of angels, and men, yet this will not hinder the intimacy and freedom of their intercourse but will rather promote it. He is thus exalted, not only for himself, but for them. He is Head over all things for their sakes, that they may be exalted and glorified; and, when they go to heaven where he is, they are exalted and glorified with him and shall not be kept at a greater distance. They shall be unspeakably more fit for it, and Christ will be in more fit circumstances to bestow on them this blessedness. Their seeing the great glory of their friend and Redeemer will not awe them to a distance and make them afraid of a near approach; but on the contrary, will most powerfully draw them near and encourage and engage them to holy freedom. They will know that he is their own Redeemer and beloved friend, the very same who loved them with a dying love and redeemed them to God by his blood. "It is I; be not afraid" (Matt. 14:27). "Fear not; . . . I am he that liveth and was dead" (Rev. 1:17–18). The nature of this glory of Christ which they shall see will be such as will draw and encourage them, for they will not only see infinite majesty and greatness, but infinite grace, condescension, gentleness, and sweetness, equal to his majesty. He appears in heaven not only as "the Lion of the tribe of Judah" (Rev. 5:5) but as "the Lamb which is in the midst of the throne." This Lamb shall be their shepherd, to "feed them, and shall lead them unto living fountains of waters" (Rev. 7:17). The sight of Christ's majesty will be no terror to them, but will only serve the more to heighten their pleasure and surprise. When Mary Magdelene was about to embrace Christ, being full of joy at seeing him again alive after his crucifixion, Christ forbids her to do it for the present, because he was not yet ascended. "Jesus saith unto her, Mary. She turned herself, and saith unto him, Rabboni; which is to say, Master. Jesus saith unto her, Touch me not; for I am not yet ascended to my Father: but go to my brethren, and say unto them, I ascend unto my Father, and your Father; and to my God, and your God" (John 20:16–17). As if he had said, "This is not the time and place for that freedom which your love to me desires. That is appointed in heaven after my ascension. I am going there, and you who are my true disciples shall, as my brethren and companions, soon be there with me in my glory." That is the place appointed for the most perfect expressions of complacence and endearment. Accordingly, the souls of departed saints in heaven find Christ manifesting those infinite riches of love towards them which he has felt from eternity; and they are enabled to express their love to him in an infinitely better manner than they could while in the body. Thus they shall be eternally encompassed by the infinitely bright, mild, and sweet beams of divine love, eternally receiving that light and forever reflecting it to the fountain.

V. They are received to a glorious fellowship with Christ in his blessedness.

The saints in heaven have communion with Christ in his glory and blessedness in heaven in the following respects:

1. They partake with him in the ineffable delights which he has in heaven in the enjoyment of his Father.

When Christ ascended to heaven, he was received to a peculiar blessedness in the enjoyment of his Father, who in his passion hid his face from him; such an enjoyment as became the relation in which he stood to the Father; and such as was a suitable reward for the great and difficult service which he had performed on earth. Then God showed him the path of life, and brought him into his presence, where is fullness of joy, and to sit on his right hand, where there are pleasures for evermore as is said of Christ (see Ps. 16:11). Then the Father made him most blessed forever; he made him exceeding glad with his countenance. The saints by their union with Christ partake of his childlike relation to the Father and are heirs with him of his happiness in the enjoyment of his Father, as seems to be intimated by the apostle and by the psalmist: "They shall be abundantly satisfied with the fatness of thy house; and thou shalt make them drink of the river of thy pleasures. For with thee is the fountain of life: in thy light shall we see light" (Ps. 36:8–9). The saints shall have pleasure in partaking with Christ in his pleasure and shall see light in his light. They shall partake with Christ of the same river of pleasure, shall drink of the water of life and of the same new wine in his Father's kingdom. That new wine is especially that joy and happiness which Christ and his true disciples shall partake of together in glory; which is the purchase of Christ's blood or the reward of his obedience unto death. Christ at his ascension into heaven received everlasting pleasures at his Father's right hand in the enjoyment of his Father's love as the reward of his own obedience unto death. But the same righteousness is reckoned both to the Head and the members; and both shall have fellowship in the same reward, each according to his distinct capacity.

That the saints in heaven thus partake with Christ in his own enjoyment of the Father manifests the transcendent excellence of their happiness and their being admitted to a vastly higher privilege in glory than the angels.

2. They partake with Christ in the glory of that dominion to which the Father has exalted him.

The saints, when they ascend to heaven and are made to sit together with Christ in heavenly places, are exalted to reign with him. They are through him made kings and priests and reign with him and in him over the same kingdom. As the Father has appointed unto him a kingdom, so he has appointed it to them. The Father has appointed the Son to reign over his own kingdom, and the Son appoints his saints to reign in his. The saints in heaven are with the angels, the King's ministers, by whom he manages the affairs of his kingdom and who are continually ascending and descending from heaven to earth and daily employed as ministering spirits to each individual member of the church below; beside the continual ascending of the souls of departed saints from all parts of the militant church. They have as much greater advantage to view the state of Christ's kingdom and the works of the new creation here than they had while in this world, as a man who ascends to the top of a high mountain has greater advantage to view the face of the earth than he had while he was in a deep valley or thick forest below, surrounded on every side with those things which impeded and limited his sight. Nor do they view them as indifferent or unconcerned spectators any more than Christ himself is an unconcerned spectator. The happiness of the saints in heaven consists very much in beholding the glory of God appearing in the work of Redemption, for it is by this chiefly that God manifests his glory, the glory of his wisdom, holiness, grace, and other perfections, to both saints and angels, as is apparent by many scriptures. Hence, undoubtedly, much of their happiness consists in beholding the progress of this work in its application, success, and the steps by which infinite power and wisdom brings it to its consummation. They are under unspeakably greater advantages to enjoy the progress of this work than we are, as they are under greater advantages to see and understand the marvelous steps which divine wisdom takes in all that is done and the glorious ends he obtains; the opposition Satan makes and how he is baffled and overthrown. They can better see the connection of one event with another and the beautiful order of all things which come to pass in the church in different ages that to us appear like confusion. Nor do they only view these things and rejoice in them as a glorious and beautiful sight, but as persons interested, as Christ is interested, as possessing these things in Christ and reigning with him in his kingdom. Christ's success in his work of redemption, in bringing home souls to himself, applying his saving benefits by his Spirit and the advancement of the kingdom of grace in the world, is the reward especially promised to him by his Father in the covenant of redemption, for the hard and difficult service which he performed while in the form of a servant. But the saints shall partake with him in the joy of this reward, for this obedience which is thus rewarded is reckoned to them as they are his members.

Thus, Abraham enjoys these things when they come to pass, which were of old promised to him, which he saw beforehand and in which he rejoiced. He will enjoy the fulfillment of the promise that all the families of the earth should be blessed in his seed when it shall be accomplished. All the ancient patriarchs who died believing in the promises of glorious things to be accomplished in this world, who had not received the promises, but saw them afar off and were persuaded of them and embraced them, do actually enjoy them when fulfilled. David saw and enjoyed the fulfillment of that promise in its due time which was made to him many hundred years before and was all his salvation and all his desire. Thus Daniel shall stand in his lot at the end of the days pointed out by his own prophecy. Thus the saints of old who died in faith, not having received the promise, are made perfect and have their faith crowned by the better things accomplished in these latter days of the gospel, which they see and enjoy in their time.

3. They have fellowship with Christ in his blessed and eternal employment of glorifying the Father.

When Christ instituted the Lord's Supper and ate and drank with his disciples at his table, giving them therein a representation and pledge of their future feasting with him and drinking new wine in his heavenly Father's kingdom, he at that time led them in their praises to God in the hymn which they sang. So, doubtless, he leads his glorified disciples in heaven. David, as the sweet psalmist of Israel, led the great congregation of God's people in their songs of praise. In this, as in innumerable other things, he was a type of Christ who is often spoken of in Scripture by the name of David. Many of the psalms which David penned were songs of praise, which he by the spirit of prophecy uttered in the name of Christ, as Head of the church and leading the saints in their praises. Christ in heaven leads the glorious assembly in their praises to God as Moses did the congregation of Israel at the Red Sea, which is implied in its being said that "they sing the song of Moses and the Lamb." John tells us that he heard a voice come out of the throne, saying, "Praise our God, all ye his servants, and ye that fear him, both small and great" (Rev. 19:5). Who can it be that utters this voice out of the throne but "the Lamb who is in the midst of the throne" calling on the glorious assembly of saints to praise his Father and their Father, his God and their God? What the consequence of this voice is, we learn in the following words: "And I heard as it were the voice of a great multitude, and as the voice of many waters, and as the voice of mighty thunderings, saying, Alleluia: for the Lord God omnipotent reigneth" (Rev. 19:6).

The subject which we have been considering may be usefully applied in the way of exhortation. Let us all be exhorted earnestly to seek after that great privilege which has been spoken of, that when we are "absent from the body, [we may] be present with the Lord" (2 Cor. 5:8). We cannot continue always in these earthly tabernacles. They are very frail and will soon decay and fall, and are continually liable to be overthrown by innumerable means. Our souls must soon leave them and go into the eternal world. Oh how infinitely great will be the privilege and happiness of those who at that time shall go to be with Christ in his glory, in the manner that has been represented! The privilege of the twelve disciples was great in being so constantly with Christ as his family in his state of humiliation. The privilege of those three disciples was great who were with him in the mount of his Transfiguration, where was exhibited to them a faint semblance of his future glory in heaven, such as they might safely behold in the present frail, feeble, and sinful state. They were greatly delighted with what they saw and were desirous of making tabernacles to dwell there and return no more down the mount. Great, also, was the privilege of Moses when he was with Christ in Mount Sinai and asked him to show him his glory, and he saw his backparts as he passed by and heard him proclaim his name. But is not that privilege infinitely greater which has now been spoken of, the privilege of being with Christ in heaven, where he sits on the throne, as the King of angels and the God of the universe, shining forth as the Sun of that world of glory—there to dwell in the full, constant, and everlasting view of his beauty and brightness, there most freely and intimately to converse with him and fully to enjoy his love, as his friends and brethren, there to share with him in the infinite pleasure and joy which he has in the enjoyment of his Father, there to sit with him on his throne, to reign with him in the possession of all things, to partake with him in the glory of his victory over his enemies and the advancement of his kingdom in the world, and to join with him in joyful songs of praise to his Father and our Father, to his God and our God, forever and ever? Is not this a privilege worth seeking after?

Here, as a powerful enforcement of this exhortation, I would improve that afflictive dispensation of God's holy providence which is the occasion of our coming together at this time—the death of that eminent servant of Jesus Christ whose funeral is this day to be attended, together with what was observable in him, living and dying.

In this dispensation of providence, God puts us in mind of our mortality and forewarns us that the time is approaching when we must be "absent from the body" and "must appear," as the apostle observes in the next verse but one to the text, "before the judgment seat of Christ; that every one may receive the things done in his body, according to that he hath done, whether it be good or bad" (2 Cor. 5:10)

In him whose death we are now called to consider and improve, we have not only an instance of mortality, but, as we have all imaginable reason to conclude, an instance of one who, being absent from the body, is present with the Lord. Of this we shall be convinced, whether we consider the nature of his experience at the time he dates his conversion, the nature and course of his inward exercises from that time forward, his outward conversation and practice in life, or his frame and behavior during the whole of that long space wherein he looked death in the face.

His convictions of sin preceding his first consolations in Christ, as appears by a written account which he has left of his inward exercises and experiences, were exceedingly deep and thorough. His trouble and sorrow arising from a sense of guilt and misery were very great and long continued, but yet sound and rational, consisting in no unsteady, violent, and unaccountable frights and perturbations of mind; but arising from the most serious considerations and a clear illumination of the conscience to discern and consider the true state of things. The light let into his mind at conversion, and the influences and exercises to which his mind was subject at that time appear very agreeable to reason and the gospel of Jesus Christ. The change was very great and remarkable, yet without any appearance of strong impressions on the imagination, of sudden flights of the affections or of vehement emotions of the animal nature. It was attended with just views of the supreme glory of the divine being, consisting in the infinite dignity and beauty of the perfections of his nature and of the transcendent excellency of the way of salvation by Christ. This was about eight years ago when he was twenty-one years of age.

Thus, God sanctified and formed for his use that vessel which he intended to make eminently a vessel of honor in his house and which he had made of large capacity, having endowed him with very uncommon abilities and gifts of nature. He was a singular instance of a ready invention, natural eloquence, easy-flowing expression, sprightly apprehension, quick discernment, strong memory, penetrating genius, close and clear thought, and piercing judgment. He had an exact taste; his understanding was, if I may so express it, of a quick, strong, and distinguishing scent.

His learning was very considerable. He had a great taste for learning and applied himself to his studies in so close a manner when he was at college that he much injured his health and was obliged on that account for a while to leave college, throw by his studies, and return home. He was esteemed one who excelled in learning in that society.

He had extraordinary knowledge of men, as well as of things, and an uncommon insight into human nature. He excelled most whom I ever knew in the power of communicating his thoughts and had a peculiar talent at accommodating himself to the capacities, tempers, and circumstances of those whom he would instruct or counsel.

He had extraordinary gifts for the pulpit. I never had an opportunity to hear him preach but have often heard him pray. I think that his manner of addressing himself to God and expressing himself before him in that duty was almost inimitable, such as I have very rarely known equaled. He expressed himself with such exact propriety and pertinency in such significant, weighty, pungent expressions, with such an appearance of sincerity, reverence, and solemnity, and so great a distance from all affectation as forgetting the presence of men and as being in the immediate presence of a great and holy God, as I have scarcely ever known paralleled. His manner of preaching, by what I have often heard of it from good judges, was no less excellent, being clear, instructive, natural, nervous, moving, searching, and convincing. He nauseated an affected noisiness and violent boisterousness in the pulpit, and yet much disrelished a flat, cold delivery when the subject required affection and earnestness.

His experiences of the holy influences of God's Spirit were not only great at his first conversion, but they were so in a continued course from that time forward. This appears from a diary which he kept of his daily inward exercises from the time of his conversion until he was disabled by the failing of his strength a few days before his death. The change which he looked upon as his conversion was not only a great change of the present views, affections, and frame of his mind, but was evidently the beginning of that work of God in his heart which God carried on in a very wonderful manner from that time to his dying day.

As his inward appearances appear to have been of the right kind and were very remarkable as to their degree, so were his outward behavior and practice agreeable. In his whole course, he acted as one who had indeed sold all for Christ, had entirely devoted himself to God, had made *his* glory his highest end, and was fully determined to spend his whole time and strength in *his* service. He was animated in religion in the right way, animated not merely nor chiefly with his tongue in professing and talking, but animated in the work and business of religion. He was not one of those who contrive to shun the cross and get to heaven in the indulgence of ease and sloth. His life of labor and self-denial, the sacrifices which he made, and the readiness and constancy with which he spent his strength and substance to promote the glory of his Redeemer are probably without a parallel in this age in these parts of the world. Much of this may be perceived by anyone who reads his printed journal, but much more has been learned by long and intimate acquaintance with him and by looking into his diary since his death, which he purposely concealed in what he published.

Not less extraordinary were his constant calmness, peace, assurance, and joy in God during the long time he looked death in the face without the least hope of recovery, continuing without interruption to the last while his illness very sensibly preyed upon his vitals from day to day and often brought him to that state in which he looked upon himself, and was thought by others, to be dying. The thoughts of approaching death never seemed in the least to damp him, but rather to encourage him and exhilarate his mood. The nearer death approached, the more desirous he seemed to be to die. He said not long before his death that "the consideration of the day of death and the Day of Judgment had a long time been peculiarly sweet" to him.

He seemed to have remarkable exercises of resignation to the will of God. He once told me that he "had longed for the outpouring of the Holy Spirit of God and the glorious times of the church and hoped they were coming; and should have been willing to have lived to promote religion at that time, if that had been the will of God." "But," said he, "I am willing it should be as it is; I would not have the choice to make for myself for ten thousand worlds."

He several times spoke of the different kinds of willingness to die, and mentioned it as an ignoble, mean kind of willingness to die, to be willing only to get rid of pain, or to go to heaven only to get honor and advancement there. His own longings for death seemed to be quite of a different kind and for nobler ends. When he was first taken with one of the last and most fatal symptoms in a consumption, he said, "Oh now the glorious time is coming! I have longed to serve God perfectly, and God will gratify these desires." At one time and another in the latter part of his illness, he uttered these expressions: "My heaven is to please God, to glorify him, to give all to him, and to be wholly devoted to his glory. That is the heaven I long for, that is my religion, that is my happiness, and always was, ever since I supposed I had any true religion. All those who are of that religion shall meet me in heaven." "I do not go to heaven to be advanced, but to give honor to God. It is no matter where I shall be stationed in heaven, whether I have a high or low seat there, but I go to love and please and glorify God. If I had a thousand souls, if they were worth anything, I would give them all to God. But I have nothing to give when all is done."

After he came to be in so low a state that he ceased to have the least expectation of recovery, his mind was peculiarly carried forth with earnest concern for the prosperity of the church of God on earth. This seemed very manifestly to arise from a pure disinterested love of Christ and a desire for his glory. The prosperity of Zion was a theme on which he dwelt much and of which he spake much, and more and more the nearer death approached. He told me when near his end that he never, in all his life, had his mind so led forth in desires and earnest prayers for the flourishing of Christ's kingdom on the earth as since he was brought so exceedingly low at Boston. He seemed much to wonder that there appeared no more of a disposition in ministers and people to pray for the flourishing of religion through the world.

But a little while before his death, he said to me as I came into the room, "My thoughts have been employed on the old dear theme, the prosperity of God's church on earth. As I waked out of sleep, I was led to cry for the pouring out of God's Spirit and the advancement of Christ's kingdom, for which the dear Redeemer died and suffered so much. It is that, especially, which makes me long for it."

A few days before his death, he desired us to sing a psalm which related to the prosperity of Zion, which he signified engaged his thoughts and desires above all things. At his desire, we sang part of the One Hundred and Second Psalm. When we had done, though he was then so low that he could scarcely speak, he so exerted himself that he made a prayer, very audibly, in which, beside praying for those present and for his own congregation, he earnestly prayed for the reviving and flourishing of religion in the world.

His own congregation especially lay much on his heart. He often spoke of them, and commonly when he did so, it was with peculiar tenderness so that his speech was interrupted and drowned with weeping.

Thus, I have endeavored to represent something of the character and behavior of that excellent servant of Christ whose funeral is now to be attended. Though I have done it very imperfectly, yet I have endeavored to do it faithfully and as in the presence and fear of God, without flattery, which surely is to be abhorred in ministers of the gospel when speaking "as messengers of the Lord of hosts."

Such reason have we to be satisfied that the person of whom I have been speaking, now he is "absent from the body," is "present with the Lord," not only so, but also with him now wears a crown of glory of distinguished brightness.

How much is there in the consideration of such an example and so blessed an end to excite us who are yet alive with the greatest diligence and earnestness to improve the time of life, that we also may go to be with Christ when we forsake the body! The time is coming, and will soon come, we know not how soon, when we must eternally take leave of all things here below to enter on a fixed, unalterable state in the eternal world. Oh, how well it is worth the while to labor, suffer, and deny ourselves, to lay up in store a good foundation of support and supply against that time! How much is such a peace as we have heard of worth at such a time! How dismal would it be to be in such circumstances, under the outward distresses of a consuming, dissolving frame, and looking death in the face from day to day, with hearts uncleansed and sin unpardoned, under a dreadful load of guilt and divine wrath, having much sorrow and wrath in our sickness, and nothing to comfort and support our minds, nothing before us but a speedy appearance before the judgment seat of an almighty, infinitely holy and angry God, and an endless eternity in suffering his wrath without pity or mercy! The person of whom we have been speaking had a great sense of this. He said, not long before his death, "It is sweet to me to think of eternity. The endlessness of it makes it sweet. But oh what shall I say to the eternity of the wicked! I cannot mention it nor think of it! The thought is too dreadful!" At another time, speaking of an heart devoted to God and his glory, he said, "Oh of what importance is it to have such a frame of mind, such an heart as this, when we come to die! It is this now that gives me peace."

How much is there, in particular, in the things which have been observed of this eminent minister of Christ to excite us who are called to the same great work of the gospel ministry to earnest care and endeavors, that we may be in like manner faithful in our work, that we may be filled with the same spirit, animated with the same pure and fervent flame of love to God, and the same earnest concern to advance the kingdom and glory of our Lord and Master and the prosperity of Zion! How lovely did these principles render him in his life, and how blessed in his end!

Oh that the things which were seen and heard in this extraordinary person—his holiness, heavenliness, labor and self-denial in life; his so remarkably devoting himself and his all, in heart and practice, to the glory of God; and the wonderful frame of mind manifested in so steadfast a manner under the expectation of death and under the pains and agonies which brought it on. May they excite in us all, both ministers and people, a due sense of the greatness of the work which we have to do in the world, of the excellency and amiableness of thorough religion in experience and practice, of the blessedness of the end of those whose death finishes such a life, and of the infinite value of their eternal reward, when "absent from the body and present with the Lord"; and effectually stir us up to constant and effectual endeavors that, in the way of such an holy life, we may at last come to so blessed an end! Amen.

John Wesley: *The Great Assize [Court Trial]*

JOHN WESLEY, THE FOUNDER of Methodism, was born at Epworth, England, on June 28, 1703, and died in London on March 2, 1791. At Oxford he was one of a band of young men conspicuous for the earnestness of their religious life, and whom the undergraduates derisively called "methodists." John Wesley was introduced to field preaching by his great contemporary, George Whitefield. The sermons of Wesley, more than in the case of any celebrated preacher, raise the question as to how it was possible for them to hold the attention of the out-of-doors throngs to which Wesley was accustomed to preach. In manner, Wesley was as calm as he was in matter. Yet his preaching was greatly used of God for the revival of Christianity in Great Britain. Most of his sermons read like quiet, fatherly, prayer-meeting addresses. This unadorned simplicity was both natural and cultivated, for he gives us his plan in preparing sermons as follows: "My design is, in some sense, to forget all that I have ever read in my life. I mean to speak in the general as if I had never read one author, ancient or modern (always excepting the inspired). I am persuaded that, on the one hand, this may be a means of enabling me more clearly to express the sentiments of my heart, while I simply follow the chain of my own thoughts, without entangling myself with those of other men; and that, on the other, I shall come with fewer weights on my mind, with less of prejudice and prepossession, either to search for myself or to deliver to others the naked truths of the gospel."

The sermon which follows, "The Great Assize," shows Wesley in a much more animated mood than in most of his pulpit deliverances. The conclusion to the sermon is a good example of the lost art of pleading with the sinner.

The Great Assize [Court Trial]

We shall all stand before the judgment seat of Christ
(Romans 14:10).

 OW *many circumstances concur* to raise the awfulness of the present solemnity! The general concourse of people of every age, sex, rank, and condition of life, willingly or unwillingly gathered together, not only from the neighboring, but from distant parts; criminals, speedily to be brought forth, and having no way to escape; officers, waiting in their various posts to execute the orders which shall be given; and the representative of our gracious sovereign, whom we so highly reverence and honor. The occasion, likewise, of this assembly adds not a little to the solemnity of it: to hear and determine causes of every kind, some of which are of the most important nature; on which depends no less than life or death, death that uncovers the face of eternity! It was, doubtless, in order to increase the serious sense of these things, and not in the minds of the vulgar only, that the wisdom of our forefathers did not disdain to appoint even several minute circumstances of this solemnity. For these also, by means of the eye or ear, may more deeply affect the heart: and when viewed in this light, trumpets, staves, apparel are no longer trifling or significant, but subservient, in their kind and degree, to the most valuable ends of society.

But, awful as this solemnity is, one far more awful is at hand. For yet a little while, and "we shall all stand before the judgment seat of Christ. For it is written, As I live, saith the Lord, every knee shall bow to me, and every tongue shall confess to God." And in that day "every one of us shall give account of himself to God" (Rom. 14:10–12).

Had all men a deep sense of this, how effectually would it secure the interests of society! For what more forcible motive can be conceived to the practice of genuine morality, to a steady pursuit of solid virtue and a uniform walking in justice, mercy, and truth? What could strengthen our hands in all that is good and deter us from all that is evil, like a strong conviction of this: "The judge standeth before the door" (James 5:9), and we are shortly to stand before him?

It may not, therefore, be improper or unsuitable to the design of the present assembly, to consider,

    I. The chief circumstances which will precede our standing before the judgment seat of Christ.

    II. The judgment itself; and

    III. A few of the circumstances which will follow it.

    I. Let us, in the first place, consider the chief circumstances which will precede our standing before the judgment seat of Christ.

    1. "God will show signs in the earth beneath," particularly he will arise "to shake terribly the earth" (Isa. 2:19). "The earth shall reel to and fro like a drunkard, and shall be removed like a cottage" (Isa. 24:20). "There shall be earthquakes" (not in divers only, but) "in all places;" not in one only, nor in a few, but in every part of the habitable world, even such as "were not since men were upon the earth, so mighty an earthquake, and so great." In one of these "every island fled away, and the mountains were not found" (Rev. 16:18,20).

Meantime, all the waters of the terraqueous globe will feel the violence of those concussions; "the sea and waves roaring" with such an agitation as had never been known before since the hour that "the fountains of the great deep were broken up" to destroy the earth, which then "stood out of the water and in the water." The air will be all storm and tempest, full of dark vapors and pillars of smoke, resounding with thunder from pole to pole, and torn with ten thousand lightnings. But the commotion will not stop in the region of air; "the powers of the heavens shall be shaken" (Matt. 24:29). "There shall be signs in the sun, and in the moon, and in the stars" (Luke

21:25), those fixed as well as those that move around them. "The sun shall be turned into darkness, and the moon into blood, before that great and notable day of the Lord come" (Acts 2:20). "The stars shall withdraw their shining," yea, and "fall from heaven," being thrown out of their orbits. And then shall be heard the universal shout, from all the companies of heaven, followed by the "voice of the archangel," proclaiming the approach of the Son of God and man, "and the trumpet of God" sounding an alarm to all that sleep in the dust of the earth. In consequence of this, all the graves shall open, and the bodies of men arise. The sea, also, shall give up the dead which are therein, and everyone shall rise with "his own body," his own in substance, although so changed in its properties as we cannot now conceive. "For this corruptible must put on incorruption, and this mortal must put on immortality" (1 Cor. 15:53). Yea, "death and hades," the invisible world, shall "deliver up the dead that are in them," so that all who ever lived and died since God created man, shall be raised incorruptible and immortal.

2. At the same time, "the Son of man . . . shall send his angels" over all the earth, "and they shall gather his elect from the four winds, from one end of heaven to the other" (Matt. 24:31). And the Lord himself shall come with clouds in his own glory and the glory of his Father, with ten thousand of his saints, even myriads of angels, and shall sit upon the throne of his glory. "And before him shall be gathered all nations; and he shall separate them one from another: and he shall set the sheep [the good] on his right hand, and the goats [the wicked] upon the left" (Matt. 25:32). Concerning this general assembly, it is that the beloved disciple speaks thus: "I saw the dead [all that had been dead], small and great, stand before God; and the books were opened [a figurative expression, plainly referring to the manner of proceeding among men]: and the dead were judged out of those things which were written in the books, according to their works" (Rev. 20:12–13).

162 + JOHN WESLEY

II. These are the chief circumstances which are recorded in the oracles of God as preceding the general judgment. We are, secondly, to consider the judgment itself, so far as it pleased God to reveal it.

1. The person by whom God will judge the world is his only-begotten Son, whose "goings forth are from everlasting;" "who is God over all, blessed forever." Unto him, being the out-beaming of his Father's glory, "the express image of his person," the Father "hath committed all judgment, because he is the Son of man"; because, though he was "in the form of God, thought it not robbery to be equal with God: but made himself of no reputation, and took upon him the form of a servant, and was made in the likeness of men"; yes, because, "being found in fashion as a man, he humbled himself [yet further], and became obedient unto death, even the death of the cross. Wherefore God also hath highly exalted Him" (Phil. 2:6–9), even in his human nature, and "ordained him," as man, to try the children of men, to be the Judge both of the quick and dead, both of those who shall be found alive at his coming and of those who were before gathered to their fathers.

2. The time, termed by the prophet "the great and the terrible day," is usually in Scripture styled "the Day of the Lord." The space from the creation of man upon the earth to the end of all things is "the day of the sons of men"; the time that is now passing is properly "our day." When this is ended, the Day of the Lord will begin. But who can say how long it will continue? "One day is with the Lord as a thousand years, and a thousand years as one day" (2 Pet. 3:8). And from this very expression some of the ancient fathers drew the inference that what is commonly called the Day of Judgment would be a thousand years; and it seems they did not go beyond the truth; very probably they did not come up to it. For if we consider the number of persons who are to be judged, and of actions which are to be inquired into, it does not appear that a thousand years will suffice for

the transactions of that day; so it may not, improbably, comprise several thousand years. But God shall reveal this also in its season.

3. With regard to the place where mankind will be judged, we have no explicit account in Scripture. An eminent writer (but not alone; many have been of the same opinion) supposes it will be on earth where the works were done, according to which they shall be judged; and that God will, in order thereto, employ the angels of his strength

> To smooth and lengthen out the boundless space,
> And spread an area for all human race.

But perhaps it is more agreeable to our Lord's own account of his coming in the clouds to suppose it will be on earth, if not "twice a planetary height." And this supposition is not a little favored by what St. Paul writes to the Thessalonians: "The dead in Christ shall rise first: then we which are alive and remain shall be caught up together with them in the clouds, to meet the Lord in the air" (1 Thess 4:16–17). So it seems most probable the great white throne will be high exalted above the earth.

4. The persons to be judged, who can count, any more than the drops of rain, or the sands of the sea? "I beheld," said St. John, "and, lo, a great multitude, which no man could number: clothed with white robes, and palms in their hands" (Rev. 7:9). How immense, then, must be the total multitude of all nations, kindreds, people, and tongues; of all that have sprung from the loins of Adam since the world began till time shall be no more! If we admit the common supposition, which seems no ways absurd, that the earth bears at any one time no less than four hundred millions of living souls, men, women, and children, what a congregation must all these generations make who have succeeded each other for seven thousand years!

> Great Xerxes' world in arms, proud Cannae's host,
> They all are here; and here they all are lost,

Their numbers swell to be discerned in vain,
Lost as a drop in the unbounded main.

Every man, every woman, every infant of days that ever breathed the vital air will then hear the voice of the Son of God start into life, and appear before him. And this seems to be the natural import of that expression, "the dead, small and great." All universally, all without exception, all of every age, sex, or degree, all that ever lived and died or underwent such a change as will be equivalent with death. For long before that day, the phantom of greatness disappears and sinks into nothing, even in the moment of death that vanishes away. Who is rich or great in the grave?

5. And every man shall there "give an account of himself to God" (Rom. 14:12), yes, a full and true account of all that he ever did while in the body, whether it was good or evil.

Nor will all the actions alone of every child of man be then brought to open view, but all their words; seeing "every idle word that men shall speak, they shall give account thereof in the day of judgment," so that "by thy words" as well as works, "thou shalt be justified, and by thy words thou shalt be condemned" (Matt. 12:36–37). Will not God then bring to light every circumstance also that accompanied every word or action, and if not altered the nature, yet lessened or increased the goodness or badness of them? And how easy is this to him who is about our bed, and about our path, and spieth out all our ways? We know the darkness is no darkness to him, "but the night shineth as the day" (Ps. 139:12).

6. Yes, he will bring to light the hidden works of darkness and the very thoughts and intents of the hearts. And no marvel, for he "searcheth the reins and understandeth all our thoughts." "All things are naked and opened unto the eyes of him with whom we have to do" (Heb. 4:13). "Hell and destruction are before the Lord, without a covering, how much more then the hearts of the children of men?" (Prov. 15:11).

7. In that day shall be discovered every inward working of every human soul: every appetite, passion, inclination, affection, with the various combinations of them, with every temper and disposition that constitute the whole complex character of each individual. So shall it be clearly and infallibly seen who was righteous and who was unrighteous, and in what degree every action, person, or character was either good or evil.

8. "Then shall the King say unto them on his right hand, Come, ye blessed of my Father: for I was an hungred, and ye gave me meat: I was thirsty, and ye gave me drink: I was a stranger, and ye took me in: naked, and ye clothed me" (Matt. 25:34–35). In like manner, all the good they did upon earth will be recited before men and angels; whatsoever they had done either in word or deed, in the name or for the sake of the Lord Jesus. All their good desires, intentions, thoughts, all their holy dispositions, will also be then remembered. It will appear that though they were unknown or forgotten among men, yet God noted them in his book. All their sufferings, likewise, for the name of Jesus, and for the testimony of a good conscience, will be displayed unto their praise from the righteous Judge, their honor before saints and angels, and the increase of that "far more exceeding and eternal weight of glory" (2 Cor. 4:17).

9. But will their evil deeds, too (since, if we take in his whole life, there is not a man on earth that liveth and sinneth not), will these be remembered in that day and mentioned in the great congregation? Many believe they will and ask "Would not this imply that their sufferings were not at an end, even when life ended, seeing they would still have sorrow, shame, and confusion of face to endure?" They ask further, "How can this be reconciled with God's declaration by the prophet, 'If the wicked will turn from all his sins that he hath committed, and keep all my statutes, and do that which is lawful and right, ... all his transgressions that he hath committed, they shall not

be mentioned unto him' (Ezek. 18:21–22)? How is it consistent with the promise which God has made to all who accept the gospel covenant, 'I will forgive their iniquity, and I will remember their sins no more' (Jer. 31:34), or as the apostle expresses it, 'I will be merciful to their unrighteousness, and their sins and their iniquities will I remember no more' ?" (Heb. 8:12).

10. It may be answered, it is apparently and absolutely necessary for the full display of the glory of God, for the clear and perfect manifestation of his wisdom, justice, power, and mercy toward the heirs of salvation, that all the circumstances of this life should be placed in open view, together with all their tempers, desires, thoughts, and intents of their hearts; otherwise, how would it appear out of what a depth of sin and misery the grace of God had delivered them? And indeed if the whole lives of all the children of men were not manifestly discovered, the whole amazing contexture of Divine Providence could not be manifested, nor should we yet be able in a thousand instances "to justify the ways of God to man," unless our Lord's words were fulfilled in their utmost sense, without any restriction or limitation: "There is nothing covered that shall not be revealed; and hid, that shall not be known" (Matt. 10:26). The abundance of God's dispensations under the sun would still appear without their reasons. And then only when God has brought to light all the hidden things of darkness, whosoever were the actors therein, will it be seen that wise and good were all his ways, that he saw through the thick cloud, and governed all things by the wise counsels of his own will, that nothing was left to chance or the caprice of men, but God disposed all strongly and sweetly and wrought all into one connected chain of justice, mercy and truth.

11. In the discovery of the divine perfections, the righteous will rejoice with joy unspeakable, far from feeling any painful sorrow or shame for any of those past transgressions which were long since blot-

ted out as a cloud and washed away by the blood of the Lamb. It will be abundantly sufficient for them that all the transgressions which they committed shall not be once mentioned unto their disadvantage; that their sins, transgressions, and iniquities shall be remembered no more to their condemnation. This is the plain meaning of the promise, and this all children of God shall find true, to their everlasting comfort.

12. After the righteous are judged, the King will turn to them upon his left hand, and they shall also be judged, every man according to his works. But not only their outward works will be brought into account, but all the evil words which they have ever spoken, yes, all the evil desires, affections, tempers which have or have had a place in their souls, and all the evil thoughts or designs which were ever cherished in their hearts. The joyful sentence of acquittal will then be pronounced upon those upon the right hand, the dreadful sentence of condemnation upon those on the left, both of which must remain fixed and unmovable as the throne of God.

III. We may, in the third place, consider a few of the circumstances which will follow the general judgment.

1. First is the execution of the sentence pronounced on the evil and the good. "These shall go away into everlasting punishment: but the righteous into life eternal" (Matt. 25:46). It should be observed it is the very same word which is used, both in the former and in the latter clause: it follows that either the punishment lasts forever, or the reward, too, will come to an end. No, never, unless God could come to an end, or his mercy and truth could fail. "Then shall the righteous shine forth as the sun in the kingdom of their Father" (Matt. 13:43) and shall drink of those rivers of pleasure which are at God's right hand for evermore. But here all description falls short, all human language fails. Only one who is caught up into the third heaven can have a just conception of it. But even such a one cannot express what he has seen, these things it is not possible for man to utter.

The wicked, meantime, shall be turned into hell, even all the people that forget God. They will be "punished with everlasting destruction from the presence of the Lord, and from the glory of his power" (2 Thess. 1:9). They will be "cast alive into a lake of fire burning with brimstone" (Rev. 19:20) originally prepared for the devil and his angels, where they will gnaw their tongues for anguish and pain. They will curse God and look upward. There the dogs of hell, pride, malice, revenge, rage, horror, despair, continually devour them. There "the smoke of their torment ascendeth up for ever and ever: and they have no rest day nor night" (Rev. 14:11). For "their worm dieth not, and the fire is not quenched" (Mark 9:44).

2. Then the heavens will be shriveled up as a parchment scroll and pass away with a great noise; they will flee from the face of him that sitteth on the throne, and there will be found no place for them. The very manner of their passing away is disclosed to us by the apostle Peter: In "the day of God, wherein the heavens being on fire shall be dissolved" (2 Pet. 3:12). The whole beautiful fabric will be overthrown by that raging element, the connection of all its parts destroyed, and every atom torn asunder from the others. By the same, "the earth also and the works that are therein shall be burned up" (2 Pet. 3:10). The enormous works of nature, the everlasting hills, mountains that have defied the rage of time and stood unmoved so many thousand years, will sink down in fiery ruin. How much less will the works of art, though of the most durable kind, the utmost effort of human industry, tombs, pillars, triumphal arches, castles, pyramids, be able to withstand the flaming conqueror! All, all will die, perish, vanish away, like a dream when one awakes!

3. It has indeed been imagined by some great and good men that as it requires that same Almighty Power to annihilate things as to create, to speak into nothing or out of nothing, so no part of an atom in the universe will be totally or finally destroyed. Rather, they suppose

that the last operation of fire, which we have yet been able to observe, is to reduce into glass what, by a smaller force, it had reduced to ashes. So, in the day God has ordained, the whole earth, if not the material heavens also, will undergo this change, after which the fire can have no further power over them. And they believe this is intimated by that expression in the Revelation made to St. John, "Before the throne there was a sea of glass like unto crystal" (Rev. 4:6). We can not now either affirm or deny this, but we shall know hereafter.

4. If it be inquired by the scoffers, the minute philosophers, how can these things be? Whence should come such an immense quantity of fire as would consume the heavens and the whole terraqueous globe? We would first remind them that this difficulty is not peculiar to the Christian system. The same opinion is almost universally held among the unbigoted heathens. But, secondly, it is easy to answer, even from our slight and superficial acquaintance with natural things, that there are abundant magazines of fire ready prepared and treasured up against the day of the Lord. How soon may a comet, commissioned by him, travel down from the most distant parts of the universe? And were it to fix upon the earth in its return from the sun, when it is some thousand times hotter than a red-hot cannon-ball, who does not see what must be the immediate consequence? But not to ascend so high as the ethereal heavens, might not the same lightnings which give shine to the world, if commanded by the Lord of nature, give ruin and utter destruction? Or to go no further than the globe itself, who knows what huge reservoirs of liquid fire are from age to age contained in the bowels of the earth? Aetna, Hecla, Vesuvius, and all the other volcanoes that belch out flames and coals of fire, what are they but so many proofs and mouths of those fiery furnaces; and at the same time so many evidences that God has in readiness wherewith to fulfill his word? Yes, were we to observe no more than the surface of the earth and the things that surround us on

every side, it is most certain (as a thousand experiments prove, beyond all possibility of denial) that we, ourselves, our whole bodies, are full of fire, as well as everything around us. Is it not easy to make this ethereal fire visible even to the naked eye and to produce thereby the very same effects on combustible matter which are produced by culinary fire? Needs there then any more than for God to unloose that secret chain whereby this irresistible agent is now bound down and lies quiescent in every particle of matter? And how soon would it tear the universal frame in pieces and involve all in one common ruin!

5. There is one circumstance more which will follow the judgment that deserves our serious consideration: "According to his promise," says the apostle, "we look for new heavens and a new earth, wherein dwelleth righteousness" (2 Pet. 3:13). The promise stands in the prophecy of Isaiah: "Behold, I create new heavens and a new earth: and the former shall not be remembered" (Isa. 65:17), so great shall the glory of the latter be! These St. John did behold in the visions of God. "I saw," said he, "a new heaven and a new earth: for the first heaven and the first earth were passed away. . . . And I heard a great voice out of [the third] heaven saying, Behold, the tabernacle of God is with men, and he will dwell with them, and they shall be his people, and God himself shall be with them, and be their God" (Rev. 21:4). Of necessity, therefore, they will all be happy. "God shall wipe away all tears from their eyes; and there shall be no more death, neither sorrow, nor crying, neither shall there be any more pain" (Rev. 21:4). "There shall be no more curse: and they shall see his face" (Rev. 22:3), shall have the nearest access to, and thence the highest resemblance of him. This is the strongest expression in the language of Scripture to denote the most perfect happiness. "And his name shall be on their foreheads" (Rev. 22:4); they shall be openly acknowledged as God's own property and his glorious nature shall most visibly shine forth in them. "And there shall be no night there; and they need

no candle, neither the light of the sun; for the Lord God giveth them light: and they shall reign for ever and ever" (Rev. 22:5).

Suffer me to add a few words to all of you who are at this present before the Lord. Should not you bear it in your minds all the day long, that a more awful day is coming? A large assembly this! But what is it to that which every eye will then behold, this general assembly of all the children of men that ever lived on the face of the whole earth! A few will stand at the judgment seat this day, to be judged touching what shall be laid to their charge; and they are now reserved in prison, perhaps in chains, till they are brought forth to be tried and sentenced. But we shall all, I that speak and you that hear, "stand before the judgment seat of Christ" (Rom. 14:10). And we are now reserved on this earth, which is not our home, in this prison of flesh and blood, perhaps many of us in chains of darkness, too, till we are ordered to be brought forth. Here a man is questioned concerning one or two acts which he is supposed to have committed. There we are to give an account of all our works from the cradle to the grave; of all our words, of all our desires and tempers, all the thoughts and intents of our hearts; of all the uses we have made of our various talents, whether of mind, body, or fortune, till God said, "Give an account of thy stewardship; for thou mayest be no longer steward" (Luke 16:2). In this count, it is possible some who are guilty may escape for want of evidence; but there is no want of evidence in that court. All men with whom you had the most secret intercourse, who were privy to all your designs and actions, are ready before your face. So are all the spirits of darkness who inspired evil designs, and assisted in the execution of them. So are all the angels of God, those eyes of the Lord that run to and fro over all the earth, who watched over your soul and labored for your good, so far as you would permit. So is your own conscience a thousand witnesses in one, now no more capable of being either blinded or silenced, but constrained to know and to speak the naked truth, touching all your thoughts, words, and actions. And is conscience as a thousand witnesses? Yes, but God is as a thousand witnesses. Oh, who can stand before the face of the great God, even our Savior Jesus Christ?

See! See! He cometh! He maketh the clouds his chariot! He rideth upon the wings of the wind! A devouring fire goeth before him, and after him a flame burneth! See! He sitteth upon his throne, clothed with light as with a garment, arrayed with majesty and honor! Behold his eyes are as a flame of fire, his voice as the sound of many waters! How will you escape? Will you call to the mountains to fall on you, the rocks to cover you? Alas, the mountains themselves, the rocks, the earth, the heavens, are just ready to flee away! Can you prevent the sentence? With what? With all the substance of your house, with thousands of gold and silver? Blind wretch! Thou camest naked from thy mother's womb, and more naked into eternity. Hear the Lord, the Judge! "Come, ye blessed of my Father, inherit the kingdom prepared for you from the foundation of the world" (Matt. 25:34). Joyful sound! How widely different from that voice which echoes through the expanse of heaven, "Depart from me, ye cursed, into everlasting fire, prepared for the devil and his angels" (Matt. 25:41)! And who is he that can prevent or retard the full execution of either sentence? Vain hope! Lo, hell is moved from beneath to receive those who are ripe for destruction. And the everlasting doors lift up their heads, that the heirs of glory may come in!

"What manner of persons ought ye to be in all holy conversation and godliness?" (2 Pet. 3:11). We know it cannot be long before the Lord will descend with the voice of the archangel and the trumpet of God, when everyone of us shall appear before him, and give an account of his own works. "Wherefore, beloved, seeing that ye look for such things," seeing ye know he will come and will not tarry, "be diligent that ye may be found of him in peace, without spot and blameless" (2 Pet. 3:14). Why should ye not? Why should one of you be found on the left hand at his appearing? He does not wish that any should perish, but that all should come to repentance; by repentance, to faith in a bleeding Lord; by faith, to spotless love; to the full image of God renewed in the heart, and producing all holiness of conversation. Can you doubt this, when you remember the Judge of all is likewise the Savior of all? Has he not bought you with his own blood, that you might not perish but have everlasting life?

Oh make proof of his mercy, rather than his justice; of his love, rather than the thunder of his power! He is not far from everyone of us; and he is now come, not to condemn, but to save the world. He stands in the midst! Sinner, does he not now, even now, knock at the door of your heart? Oh, that you may know, at least in this your day, the things that belong unto your peace. Oh, that you may now give yourselves to him who gave himself for you, in humble faith, in holy, active, patient love! So shall you rejoice with exceeding joy in his day, when he cometh in the clouds of heaven!

George Whitefield: *Repentance*

GEORGE WHITEFIELD, PRINCE OF THE FIELD PREACHERS, was born at Gloucester, England, in 1714 and died at Newburyport, Massachusetts, 1770. As a boy at school he very early evinced dramatic and elocutionary powers and, when doing the work of a common drawer in his mother's tavern at Gloucester, composed several sermons. Because of his manifest gifts and religious inclination, he was sent to Oxford at the age of eighteen. There he fell in with the Wesleys and joined the "Holy Club." Although Whitefield had prayed a thousand times that the pulpit might not be his destiny, he was ordained by the Bishop of Gloucester in 1736. Of his first sermon he says, "Some few mocked, but most for the present seemed struck."

At the urgent call of the Wesleys, Whitefield went out to Georgia in 1738. There he founded the orphan home for the support of which he traveled through the colonies and up and down in Great Britain. Probably no preacher since the days of St. Paul was as great a traveler as Whitefield, for he made thirteen trips across the Atlantic, in a day when the voyage was often of two or three months' duration. On the return from his second trip to America, he found that the Wesleys had gone over to Arminianism and withdrew from their fellowship because of his rigid Calvinism. When the news reached London of the death of Whitefield in America, a follower of Whitefield went up to John Wesley after one of his sermons and asked him if he expected to see Whitefield in heaven. Wesley said he did not. "Ah," said the woman, "I thought you would say that!" "But wait, madam," added Wesley, "when I get to heaven, George Whitefield will be so near the throne that a poor sinner like me will never get a glimpse of him."

During his itinerating trips in America, the Bermudas, and Great Britain, Whitefield was constantly preaching. His "short allowance" was once every weekday and three times on Sunday. Whitefield first discovered the deep emotions he could stir in the hearts of his hearers when he was preaching to the thousands of miners in the fields near Bristol and saw the white channels in their black faces made by the tears coursing down their cheeks. Wherever he preached, Whitefield left an unforgettable impression behind him. Not only the masses of the common people who heard him gladly, but philosophers like Hume and Franklin, and actors like Foote and Garrick pay tribute to his wonderful power as a preacher. Preaching once in a drawing room to the aristocracy of London, he so graphically described a blind man on the verge of a precipice that the worldly Chesterfield cried out, "For heaven's sake, Whitefield, save him!" David Garrick envied him the ability to pronounce the word "Mesopotamia" in a way that swept the deepest chords of emotion. He must have possessed a marvelous voice, for Franklin, by walking around the place where he was preaching, estimated that he could have been heard easily by thirty thousand persons. At the famous Moorfields fairs, the shows were deserted by the people as they thronged to hear the great preacher.

Perhaps the best-known tribute to the eloquence of Whitefield is the story of how Franklin went once to hear him in Philadelphia, determined that he would give nothing for his collection and thus prove himself above the weakness of his fellow countrymen. As Whitefield proceeded, Franklin relented and decided to give what coppers he had; then the silver, and then the gold; and when the plate was passed, Franklin poured all he possessed into it and then asked a friend near him to loan more.

Whitefield's published sermons give no conception of the sway he cast over the thousands who heard him. They are not marked for their logic nor for their deep penetration or subtle analysis. But always they ring with the note of earnestness. The second personal pronoun is constantly employed, and it is evident from the beginning that Whitefield has in view the one end, the salvation of the souls of those who heard him. His sermon on "Repentance" is a good example of how Whitefield wrestled with souls.

Repentance

"Except ye repent, ye shall all likewise perish" (Luke 13:3).

WHEN *we consider* how heinous and aggravating our offenses are in the sight of a just and holy God, that they bring down his wrath upon our heads, and occasion us to live under his indignation; how ought we thereby to be deterred from evil, or at least engaged to study to repent thereof and not commit the same again! But man is so thoughtless of an eternal state, and has so little consideration of the welfare of his immortal soul, that he can sin without any thought that he must give an account of his actions at the Day of Judgment. If he, at times, has any reflections on his behavior, they do not drive him to true repentance. He may, for a short time, refrain from falling into some gross sins which he had lately committed; but then, when the temptation comes again with power, he is carried away with the lust; and thus he goes on promising and resolving, and in breaking both his resolutions and his promises, as fast almost as he has made them. This is highly offensive to God; it is mocking of him. My brethren, when grace is given us to repent truly, we shall turn wholly unto God; and let me beseech you to repent of your sins, for the time is hastening when you will have neither time nor call to repent; there is none in the grave, whither we are going. But do not be afraid, for God often receives the greatest sinner to mercy through the merits of Christ Jesus. This magnifies the riches of his free grace; and should be an encouragement for you, who are great and notorious sinners, to repent, for he will have mercy upon you, if you through Christ return unto him.

St. Paul was an eminent instance of this. He speaks of himself as "the chief of sinners," and he declares how God showed mercy unto him. Christ loves to show mercy unto sinners, and if you repent, he will have mercy upon you. But as no word is more mistaken than that of repentance, I shall:

I. Show you what the nature of repentance is.

II. Consider the several parts and causes of repentance.

III. I shall give you some reasons, why repentance is necessary to salvation. And

IV. Exhort all of you, high and low, rich and poor, one with another, to endeavor after repentance.

I. Repentance, my brethren, in the first place, as to its nature, is the carnal and corrupt disposition of men being changed into a renewed and sanctified disposition. A man who has truly repented is truly regenerated: it is a different word for one and the same thing. The motley mixture of the beast and devil is gone: there is a new creation wrought in your hearts. If your repentance is true, you are renewed throughout, both in soul and body; your understandings are enlightened with the knowledge of God, and of the Lord Jesus Christ; and your wills, which were stubborn, obstinate, and hated all good, are obedient and conformable to the will of God. Indeed, our deists tell us that man now has a free will to do good, to love God, and to repent when he will. But indeed, there is no free will in any of you, but to sin; nay, your free will leads you so far that you would, if possible, pull God from his throne. This may, perhaps, offend the Pharisees; but (it is the truth in Christ which I speak, I lie not) every man by his own natural will hates God. But when you are turned unto the Lord by evangelical repentance, then your will is changed; then your consciences, now hardened and benumbed, shall be quickened and awakened; then your hard hearts shall be melted, and your unruly affections shall be crucified. Thus, by that repentance, the whole soul will be changed; you will have new inclinations, new desires, and new habits.

You may see how vile we are by nature, that it requires so great a change to be made upon us, to recover us from this state of sin, and therefore the consideration of our dreadful state should make us earnest with God to change our conditions, and that change true repentance implies. Therefore, my brethren, consider how hateful your ways are to God, while you continue in sin; how abominable you are unto him, while you run into evil. You cannot be said to be Christians while you are hating Christ and his people; true repentance will entirely change you, the bias of your souls will be changed; then you will delight in God, in Christ, in his Law, and in his people. You will then believe that there is such a thing as inward feeling, though now you may esteem it madness and enthusiasm; you will not then be ashamed of becoming fools for Christ's sake; you will not regard being scoffed at; it is not then their pointing after you and crying, "Here comes another troop of his followers," will dismay you. No, your soul will abhor such proceedings. The ways of Christ and his people will be your whole delight.

It is the nature of such repentance to make a change, and the greatest change as can be made here in the soul. Thus you see what repentance implies in its own nature; it denotes an abhorrence of all evil, and a forsaking of it. I shall now proceed,

II. To show you the parts of it, and the causes concurring thereto.

The parts are, sorrow, hatred, and an entire forsaking of sin.

Our sorrow and grief for sin must not spring merely from a fear of wrath; for if we have no other ground but that, it proceeds from self-love, and not from any love to God; and if love to God is not the chief motive of your repentance, your repentance is in vain, and not to be esteemed true.

Many in our days think their crying, "God forgive me!" or, "Lord have mercy upon me!" or "I am sorry for it!" is repentance, and that God will esteem it as such: but, indeed, they are mistaken. It is not the drawing near to God with our lips, while our hearts are far from him, which he regards. Repentance does not come by fits and starts; no, it is one continued act of our lives; for as we daily commit sin, so we need a daily repentance before God, to obtain forgiveness for those sins we commit.

It is not your confessing yourselves to be sinners, it is not knowing your condition to be sad and deplorable, so long as you continue in your sins: your care and endeavors should be to get the heart thoroughly affected therewith that you may feel yourselves to be lost and undone creatures, for Christ came to save such as are lost. If you are enabled to groan under the weight and burden of your sins, then Christ will ease you and give you rest.

Until you are thus sensible of your misery and lost condition, you are a servant to sin and to your lusts, under the bondage and command of Satan, doing his drudgery: thou art under the curse of God, and liable to his judgment. Consider how dreadful thy state will be at death, and after the Day of Judgment, when you will be exposed to such miseries which the ear has not heard, neither can the heart conceive, and that to all eternity, if you die impenitent.

But I hope better things of you, my brethren, though I thus speak, things which accompany salvation. Go to God in prayer, and be earnest with him, that by his Spirit he would convince you of your miserable condition by nature, and make you truly sensible thereof. Oh be humbled, be humbled, I beseech you, for your sins! Having spent so many years in sinning, what canst thou do less, than be concerned to spend some hours in mourning and sorrowing for the same, and be humbled before God?

Look back into your lives, call to mind thy sins, as many as possibly thou canst, the sins of thy youth, as well as of thy riper years. See how you have departed from a gracious Father, and wandered in the way of wickedness, in which you have lost yourselves, the favor of God, the comforts of his Spirit, and the peace of your own consciences. Then go and beg pardon of the Lord, through the blood of the Lamb, for the evil thou hast committed, and for the good thou hast omitted. Consider, likewise, the heinousness of thy sins; see what very aggravating circumstances thy sins are attended with, how you have abused the patience of God, which should have led you to repentance; and when thou findest thy heart hard, beg of God to soften it, cry mightily unto him, and he will take away thy stony heart, and give thee a heart of flesh.

Resolve to leave all thy sinful lusts and pleasures; renounce, forsake, and abhor thy old sinful course of life, and serve God in holiness and righteousness all the remaining part of life. If you lament and bewail past sins and do not forsake them, your repentance is in vain; you are mocking God, and deceiving your own soul. You must put off the old man, with his deeds, before you can put on the new man, Christ Jesus.

You, therefore, who have been swearers and cursers; you, who have been harlots and drunkards; you, who have been thieves and robbers; you, who have hitherto followed the sinful pleasures and diversions of life, let me beseech you, by the mercies of God in Christ Jesus, that you would no longer continue therein, but that you would forsake your evil ways, and turn unto the Lord. For he waits to be gracious to you, he is ready, he is willing to pardon you of all your sins: but do not expect Christ to pardon you of sin when you run to it, and will not abstain from complying with the temptations. But if you will be persuaded to abstain from evil and choose the good, to return to the Lord and repent of your wickedness, he has promised he will abundantly pardon you, he will heal your backslidings, and will love you freely. Resolve now this day to have done with your sins forever; let your old ways and you be separated; you must resolve against it, for there can be no true repentance without a resolution to forsake it. Resolve for Christ, resolve against the devil and his works, and go on fighting the Lord's battles against the devil and his emissaries; attack him in the strongest holds he has, fight him as men, as Christians, and you will soon find him to be a coward; resist him, and he will fly from you. Resolve, through grace to do this, and your repentance is half done; but then take care that you do not ground your resolutions on your own strength, but in the strength of the Lord Jesus Christ. He is the way, he is the truth, and he is the life; without his assistance you can do nothing, but through his grace strengthening thee, thou wilt be enabled to do all things. The more thou art sensible of thy own weakness and inability, the more ready Christ will be to help thee; and what can all the men of the world do to thee when Christ is for thee? Thou wilt not regard what they say against thee, for thou wilt have the testimony of a good conscience.

Resolve to cast thyself at the feet of Christ in subjection to him, and throw thyself into the arms of Christ for salvation by him. Consider, my dear brethren, the many invitations he has given you to come unto him, to be saved by him. God has "laid on him the iniquity of us all" (Isa. 53:6). Oh let me prevail with you, above all things, to make choice of the Lord Jesus Christ, resign yourselves unto him, take him, oh take him upon his own terms; and whoever thou art, however great a sinner thou hast been, this evening, in the name of the great God, do I offer Jesus Christ unto thee; as thou valuest thy life and soul, refuse him not, but stir up thyself to accept the Lord Jesus. Take him wholly as he is, for he will be applied wholly unto you, or else not at all. Jesus Christ must be your whole wisdom, Jesus Christ must be your whole righteousness, Jesus Christ must be your whole sanctification, or he will never be your eternal redemption.

What though you have been ever so wicked and profligate, yet if you will now abandon your sins, and turn unto the Lord Jesus Christ, thou shalt have him given to thee, and all thy sins shall be freely forgiven. Oh why will you neglect the great work of your repentance?

Do not defer the doing of it one day longer, but today, even now, take Christ who is freely offered to you.

Now, as to the causes hereof, the first cause is God; he is the author, "we are born . . . of God" (John 1:13), God has begotten us, even God, the Father of our Lord Jesus Christ. It is he who stirs us up to will and to do of his own good pleasure. Another cause is God's free grace. It is owing to the "riches of his free grace," my brethren, that we have been prevented from going down to hell long ago; it is because the compassions of the Lord fail not; they are new every morning, and fresh every evening.

Sometimes the instruments are very unlikely: a poor, despised minister or member of Jesus Christ may, by the power of God, be made an instrument in the hands of God, of bringing you to true evangelical repentance. This may be done to show that the power is not in men, but that it is entirely owing to the good pleasure of God. If there has been any good done among any of you by preaching the word, as I trust there has, though it were preached in a field, if God has met and owned us, and blessed his word, though preached by an enthusiastic babbler, a boy, a madman; I do rejoice, yes, and will rejoice, let foes say what they will. I shall now,

III. Show the reasons why repentance is necessary to salvation.

And this, my brethren, is plainly revealed to us in the word of God: The soul that does not repent and turn unto the Lord, shall die in its sins, and their blood shall be required at their own hands. It is necessary, as we have sinned, we should repent; for a holy God could not, nor ever can or will, admit anything that is unholy into his presence. This is the beginning of grace in the soul; there must be a change in heart and life before there can be a dwelling with a holy God. You cannot love sin and God, too; you cannot love God and mammon. No unclean person can stand in the presence of God; it is contrary to the holiness of his nature. There is a contrariety between the holy nature of God and the unholy nature of carnal and unregenerate men.

What communication can there be between a sinless God and creatures full of sin, between a pure God and impure creatures? If you were to be admitted into heaven with your present tempers, in your impenitent condition, heaven itself would be a hell to you; the songs of angels would be as enthusiasm, and would be intolerable to you. Therefore, you must have these tempers changed; you must be holy as God is. He must be your God here, and you must be his people, or you will never dwell together to all eternity. If you hate the ways of God and cannot spend an hour in his service, how will you think to be easy in all eternity, in singing praises to him that sits upon the throne, and to the Lamb forever?

This is to be the employment, my brethren, of all those who are admitted into this glorious place, where neither sin nor sinner is admitted, where no scoffer ever can come without repentance from his evil ways, a turning unto God, and a cleaving unto him. This must be done before any can be admitted into the glorious mansions of God, which are prepared for all that love the Lord Jesus Christ in sincerity and truth; repent then of all your sins. Oh my dear brethren, it makes my blood run cold to think that any of you should not be admitted into the glorious mansions above. If it were in my power, I would place all of you, yes you, my scoffing brethren, and the greatest enemy I have on earth, at the right hand of Jesus; but this I cannot do. However, I advise and exhort you with all love and tenderness to make Jesus your refuge. Fly to him for relief. Jesus died to save such as you; he is full of compassion, and if you go to him, as poor, lost, undone sinners, Jesus will give you his Spirit. You shall live and reign, and reign and live, you shall love and live, and live and love, with this Jesus to all eternity.

IV. I am to exhort all of you, high and low, rich and poor, one with another, to repent of all your sins, and turn unto the Lord.

I shall speak to each of you; for you have either repented, or you have not; you are believers in Christ Jesus, or unbelievers.

First, you who never have truly repented of your sins, and never have truly forsaken your lusts, be not offended if I speak plainly to you; for it is love, love to your souls, that constrains me to speak. I shall lay before you your danger, and the misery to which you are exposed, while you remain impenitent in sin. And oh that this may be a means of making you fly to Christ for pardon and forgiveness.

While thy sins are not repented of, thou art in danger of death; and if you should die, you would perish forever. There is no hope of any who live and die in their sins, but that they will dwell with devils and damned spirits to all eternity. And how do we know we shall live much longer? We are not sure of seeing our own habitations this night in safety. What do you mean then being at ease and pleasure while your sins are not pardoned? As sure as ever the word of God is true, if you die in that condition, you are shut out of all hope and mercy forever, and shall pass into baseless and endless misery.

What are all thy pleasures and diversions worth? They last but for a moment; they are of no worth, and but of short continuance. And sure it must be gross folly, eagerly to pursue those sinful lusts and pleasures which war against the soul, which tend to harden the heart, and keep us from closing with the Lord Jesus. Indeed, these are destructive of our peace here and, without repentance, will be of our peace hereafter.

Oh the folly and madness of this sensual world; if there were nothing in sin but present slavery, it would keep an ingenuous spirit from it. But to do the devil's drudgery! If we do that, we shall have his wages, which is eternal death and condemnation. Oh, consider this, my guilty brethren, you who think it no crime to swear, whore, drink or scoff and jeer at the people of God. Consider how your voices will then be changed, and you, that counted their lives madness, and their end without honor, shall howl and lament at your own madness and folly, that should bring you to so much woe and distress! Then you will lament and bemoan your own dreadful condition: but it will be of no signification; for he that is now your merciful Savior, will then become your inexorable Judge. Now he is easy to be entreated; but then, all your tears and prayers will be in vain, for God has allotted to every man a day of grace, a time of repentance, which, if he does not improve, but neglects and despises the means which are offered to him, he cannot be saved.

Therefore, while you are going on in a course of sin and unrighteousness, I beseech you, my brethren, to think of the consequence that will attend your thus misspending your precious time. Your souls are worth being concerned about, for if you can enjoy all the pleasures and diversions of life, at death you must leave them; that will put an end to all your worldly concerns. And will it not be deplorable to have your good things here, all your earthly, sensual, devilish pleasures, which you have been so much taken up with, all over; and the thought of how trifling a concern thou hast lost eternal welfare, will gnaw at your very soul.

Thy wealth and grandeur will stand in no stead; thou canst carry nothing of it into the other world. Then the consideration of thy uncharitableness to the poor, and the ways thou didst take to obtain thy wealth, will be a very hell unto thee.

Now you enjoy the means of grace, as the preaching of his word, prayer, and sacraments; and God has sent his ministers out into the fields and highways to invite, to woo you to come in. But they are tiresome to thee, thou hadst rather be at thy pleasures. Ere long, my brethren, they will be over, and you will be no more troubled with them; but then you would give ten thousand worlds for one moment of that merciful time of grace which thou hast abused. Then thou wilt cry for a drop of that precious blood which now you trample under your feet; then you will wish for one more offer of mercy, for Christ and his free grace to be offered to you again. But your crying will be in vain, for as you would not repent here, God will not give you an opportunity to repent hereafter. If you would not in Christ's time, you shall not in your own. In what a dreadful condition will you then be? What horror and astonishment will possess your souls? Then all thy lies and oaths, thy scoffs and jeers at the people of God; all thy filthy and unclean thoughts and actions; thy misspent time in balls, plays, and assemblies; thy spending whole evenings at cards, dice, and masquerades; thy frequenting of taverns and alehouses; thy worldliness, covetousness, and thy uncharitableness, will be brought at once to thy remembrance, and at once charged upon thy guilty soul. How can you bear the thoughts of these things? Indeed, I am full of compassion towards you, to think that this should be the portion of any who now hear me. These are truths, though awful ones, my brethren; these are the truths of the gospel; and if there were not a necessity for thus speaking, I would willingly forbear, for it is not a pleasing subject to me, any more than it is to you; but it is my duty to show you the dreadful consequences of continuing in sin. I am only now acting the part of a skillful surgeon, that searches a wound before he heals it. I would show you your danger first; that deliverance may be the more readily accepted by you.

Consider that however you may be for putting the evil day away from you, and are now striving to hide your sins, at the Day of Judgment there shall be a full discovery of all. Hidden things on that day shall be brought to light; and after all thy sins have been revealed to the whole world, then you must depart into everlasting fire in hell, which will not be quenched night and day; it will be without intermission, without end. Oh then, what stupidity and senselessness has possessed your hearts, that you are not frighted from your sins. The fear of Nebuchadnezzar's fiery furnace made men do anything to avoid it; and shall not an everlasting fire make men, make you, do anything to avoid it?

Oh that this would awaken and cause you to humble yourselves for your sins, and to beg pardon for them, that you might find mercy in the Lord.

Do not go away, let not the devil hurry you away before the sermon is over; but stay, and you shall have Jesus offered to you, who has made full satisfaction for all your sins.

Let me beseech you to cast away your transgressions, to strive against sin, to watch against it, and to beg power and strength from Christ, to keep down the power of those lusts that hurry you on in your sinful ways.

But if you will not do any of these things, if you are resolved to sin on, you must expect eternal death to be the consequence; you must expect to be seized with horror and trembling, with horror and amazement, to hear the dreadful sentence of condemnation pronounced against you. Then you will run, and call upon the mountains to fall on you, to hide you from the Lord, and from the fierce anger of his wrath.

Had you now a heart to turn from your sins unto the living God, by true and unfeigned repentance, and to pray unto him for mercy, in and through the merits of Jesus Christ, there were hope. But at the Day of Judgment, thy prayers and tears will be of no signification; they will be of no service to thee; the Judge will not be entreated by thee; as you would not hearken to him when he called unto thee, but despised both him and his ministers, and would not leave your iniquities. Therefore, on that day, he will not be entreated, notwithstanding all thy cries and tears; for God himself has said, "Because I have called, and you refused; I have stretched out my hand, and no man regarded; but ye have set at nought all my counsel, and would none of my reproof: I also will laugh at your calamity; I will mock when your fear cometh . . . as desolation, and your destruction cometh as a whirlwind; when distress and anguish cometh upon you. Then shall they call upon me, but I will not answer; they shall seek me early, but they shall not find me" (Prov. 1:24–28).

Now, you may call this enthusiasm and madness; but at that great day, if you repent not of your sins here, you will find by woeful experience that your own ways were madness indeed. But God forbid it should be left undone till then: seek after the Lord while he is to be found; call upon him while he is near, and you shall find mercy; repent this hour, and Christ will joyfully receive you.

What do you say? Must I go to my Master, and tell him you will not come unto him, and will have none of his counsels? No; do not send me on so unhappy an errand: I cannot, I will not tell him any such thing. Shall not I rather tell him, you are willing to repent and to be converted, to become new men, and to take up a new course of life? This is the only wise resolution you can make. Let me tell my Master, that you will come unto and will wait upon him: for if you do not, it will be your ruin in time, and to eternity.

You will at death wish you had lived the life of the righteous, that you might have died his death. Be advised then; consider what is before you: Christ and the world, holiness and sin, life and death. Choose now for yourselves; let your choice be made immediately, and let that choice be your dying choice.

If you would not choose to die in your sins, to die drunkards, to die adulterers, to die swearers and scoffers, live not out this night in the dreadful condition you are in. Some of you, it may be, may say, "You have no power, you have no strength." But have you not been lacking yourselves in such things that were within your power? Have you not as much power to go to hear a sermon, as to go into a play house, or to a ball, or to a masquerade? You have as much power to read the Bible, as to read plays, novels, and romances; and you can associate as well with the godly, as with the wicked and profane; this is but an idle excuse, my brethren, to go on in your sins. If you will be found in the means of grace, Christ has promised he will give you strength. While Peter was preaching, the Holy Ghost fell on all that heard the word: how then should you be found in the way of your duty! Jesus Christ will then give thee strength; he will put his Spirit within thee; thou shalt find he will be thy wisdom, thy righteousness, thy sanctification, and thy redemption. Do but try what a gracious, kind, and loving Master he is. He will be a help to thee in all thy burdens: and if the burden of sin be on thy soul, go to him as weary and heavy laden, and thou shalt find rest.

Do not say that your sins are too many and too great to expect to find mercy. No, be they ever so many, or ever so great, the blood of the Lord Jesus Christ will cleanse you from all sins. God's grace, my brethren, is free, rich, and sovereign. Manasseh was a great sinner, and yet he was pardoned; Zaccheus was gone far from God, and went out to see Christ, with no other view but to satisfy his curiosity; and yet Jesus met him, and brought salvation to his house. Manasseh was an idolater and murderer, yet he received mercy; the other was an oppressor and extortioner, who had gotten riches by fraud and deceit, and by grinding the faces of the poor: so did Matthew, too, and yet they found mercy.

Have you been blasphemers and persecutors of the saints and servants of God? So was St. Paul, yet he received mercy. Have you been common harlots, filthy and unclean persons? So was Mary Magdalene, and yet she received mercy. Hast thou been a thief? The thief upon the cross found mercy. I despair of none of you, however vile and profligate you have been; I say, I despair of none of you, especially when God has had mercy on such a wretch as I am.

Remember the poor publican, how he found favor with God, when the proud, self-conceited Pharisee, who, puffed up with his own righteousness, was rejected. And if you will go to Jesus as the poor publican did, under a sense of your own unworthiness, you shall find favor as he did: there is virtue enough in the blood of Jesus to pardon greater sinners than he has yet pardoned. Then be not discouraged, but come unto Jesus, and you will find him ready to help in all thy distresses, to lead thee into all truth, to bring thee from darkness to light, and from the power of Satan unto God.

Do not let the devil deceive you by telling you that all your delights and pleasures will be over. No; this is so far from depriving you of all pleasure, that it is an inlet unto unspeakable delights, peculiar to all who are truly regenerated. The new birth is the very beginning of a life of peace and comfort; and the greatest pleasantness is to be found in the ways of holiness. Solomon, who had experience of all other pleasures, said of the ways of godliness, "All her ways are ways of pleasantness, and all her paths are peace" (Prov. 3:17). Then surely you will not let the devil deceive you; it is all he wants, it is what he aims at, to make religion appear to be melancholy, miserable, and enthusiastic. Let him say what he will; give no ear to him, regard him not, for he always was and will be a liar.

What entreaties, shall I use to make you come unto the Lord Jesus Christ? The little love I have experienced since I have been brought from sin to God is so great, that I would not be in a natural state for ten thousand worlds, and what I have felt is but little to what I hope to feel. That little love which I have experienced is a sufficient buoy against all the storms and tempests of this boisterous world; and let men and devils do their worst, I rejoice in the Lord Jesus, yes, and I will rejoice.

And oh, if you repent and come to Jesus, I would rejoice on your accounts, too: and we should rejoice together to all eternity, when once passed on the other side of the grave. Oh, come to Jesus. The arms of Jesus Christ will embrace you; he will wash away all your sins in his blood, and will love you freely.

Come, I beseech you to come unto Jesus Christ. Oh that my words would pierce to the very soul! Oh, that Jesus Christ was formed in you! Oh that you would turn to the Lord Jesus Christ, that he might have mercy upon you!

I would speak till midnight—yes, I would speak till I could speak no more, so it might be a means to bring you to Jesus. Let the Lord Jesus enter your souls, and you shall find peace which the world can neither give nor take away. There is mercy for the greatest sinner among you; go unto the Lord as sinners, helpless and undone without it, and then you shall find comfort in your souls, and be admitted at last among those who sing praises to the Lord to all eternity.

Now, my brethren, let me speak a word of exhortation to those of you, who are already brought to the Lord Jesus, who are born again, who do belong to God, to whom it has been given to repent of your sins, and are cleansed from their guilt; and that is, Be thankful to God for his mercies towards you. Oh admire the grace of God, and bless his name forever! Are you made alive in Christ Jesus? Is the life of God begun in your souls, and have you the evidence thereof? Be thankful for this unspeakable mercy to you; never forget to speak of his mercy. And as your life was formerly devoted to sin, and to the pleasures of the world, let it now be spent wholly in the ways of God; and oh embrace every opportunity of doing and receiving good. Whatever opportunity you have, do it vigorously, do it speedily, do not defer it. If thou seest one hurrying on to destruction, use the utmost of thy endeavor to stop him in his course. Show him the need he has of repentance, and that without it he is lost forever; do not regard his despising you; still go on to show him his danger. If thy friends mock and despise, do not let that discourage you. Hold on, hold out to the end, so you shall have a crown which is immutable, and that fadeth not away.

Let the love of Jesus to you, keep you also humble; do not be high-minded, keep close unto the Lord, observe the rules which the Lord Jesus Christ has given in his word, and let not the instructions be lost which you are capable of giving. Oh consider what reason you have to be thankful to the Lord Jesus Christ for giving you that repentance you yourselves had need of; a repentance which worketh by love. Now you find more pleasure in walking with God one hour, than in all your former carnal delights, and all the pleasures of sin. Oh! The joy you feel in your own souls, which all the men of this world and all the devils in hell, though they were to combine together, could not destroy. Then fear not their wrath or malice, for through many tribulations we must enter into glory.

A few days, weeks, or years more, and then you will be beyond their reach. You will be in the heavenly Jerusalem; there is all harmony and love, there is all joy and delight; there the weary are at rest.

Now we have many enemies, but at death they are all lost; they cannot follow us beyond the grave: and this is a great encouragement to us not to regard the scoffs and jeers of the men of this world.

Oh let the love of Jesus be in your thoughts continually. It was his dying that brought you life; it was his crucifixion that paid the satisfaction for your sins; his death, burial, and resurrection that completed the work; and he is now in heaven, interceding for you at the right hand of his Father. And can you do too much for the Lord Jesus Christ, who has done so much for you? His love to you is unfathomable. Oh the height, the depth, the length, and breadth, of this love, that brought the King of glory from his throne to die for such rebels as we are, when we had acted so unkindly against him, and deserved nothing but eternal damnation. He came down and took our nature upon him; he was made of flesh, and dwelt among us; he was put to death on our account; he paid our ransom. Surely, this should make us love the Lord Jesus Christ; should make us rejoice in him, and not do as too many do, and as we ourselves have too often, crucify this Jesus fresh. Let us do all we can, my dear brethren, to honor him.

Come, all of you, come, and behold him stretched out for you; see his hands and feet nailed to the cross. Oh come, come, my brethren, and nail your sins thereto; come, come and see his side pierced; there is a fountain open for sin, and for uncleanness; oh wash, wash, and be clean: come and see his head crowned with thorns, and all for you. Can you think of a panting, bleeding, dying Jesus, and not be filled with pity towards him? He underwent all this for you. Come to him by faith; lay hold on him; there is mercy for every soul of you that will come unto him. Then do not delay; fly into the arms of this Jesus, and you shall be made clean in his blood.

Oh, what shall I say to you, to make you come to Jesus? I have showed you the dreadful consequences of not repenting of your sins; and if, after all I have said, you are resolved to persist, your blood will be required at your own hands; but I hope better things of you, and things that accompany salvation. Let me beg of you to pray in good earnest for the grace of repentance. I may never see your faces again; but at the Day of Judgment I will meet you. There you will either bless God that ever you were moved to repentance; or else this sermon, though in a field, will be as a swift witness against you. Repent, repent, therefore, my dear brethren, as John the Baptist, and our blessed Redeemer himself earnestly exhorted, and turn from your evil ways, and the Lord will have mercy on you.

Show them, oh Father, wherein they have offended thee; make them to see their own vileness, and that they are lost and undone without true repentance. Oh give them that repentance, we beseech thee, that they may turn from sin unto thee, the living and true God. These things, and whatever else thou seest needful for us, we entreat that thou would bestow upon us, on account of what dear Jesus Christ has done and suffered; to whom, with thyself and the Holy Spirit, three persons and one God, be ascribed, as is most due, all power, glory, might, majesty, and dominion, now, henceforth, and forevermore. Amen.

Samuel Davies: *The General Resurrection*

SAMUEL DAVIES, ONE OF THE GREAT preachers of colonial America, was born in Pennsylvania in 1724, and died at Princeton, New Jersey, in 1761. He was ordained as a Presbyterian minister and settled at Hanover, near Richmond, Virginia. In 1753, Dr. Davies was chosen to go abroad with the Reverend Gilbert Tennant to solicit funds for the College of New Jersey, now Princeton University. When Davies was in England, King George II heard of his fame and invited him to preach in the royal chapel. Davies noticed the king talking and smiling with those near him during the sermon, and pausing in his discourse, fixed his eyes on the monarch and said, "When the lion roars, the beasts of the forest all tremble, and when King Jesus speaks the princes of the earth should keep silence." The comments of the king were declared to have been expressions of wonder and delight at the eloquence of the preacher. At all events, King George made a handsome donation to the college fund, and when he died Davies preached a sermon upon his character and death. In 1759, Dr. Davies was chosen to succeed Jonathan Edwards as president of Princeton.

Davies wrote out his sermons with great care, but in the delivery of them he was free and eloquent. Commenting on his own preaching, he said: "Perhaps once in three or four months I preach in some measure as I could wish, that is, I preach as in the sight of God and as if I were to step from the pulpit to the supreme tribunal. I feel my subject. I melt into tears or shudder with horror when I denounce the terrors of the Lord. I glow, I soar in sacred ecstasies when the love of Jesus is my theme, and, as Mr. Richard Baxter was wont to express it, in lines more striking to me than all the fine poetry in the world,

'I preached as never sure to preach again;
And as a dying man to dying men.'"

The General Resurrection and the Last Judgment are themes which have stirred the souls of great preachers ever since St. Paul made Felix tremble as he reasoned with him of righteousness and temperance and judgment to come. In Dr. Davies' powerful sermon, "The General Resurrection," the most striking and effective portion is where he describes the reluctant soul of the wicked, joined to its body in the day of resurrection, denouncing the body as the cause of its failure in time and its misery in eternity.

The General Resurrection

"The hour is coming, in the which all that are in the graves shall hear his voice, and shall come forth; they that have done good, unto the resurrection of life; and they that have done evil, unto the resurrection of damnation" (John 5:28–29).

 VER since sin entered into the world and death by sin, this earth has been a vast graveyard, or burying place, for her children. In every age, and in every country, that sentence has been executing, "Dust thou art, and unto dust shalt thou return" (Gen. 3:19). The earth has been arched with graves, the last lodgings of mortals, and the bottom of the ocean paved with the bones of men. Human nature was at first confined to one pair, but how soon and how wide did it spread! How inconceivably numerous are the sons of Adam! How many different nations on our globe contain many millions of men even in one generation! And how many generations have succeeded one another in the long run of near six thousand years! Let imagination call up this vast army: children that just light upon our globe, and then wing their flight into an unknown world; the gray-headed that have had a long journey through life; the blooming youth, and the middle-aged; let them pass in review before us from all countries and from all ages, and how vast and astonishing the multitude! If the posterity of one man (Abraham) by one son was, according to the divine promise, as the stars of heaven or as the sand by the seashore, innumerable, what numbers can compute the multitudes that have sprung from all the patriarchs, the sons of Adam and Noah! But what is become of them all? Alas! they are turned into earth, their original element; they are all imprisoned in the grave, except the present generation, and we are dropping one after another in quick succession into that place appointed for all living.

There has not been perhaps a moment of time for five thousand years, but what someone or other has sunk into the mansions of the dead. In some fatal hours, by the sword of war or the devouring jaws of earthquakes, thousands have been cut off and swept away at once and left in one huge, promiscuous carnage. The greatest number of mankind beyond comparison are sleeping under ground. There lies beauty moldering into dust, rotting into stench and loathsomeness, and feeding the vilest worms. There lies the head that once wore a crown, as low and contemptible as the meanest beggar. There lie the mighty giants, the heroes and conquerors, the Samsons, the Ajaxes, the Alexanders, and the Caesars of the world! There they lie stupid, senseless, inactive, and unable to drive off the worms that riot on their marrow, and make their houses in those sockets where the eyes sparkled with living luster. There lie the wise and the learned, as rotten, as helpless as the fool. There lie some that we once conversed with, some that were our friends, our companions; and there lie our fathers and mothers, our brothers and sisters.

And shall they lie there always? Shall this body, this curious workmanship of heaven, so wonderfully and fearfully made, always lie in ruins, and never be repaired? Shall the wide-extended valleys of dry bones never more live? This we know, that "it is not a thing impossible with God to raise the dead." He that could first form our bodies out of nothing is certainly able to form them anew, and repair the wastes of time and death. But what is his declared will in this case? On this the matter turns; and this is fully revealed in my text. "The hour is coming, when all that are in the graves, all that are dead, without exception, "shall hear [the] voice [of the Son of God], and shall come forth" (John 5:28–29).

And for what end shall they come forth? Oh! For very different purposes: some to "the resurrection of life," and some to "the resurrection of damnation" (v. 29).

And what is the ground of this vast distinction? Or what is the difference in character between those who shall receive so different a doom? It is this: They that have done good shall rise to life, and they that have done evil to damnation. It is this, and this only, that will then be the rule of distinction.

I would avoid all art in my method of handling this subject, and intend only to illustrate the several parts of the text. "All that are in the graves shall hear his voice, and shall come forth; they that have done good, unto the resurrection of life; and they that have done evil, unto the resurrection of damnation" (John 5:28–29).

I. They that are in the graves shall hear his voice. The voice of the Son of God here probably means the sound of the archangel's trumpet, which is called his voice, because sounded by his orders and attended with his all-quickening power. This all-awakening call to the tenants of the grave we frequently find foretold in Scripture. I shall refer you to two plain passages. "Behold," says St. Paul, "I show you a mystery;" an important and astonishing secret, "we shall not all sleep," that is, mankind will not all be sleeping in death when that day comes. There will be a generation then alive upon the earth, and though they cannot have a proper resurrection, yet they shall pass through a change equivalent to it. "We shall all be changed," says he, "in a moment, in the twinkling of an eye, at the last trump: for the trumpet shall sound, it shall give the alarm and no sooner is the awful clangor heard than all the living shall be transformed into immortals. "And the dead shall be raised incorruptible," and "we who are then alive," shall be changed (1 Cor. 15:51-52). This is all the difference, they shall be raised incorruptible, and we shall be changed. This awful prelude of the trumpet is also mentioned again: "We which are alive and remain unto the coming of the Lord shall not prevent them which are asleep." We shall not be beforehand with them in meeting our descending Lord, "For the Lord himself shall descend from heaven with a shout, with the voice of the archangel, and with the trump of God:" that is, with a godlike trump, such as it becomes his majesty to sound, "and the dead in Christ shall rise first" (1 Thess. 4:16), that is, before the living shall be caught up in the clouds to meet the Lord in the air. When they are risen, and the living transformed, they shall ascend together to the place of judgment.

My brethren, realize the majesty and terror of this universal alarm. The dead are sleeping in the silent grave; the living are thoughtless and unapprehensive of the grand event, or intent on other pursuits; some of them asleep in the dead of night; some of them dissolved in sensual pleasures, eating and drinking, marrying and giving in marriage; some of them planning or executing schemes for riches or honors; some in the very act of sin; the generality stupid and careless about the concerns of eternity, and the dreadful day just at hand. A few here and there are conversing with their God, and "looking for that blessed hope, and the glorious appearing of the great God and our Savior" (Titus 2:13), when the course of nature runs on uniformly and regularly as usual, and infidel scoffers are taking umbrage from thence to ask, "Where is the promise of his coming? for since the fathers fell asleep, all things continue as they were from the beginning of the creation" (2 Pet. 3:4). Oh what a surprise will this be to a thoughtless world! Should this alarm burst over our heads this moment, into what a terror would it strike many in this assembly? Such will be the terror, such the consternation, when it actually comes to pass. Sinners will be the same timorous, self-condemned creatures then, as they are now. And they will not be able to stop their ears, who are deaf to all the gentler calls of the gospel now. Then the trump of God will constrain them to hear and fear, to whom the ministers of Christ now preach in vain. Then they must all hear, for,

II. My text tells you, "all that are in the graves," all without exception, "shall hear his voice." Now the voice of mercy calls, reason pleads, conscience warns, but multitudes will not hear. But this is a voice which shall, which must reach every one of the millions of mankind, and not one of them will be able to stop his ears. Infants and giants, kings and subjects, all ranks, all ages of mankind shall hear the call. The living shall start and be changed, and the dead rise at the sound. The dust that was once alive and formed a human body, whether it flies in the air, floats in the ocean, or vegetates on earth, shall hear the new-creating fiat. Wherever the fragments of the human frame are scattered, this all-penetrating call shall reach and speak them into life. We may consider this voice as a summons, not only to dead bodies to rise, but also to souls that once animated them, to appear and be reunited to them, whether in heaven or hell. To the grave, the call will be, "Arise, ye dead, and come to judgment;" to heaven, ye "spirits of just men made perfect" (Heb. 12:23); "descend to the world whence you originally came and assume your new-formed bodies": to hell, "Come forth and appear, ye damned ghosts, ye prisoners of darkness, and be again united to the bodies in which you once sinned, that in them ye may now suffer." Thus will this summons spread through every corner of the universe; and heaven, earth and hell, and all their inhabitants, shall hear and obey. Devils, as well as sinners of our race, will tremble at the sound; for now they know they can plead no more as they once did, "Torment us not before the time," for the time is come, and they must mingle with the prisoners at the bar. And now when all that are in the graves hear this all-quickening voice,

III. They "shall come forth." Now I think I see, I hear the earth heaving, charnel houses rattling, tombs bursting, graves opening. Now the nations under ground begin to stir. There is a noise and a shaking among the dry bones. The dust is all alive and in motion, and the globe breaks and trembles as with an earthquake, while this vast army is working its way through and bursting into life. The ruins of human bodies are scattered far and wide, and have passed through many and surprising transformations. A limb in one country, and another in another; here the head and there the trunk, and the ocean rolling between. Multitudes have sunk in a watery grave, been swallowed up by the monsters of the deep, and transformed into a part of their flesh. Multitudes have been eaten by beasts and birds of prey and incorporated with them; and some have been devoured by their fellow men in the rage of a desperate hunger or of unnatural cannibal appetite, and digested into a part of them. Multitudes have moldered into dust, and this dust has been blown about by winds, washed away with water, petrified into stone, or been burnt into brick to form dwellings for their posterity. Or this dust has grown up in grain, trees, plants, and other vegetables, which are the support of man and beast, and are transformed into their flesh and blood. But through all these various transformations and changes, not a particle that was essential to one human body has been lost, or incorporated with another human body, so as to become an essential part of it. And as to those particles that were not essential, they are not necessary to the identity of the body or of the person; and therefore we need not think they will be raised again. The omniscient God knows how to collect, distinguish, and compound all those scattered and mingled seeds of our mortal bodies. And now at the sound of the trumpet, they shall all be collected, wherever they were scattered; all properly sorted and united, however they were confused; atom to its fellow-atom, bone to its fellow-bone. Now I think you may see the air darkened with fragments of bodies flying from country to country to meet and join their proper parts.

Then, my brethren, your dust and mine shall be reanimated and organized; "and though after my skin worms destroy this body, yet in my flesh shall I see God" (Job 19:26).

And what a vast improvement will the frail nature of man then receive? Our bodies will then be substantially the same; but how different in qualities, in strength, in agility, in capacities for pleasure or pain, in beauty or deformity, in glory or terror, according to the moral character of the persons to whom they belong. Matter, we know, is capable of prodigious alterations and refinements; and there it will appear in the highest perfection. The bodies of the saints will be formed glorious, incorruptible, without the seeds of sickness and death. The glorified body of Christ, which is undoubtedly carried to the highest perfection that matter is capable of, will be the pattern after which they shall be formed. "[He] will change our vile body," says St. Paul, "that it may be fashioned like unto his glorious body" (Phil. 3:21). "Flesh and blood," in their present state of grossness and frailty, "cannot inherit the kingdom of God; neither doth corruption inherit incorruption. . . . For this corruptible shall have put on incorruption, and this mortal shall have put on immortality" (1 Cor. 15:50,53). And how vast the change, how high the improvement from this present state! "It is sown in corruption; it is raised in incorruption: it is sown in dishonour; it is raised in glory; it is sown in weakness; it is raised in power" (1 Cor. 15:42–43). Then will the body be able to bear up under the "exceeding great and eternal weight of glory"; it will no longer be a clog or an encumbrance to the soul, but a proper instrument and assistant in all the exalted services and enjoyments of the heavenly state.

The bodies of the wicked will also be improved, but their improvements will all be terrible and vindictive. Their capacities will be thoroughly enlarged, but then it will be that they may be made capable of greater misery; they will be strengthened, but it will be that they may bear the heavier load of torment. Their sensations will be more quick and strong, but it will be that they may feel the more exquisite pain. They will be raised immortal that they may not be consumed by everlasting fire, or escape punishment by dissolution or annihilation. In short, their augmented strength, their enlarged capacities, and their immortality will be their eternal curse; and they would willingly exchange them for the fleeting duration of a fading flower or the faint sensations of an infant. The only power they would rejoice in is that of self-annihilation.

Now when the bodies are completely formed and fit to be inhabited, the souls that once animated them are collected from heaven and hell, re-enter, and take possession of their old mansions. They are united in bonds which shall never more be dissolved; and the moldering tabernacles are now become everlasting habitations.

With what joy will the spirits of the righteous welcome their old companions from their long sleep in the dust, and congratulate their glorious resurrection! How will they rejoice to re-enter their old habitations, now so completely repaired and highly improved! To find those bodies which were once their encumbrance, once frail and mortal, in which they were imprisoned, and languished, once their temptation, tainted with the seeds of sin, now their assistants and co-partners in the business of heaven, now vigorous, incorruptible, and immortal, now free from all corrupt mixtures, and shining in all the beauties of perfect holiness! In these bodies they once served their God with honest though feeble efforts, conflicted with sin and temptation, and passed through all the united trials and hardships of mortality and the Christian life. But now they are united to them for more exalted and blissful purposes. The lungs that once heaved with penitential sighs and groans shall now shout forth their joys and the praises of their God and Savior. The hearts once broken with sorrows shall now be bound up for ever, and overflow with immortal pleasures. Those very eyes that ran down with tears and beheld many a tragic sight, shall now behold the "King in his beauty" (Isa. 33:17), shall behold the Savior whom, though unseen, they loved, and all the glories of heaven; and "God shall wipe away all their tears" (Rev. 7:17). All the senses, which were once avenues of pain, shall now be inlets of the most exalted pleasure. In short, every organ, every member shall be employed in the most noble services and enjoyments, instead of the sordid and laborious drudgery and the painful sufferings of the present state. Blessed change indeed! Rejoice, ye children of God, in the prospect of it.

But how shall I glance a thought upon the dreadful case of the wicked in that tremendous day! While their bodies burst from their graves, the miserable spectacles of horror and deformity, see the millions of gloomy ghosts that once animated them, rise like pillars of smoke from the bottomless pit! With what reluctance and anguish do they re-enter their old habitations! Oh what a dreadful meeting! What shocking salutations! "And must I be chained to thee again, (may the guilty soul say) oh thou accursed, polluted body, thou system of deformity and terror! In thee I once sinned, by thee I was once ensnared, debased, and ruined. To gratify thy vile lusts and appetites, I neglected my own immortal interests, degraded my native dignity, and made myself miserable forever. And hast thou now met me to torment me forever? Oh that thou hadst still slept in the dust, and never been repaired again! Let me rather be condemned to animate a toad or serpent than that odious body once defiled with sin, and the instrument of my guilty pleasures, now made strong and immortal to torment me with strong and immortal pains. Once indeed I received sensations of pleasure from thee, but now thou art transformed into an engine of torture. No more shall I through thine eyes behold the cheerful light of the day, and the beautiful prospects of nature, but the thick glooms of hell, grim and ghastly ghosts, heaven at an impassable distance, and all the horrid sights of woe in the infernal regions. No more shall thine ears charm me with the harmony of sounds, but terrify and distress me with the echo of eternal groans, and the thunder of almighty vengeance! No more shall the gratification of thine appetites afford me pleasure, but thine appetites, forever hungry, forever unsatisfied, shall eternally torment me with their eager, importunate cravings. No more shall thy tongue be employed in mirth, jest, and song, but complain, groan, blaspheme, and roar forever. Thy feet, that once walked in the flowery, enchanted paths of sin, must now walk on the dismal burning soil of hell. Oh my wretched companion! I parted with thee with pain and reluctance in the struggles of death, but now I meet with greater terror and agony. Return to thy bed in the dust; there to sleep and rot, and let me never see thy shocking visage more." In vain the petition! The reluctant soul must enter its prison, from whence it shall never more be dismissed. And if we might indulge imagination so far, we might suppose the body begins to recriminate in such language as this: "Come, guilty soul, enter thy old mansion. If it be horrible and shocking, it is owing to thyself. Was not the animal frame, the brutal nature, subjected to thy government, who art a rational principle? Instead of being debased by me, it became thee to have not only retained the dignity of thy nature, but also to have exalted mine, by nobler employments and gratifications worthy an earthly body united to an immortal spirit. Thou mightest have restrained my members from being the instruments of sin, and made them the instruments of righteousness. My knees would have bowed at the throne of grace, but thou didst not affect that posture. Mine eyes would have read, and mine ears heard the word of life; but thou wouldest not set them to that employ, or wouldest not attend to it. And now it is but just the body thou didst prostitute to sin should be the instrument of thy punishment. Indeed, I wish I could relapse into senseless earth as I was, and continue in that insensibility forever—but didst thou not hear the all-rousing trumpet just now? Did it not even shake the foundations of thy infernal prison? It was that call that awakened me, and summoned me to meet thee, and I could not resist it. Therefore come, miserable soul, take possession of this frame, and let us prepare for everlasting burning. Oh that it were now possible to die! Oh that we could be again separated, and never be united more! Vain wish; the weight of mountains, the pangs of hell, the flames of unquenchable fire, can never dissolve these chains which now bind us together!"

But for what end do these sleeping multitudes rise? For what purposes do they come forth? My text will tell you.

IV. They "shall come forth; they that have done good, unto the resurrection of life; and they that have done evil unto the resurrection of damnation" (John 5:28–29). They are summoned from their graves to stand at the bar, and brought out of prison by angelic guards to pass their last trial. And as in this impartial trial they will be found to be persons of very different characters, the righteous Judge of the earth will accordingly pronounce their different doom.

See a glorious "multitude, which no man could number" (Rev. 7:9), openly acquitted, pronounced blessed, and welcomed into "the kingdom prepared for [them] from the foundation of the world" (Matt. 25:34). Now they enter upon a state which deserves the name of life. They are all vital, all active, all glorious, all happy. They "shine as the brightness of the firmament: as the stars for ever and ever" (Dan. 12:3). All their faculties overflow with happiness. They mingle with the glorious company of angels; they behold that Savior whom unseen they loved; they dwell in eternal intimacy with the Father of their spirits; they are employed with ever new and growing delight in the exalted services of the heavenly sanctuary. They shall nevermore fear nor feel the least touch of sorrow, pain, or any kind of misery, but shall be as happy as their natures can admit through an immortal duration. What a glorious new creation is here! What illustrious creatures formed of the dust! And shall any of us join in this happy company? Oh shall any of us, feeble, dying, sinful creatures share in their glory and happiness? This is a most interesting inquiry, and I would have you think of it with trembling anxiety; and I shall presently answer it in its place. The prospect would be delightful, if our charity could hope that this will be the happy end of all the sons of men. But, alas! Multitudes, and we have reason to fear the far greater number, shall come forth, not to the resurrection of life, but to the resurrection of damnation! What terror is in the sound! If audacious sinners in our world make light of it, and pray for it on every trifling occasion, their infernal brethren that feel its tremendous import are not so hardy, but tremble and groan, and can trifle with it no more.

Let us realize the miserable doom of this class of mankind. See them bursting into life from their subterranean dungeons, hideous shapes of deformity and terror, expressive of the vindictive design for which their bodies are repaired, and of the boisterous and malignant passions that ravage their souls. Horror throbs through every vein, and glares wild and furious in their eyes. Every joint trembles, and every countenance looks downcast and gloomy. Now they see that tremendous day of which they were warned in vain, and shudder at those terrors of which they once made light. They immediately know the grand business of the day, and the dreadful purpose for which they are roused from their slumbers in the grave: to be tried, to be convicted, to be condemned, and to be dragged away to execution. Conscience has been anticipating the trial in a separate state; and no sooner is the soul united to the body, than immediately conscience ascends its throne in the breast, and begins to accuse, to convict, to pass sentence, to upbraid, and to torment. The sinner is condemned, condemned at his own tribunal, before he arrives at the bar of his Judge. The first act of consciousness in his new state of existence is a conviction that he is condemned, an irrevocably condemned creature. He enters the court, knowing beforehand how it will go with him. When he finds himself ordered to the left hand of his Judge, when he hears the dreadful sentence thundered out against him, "Depart from me, accursed," it was but what he expected. Now he can flatter himself with vain hopes, and shut his eyes against the light of conviction, but then he will not be able to hope better; then he must know the worst of his case. The formality of the judicial trial is necessary for the conviction of the world, but not for his; his own conscience has already determined his condition. However, to convince others of the justice of his doom, he is dragged and guarded from his grave to the judgment seat by fierce, unrelenting devils, now his tempters, but then his tormentors. With what horror does he view the burning throne and the frowning face of his Judge, that Jesus whom he once disregarded, in spite of all his dying love and the salvation he offered! How does he wish for a covering of rocks and mountains to conceal him from his angry eye!—but all in vain. Appear he must. He is ordered to the left among the trembling criminals; and now the trial comes on. All his evil deeds and all his omissions of duty, are now produced against him. All the mercies he abused, all the chastisements he despised, all the means of grace he neglected or misimproved, every sinful, and even every idle word, even his most secret thoughts and dispositions, are all exposed, and brought into judgment against him. And when the Judge puts it to him, "Is it not so, sinner? Are not these charges true?" conscience obliges him to confess and cry out, "Guilty! Guilty!" And now the trembling criminal being plainly convicted and left without all plea and all excuse, the supreme Judge, in stern majesty and inexorable justice, thunders out the dreadful sentence, "Depart from me, ye cursed, into everlasting fire, prepared for the devil and his angels" (Matt. 25:41). Oh tremendous doom! Every word is big with terror, and shoots a thunderbolt through the heart. "Depart: away from my presence; I cannot bear so loathsome a sight. I once invited thee to come to me, that thou mightest have life, but thou wouldst not regard the invitation; and now thou shalt never hear that inviting voice more. Depart from me, the only fountain of happiness, the only proper good for an immortal mind." "But, Lord," (we may suppose the criminal to say) "if I must depart, bless me before I go." "No," says the angry Judge, "depart accursed; depart with my eternal and heavy curse upon thee; the curse of that power that made thee; a curse dreadfully efficacious, that blasts whatever it falls upon like flashes of consuming irresistible lightning." "But if I must go away under thy curse, (the criminal may be supposed to say), yet that be all my punishment; let me depart to some agreeable, or at least tolerable recess, where I may meet with something to mitigate the curse." "No, depart into fire; there burn in all the excruciating tortures of that outrageous element." "But, Lord, if I must make my bed in fire, oh let it be a transient blaze, that will soon burn itself out, and put an end to my torment." "No, depart into everlasting fire; there burn without consuming, and be tormented without end." "But, Lord, grant me (cries the poor wretch) at least the mitigation of friendly, entertaining, and sympathizing company; or, if this cannot be granted, grant me this small, this almost no request, to be doomed to some solitary corner in hell, where I shall be punished only by my own conscience and thine immediate hand. But oh deliver me from these malicious, tormenting devils; banish me into some apartment in the infernal pit far from their society." "No, depart into everlasting fire prepared for the devil and his angels: thou must make one of their wretched crew forever; thou didst join with them in sinning, and now must share in their punishment: thou didst submit to them as thy tempters, and now thou must submit to them as thy tormentors."

The sentence being pronounced, it is immediately executed. "These shall go away into everlasting punishment." Devils drag them away to the pit, and push them down headlong. There they are confined in chains of darkness, and in a lake burning with fire and brimstone, forever, forever! In that dreadful word lies the emphasis of torment; it is a hell in hell. If they might be released from pain, though it were by annihilation after they have wept away ten thousand millions of ages in extremity of pain, it would be some mitigation, some encouragement. But, alas! When as many millions of ages are passed as the stars of heaven, or the sands of the seashore, or the atoms of dust in this huge globe of earth, their punishment is as far from an end as when the sentence was pronounced upon them. Forever! There is no exhausting of that word; and when it is affixed to the highest degree of misery, the terror of the sound is utterly insupportable. See, sirs, what depends upon time, that span of time we may enjoy in this fleeting life. Eternity! awful, all-important eternity, depends upon it.

All this while, conscience tears the sinner's heart with the most tormenting reflections. "Oh what a fair opportunity I once had for salvation, had I improved it! I was warned of the consequences of a life of sin and carelessness; I was told of the necessity of faith, repentance, and universal holiness of heart and life; I enjoyed a sufficient space for repentance, and all the necessary means of salvation, but, fool that I was, I neglected all, I abused all; I refused to part with my sins; I refused to engage seriously in religion, and to seek God in earnest; and now I am lost forever, without hope. Oh for one of those months, one of those weeks, or even so much as one of those days or hours I once trifled away; with what earnestness, with what solicitude would I improve it! But all my opportunities are past, beyond recovery, and not a moment shall be given me for this purpose any more. Oh what a fool was I to sell my soul for such trifles! To set so light by heaven, and to fall into hell through mere neglect and carelessness!" Ye impenitent, unthinking sinners, though you may now be able to silence or drown the clamors of your consciences, yet the time, or rather the dread eternity is coming, when they will speak in spite of you; when they will speak home, and be felt by the most hardened and remorseless heart. Therefore now regard their warnings while they may be the means of your recovery.

You and I, my brethren, are concerned in the solemn transaction of the day I have been describing. You and I shall either be changed in a moment, in the twinkling of an eye, or while moldering in the grave, we shall hear the voice of the Son of God, and come forth, either to the resurrection of life, or to the resurrection of damnation. And which, my brethren, shall be our doom? And now who is for life, and who for damnation among you? These characters are intended to make the distinction among you, and I pray you apply them for that purpose.

As for such of you, who, amid all your lamented infirmities, are endeavoring honestly to do good, and grieved at heart that you can do no more, you must also die; you must die, and feed the worms in the dust. But you shall rise gloriously improved, rise to an immortal life, and in all the terrors and consternation of that last day, you will be secure, serene, and undisturbed. The almighty Judge will be your friend, and that is enough. Let this thought disarm the king of terrors, and give you courage to look down into the grave, and forward to the great rising day. Oh what a happy immortality opens its glorious prospects beyond the sight before you! After a few struggles more in this state of warfare, and resting a while in the bed of death, at the regions of eternal blessedness you will arrive, and take up your residence there forever.

But are there not some here who are conscious that these favorable characters do not belong to them? That know that well-doing is not the business of their life, but that they are workers of iniquity? I tell you plainly, and with all the authority the word of God can give, that if you continue such, you shall rise to damnation. That undoubtedly will be your doom, unless you are greatly changed and reformed in heart and life. And will this be no excitement to vigorous endeavors? Are you proof against the energy of such a consideration? Ye careless sinners, awake out of your security, and prepare for death and judgment! This fleeting life is all the time you have for preparation, and can you trifle it away? Your all, your eternal all is set upon the single cast of life, and you must stand the hazard of the die. You can make but one experiment, and if that fails, through your sloth or mismanagement, you are irrecoverably undone forever. Therefore, by the dread authority of the great God, by the terrors of death, and the great rising day, by the joys of heaven and the torments of hell, and by the value of your immortal souls, I entreat, I charge, I adjure you to awake out of your security, and improve the precious moments of life. The world is dying all around you. And can you rest easy in such a world, while unprepared for eternity? Awake to righteousness now, at the gentle call of the gospel, before the last trumpet give you an alarm of another kind.

Rowland Hill: *Glorious Displays of Gospel Grace*

ROWLAND HILL WAS BORN on August 12, 1744, at Hawkeston, England, and died on April 11, 1833. He was the son of Sir Robert Hill. At Cambridge he came under the influence of Whitefield and became, like Whitefield, a great open-air preacher. He built with his own money Surrey Chapel in London and was heard by great throngs in his church and on his itinerating tours through the country. He left behind him an impression of great natural eloquence. Sheridan said of him: "I hear Rowland Hill because his ideas come hot from the heart"; and Robert Hall: "No man has ever drawn, since the days of our Savior, such sublime images from nature." There are many anecdotes of his wit, which sometimes verged on buffoonery. He gave free rein to the feeling of the moment and sometimes offended against good taste. On a wet day, a number of persons took shelter in his chapel during a heavy shower while he was in the pulpit. Seeing them come in, Hill said: "Many people are greatly blamed for making their religion a cloak, but I do not think those are much better who make it an umbrella." When asked once why he did not preach to the elect, he said from the pulpit: "I don't know them, or I would preach to them. Have the goodness to mark them with a piece of chalk, and then I'll talk to them."

In his sermon on the "Displays of Gospel Grace," Rowland Hill, after paying tribute to the mighty works done by Whitefield, challenges the formal and literary preachers to produce a like effect, saying: "Let us try how some of these rationalists in religion (as they *humbly* wish to be thought) would be likely to succeed on a similar occasion. Let them seek for some other colliery of the like description; there, take one of their nicely composed paper-pop-guns and read it among the multitude. I would willingly and gladly carry their stools behind them to see what sort of figures they would cut in their attempts to reform. I hate such silly pride, and it is best corrected by the lash of ridicule and contempt."

Glorious Displays of Gospel Grace

"This gospel of the kingdom shall be preached in all the world for
a witness unto all nations: and then shall the end come" (Matt. 24:14).

 F *ever my mind felt the solemn weight* of those words of
the good old patriarch, "This is none other but the
house of God, and this is the gate of heaven" (Gen.
28:17), it is on this present occasion. Can we suppose that so many of
God's ministers and people should find it in their hearts to assemble
together on such a glorious design, and he not be present with them?
Oh surely not! We believe him to be in the midst of us. Nor can anything short of his special presence crown our labors with success.
What a mercy then that we live in a day in which the Lord's promise
is, we hope, to be remarkably verified, "Lo, I am with you alway, even
unto the end of the world" (Matt. 28:20).

Matters of salvation are of infinite importance. The glory of
bringing souls to Christ is the greatest honor God can confer upon
us. The salvation of one soul is of more worth than a thousand
worlds. My dearest brethren in the ministry, may God fill us with the
like ardent desires to those which warmed the apostle's heart, when
he was constrained to declare to his Galatian hearers that "he travailed in birth again till Christ was formed in them" (see Gal. 4:19).
And while you thus assemble upon the business of sending the
gospel to heathen nations, may you on your departure, beloved
brethren, from this our British Jerusalem, be so filled with the spirit
and power from above that you may be a thousand times more successful, not only in promoting good among those whom you are
more immediately concerned to serve in the ministry of the word,
but also for the conversion of the poor heathen in your neighborhood. Oh, what crowds of heathens, and worse than heathens, though

under the Christian name, are everywhere to be found among us! And why may we not expect that such a fire shall now be kindled as that not only wonders be done among the nations that know not God, but that even in our own land it shall be our portion also to be indulged with a remarkable revival of the power of religion, "when the times of refreshing shall come from the presence of the Lord" (Acts 3:19).

What littleness and insignificance are stamps upon all the things of time and sense, when compared to such blessings as these! What avail the things that are temporal in comparison of those that are eternal? Here are glories that words can never reach, nor tongue express, and I wonder not at the sensations of one happy mind, who, though quite in the agonies of dissolving nature, and beyond the power of giving an intelligible answer to any question asked, yet, with a hope full of immortality though in the jaws of death, felt such blessedness upon his mind as constrained him to lift up his arms in triumph, and with a very heaven on his countenance thrice to repeat, "Oh the glories! Oh the glories! Oh the glories!"

Now to be made the happy instruments of conveying so much felicity, in such solemn circumstances as this dying man felt, what an honor! While we live, may God fill our hearts with these surprising glories; that they may be our cordial in our departing moments; and may divine mercy teach a world of sinners to seek the fame!

We shall not then blush at what the world calls the irregularity of our conduct. When an apostolic warmth of zeal shall make every minister a missionary around his own neighborhood, and when, touched with the sacred tenderness of Christian compassion, he can never be contented while on earth to leave a single sinner within his reach unconverted to God.

A poor sinner in her dying moments, requesting that a despised servant of Jesus Christ might visit her before her departure, heard someone ridicule her choice, that she should call in one of such a methodistical character, a common street-preacher and field-preacher. Roused with zeal and gratitude to God for the instrument of her conversion, she said to those who stood around her, "Let who will despise him. I will thank him before men and angels that he went out into the streets and lanes of our city to bring my lost, wandering soul to God." I drop the hint to encourage you, my brethren in the blessed work of field preaching, that we may be instant in season and out of season, and do the work of an evangelist. But I am now to follow the plan designed from the text, Lord help me! The word before us gives us to understand that as wonders have in former ages been done by the gospel, so in future still greater glories shall be accomplished. Nor in our day "the Lord's hand is not shortened that it cannot save; neither his ear heavy, that it cannot hear" (Isa. 59:1). No, the longer we live, the manifestation of still greater glories ought to be expected; for the time is still to come when the "earth shall be filled with the knowledge of the glory of the Lord, as the waters cover the sea" (Hab. 2:14). Yes, "the kingdoms of this world are become the kingdoms of our Lord, and of his Christ" (Rev. 11:15). Saints and angels wait with holy impatience to rend the vault of heaven at the arrival of the time when that song, more universally than ever, shall be sung, "Alleluiah: for the Lord God omnipotent reigneth. . . . King of kings and Lord of lords" (Rev. 19:6,16).

I mean not merely to show that the gospel of the kingdom was preached in all ages since the fall of man, but more especially to note the outpourings of the Spirit in different ages, under the divine manifestation of mercy to mankind, that our hearts may be enlarged and our hopes quickened on this present occasion.

No sooner had our first parents brought sin into the world by their transgression, and scarcely had divine justice pronounced the curse, when sovereign mercy dropped the gracious promise, the seed of the woman shall bruise the serpent's head (see Gen. 3:15). Thus was the gospel first preached in paradise itself. They, to whom it was preached, we trust lived upon the promise given and looked with long expectation after it. They even seemed to conclude they had obtained the accomplishment when Eve, upon the birth of her first son, to render the passage more literally, cried, "I have gotten a man, the Lord."

This we may call the first spring of mercy to fallen man, but we find it awfully limited to a narrow channel throughout the antediluvian world, while such floods of iniquity overspread the face of the earth that God himself is described as repenting that he had made man, yes, as being on this account grieved at his heart (see Gen. 6:6). In the family of Noah alone was the knowledge and fear of God preserved.

But now the stream that began to flow from the most early period of time gradually increases and continues upon the increase like a spreading river, till its wide, extended currents open themselves into the bosom of the ocean.

God separated Abraham and his family early for that purpose. The faith of the renowned patriarch was strong and clear, respecting the person and glories of Christ. Faith is a long-sighted grace, for, notwithstanding the distance of time, he "rejoiced to see [Christ's] day: he saw it and was glad" (John 8:56). Paul declares that the same faith which justified Abraham justifies believers in Jesus in all ages; that the blessings of the same salvation are to be imparted to us also, if blessed with the same faith that dwelt in him, who is the father of the faithful. And indeed, all the great works done by the worthies of old are described in the eleventh of Hebrews as done by faith in the Lord Jesus, which alone rendered them acceptable in the sight of God, for "without faith it is impossible to please him" (Heb. 11:6).

We next notice other revivals that succeeded: Caleb the son of Jephunneh and Joshua the son of Nun stand highly recorded in sacred writ. Though sin kept the generation of their contemporaries from the promised land—they rotted through unbelief in the wilderness —yet nothing could affect the lives of these men of renown, or prevent them from possessing their desired Canaan. Great was the revival of religion in their days, and much good was done by their instrumentality. God was eminently with them and they acknowledged him in all their ways. No Canaanitish foe could prevent their glorious progress; they were conquerors, more than conquerors, because they believed on their God. And cannot God give the like precious faith in the present undertaking? When God says, "Let there be light," is it in the power of all hell to create darkness? When he says, "Arise, shine," shall not omnipotence prevail? We triumph while we believe in God. "If God be for us, who can be against us?" (Rom. 8:31).

Once my mind had its doubts respecting a mission to the heathen. Unbelief said there were a thousand difficulties in the way. I thank God that my soul was made to blush when that text was brought to my recall, "God is able of these stones to raise up children unto Abraham" (Matt. 3:9). Now what is so inanimate as a stone? Had the metaphor been taken from trees, or any other part of the vegetable creation, there we might have discovered the existence at least of vegetable life; but what power can command stones to live but the power of the living God?

Time would fail us to trace the like divine displays of grace, through the regency of Samuel and the first part of the reign of Saul, and the increasing glories which rested on the church of God while the scepter was entrusted in David's hands. We hasten to the time of Solomon. Then the reflected light given through that dispensation shone with its fullest splendor, but, like the shining of the moor which gradually withdraws her humble light till she totally disappears and hides herself behind the sun, so we shall find that these gracious revivals gradually declined, till Jesus the Sun of Righteousness arose, creating the gospel day of grace and adorning it with all the glories of his great salvation.

Solomon's reign was filled with wonders. We trace however, but the more pure and chaste part of his history while the Lord was truly with him.

He began his reign with divine communications with his God, and while he maintained communion with Him he prospered; his noblest wish was to build the temple. It was during that period that the heart of this prince was fully devoted to the Lord. His wisdom, his riches, and his honors were entirely dedicated to promote the glory of his God; with zeal he completes the work which God had given him to perform. And now the temple is to be dedicated to him for whose service it was built. Oh what a day is this, when all Israel appears before the Lord like a multitude which no man could number. The king himself leads the devotions of his people, and God miraculously declares his approbation of the solemn work, while flakes of holy fire descend on the sacrifice already prepared for the divine service, and the glory of God fills all the temple and constrains the people to rejoice with reverence and godly fear.

Can we suppose that a mere outward and visible manifestation of the glory of God was all that the great majesty of heaven designed hereby? Oh surely no! He that is as a refiner's fire to the hearts of his people was now doubtless working upon their hearts also, by his invisible agency, that he might prepare them for himself and then take them to his glory. In short, does not this appear as the great Pentecost of the Old Testament church, similar in its nature and effects to that recorded in the New Testament, when cloven tongues of fire rested upon the heads of the apostles, a visible sign of their preparation for their important ministry, that through their instrumentality great grace might rest upon the hearts of thousands, to prepare them for glory?

Oh! What views further open to our minds, when we meditate on the multitudes of glorified spirits already brought to God under these different outpourings of the spirit of grace. They are long ago safely landed, and are waiting with holy joy for those who are now coming, and for others who shall yet come, till God shall have accomplished the number of his elect and finished his great work of the salvation of millions of mankind.

Now a long night ensues. Through a space of nearly seven hundred years we read in the inspired records (excepting what is referred to in the Forty-fourth Psalm and some other places) but of one revival of the power of the glorious faithfulness of the Jewish church in days of dreadful persecution of religion, and that was under the government of Ezra and Nehemiah on the return of Israel from their Babylonish captivity. Let us a little investigate the glories of that revival. The people had polluted themselves by their unlawful connections while captives in an heathen land, and even after their return from the captivity. These by the command of God were to be renounced, and yet what dearer to nature than the wife of a man's bosom? But Ezra, the holy reformer, was at a point with the people. The command was explicit: wives taken unlawfully are now to be rejected, and they yield obedience to what nature would call this severe injunction of the Lord.

Whatever may be dear to us, may our Lord and God be dearer still! Yes, dearer and dearer day by day! Oh that Christ may find out for us in this present work, those who can forsake houses, lands, brothers, sisters, husbands, wives, and all for his dear sake! And why should any refuse to forsake such low things as these for him, who forsook his heaven, his glory, and hid not his face from shame and spitting, and at last laid down his life to ransom us from the hell that sin most righteously deserves, that he might make us partakers with himself of blessedness in eternal glory? I will make a few observations further on this last revival of religion before the coming of our Lord. The word of God was again brought forth into public notice.

Ezra the scribe stands on a pulpit of wood, from the sun rising till the noonday. For six hours at one time, he reads and expounds the word of God, assisted by twelve others of the princes of Israel, six of them standing on the one side and six of them on the other. "They read in the book in the law of God distinctly, and gave the sense, and caused them to understand the reading" (Neh. 8:8). Nor were they tired with the length of the sermon; no, a weeping congregation will not speedily be weaned of the word of God. It was a strong evidence on their behalf that God was with them of a truth, that their hearts were melted before the Lord and their eyes were a fountain of tears.

Oh what a refreshing sight would it be to us, my brethren, if such were the state of our congregations to manifest such tenderness of heart and such readiness at once to obey all that they hear from the sacred word of truth! I am sure no sight is so glorious as the presence of God upon a worshipping congregation; nor anything so animating to the heart of a minister as when he perceives that the word he preaches comes to the hearts of the hearers, with "the demonstration of the Spirit and of power" (1 Cor. 2:4).

After this period till the coming of Christ a gross darkness for the most part covered the earth. Religion seemed sunk into formality, while the institutions of God at the same time were wretchedly blended with the inventions of men.

The spirit of prophecy was now totally withdrawn; no zealous reformers made their appearances, nor were any indications given of the people lamenting over their deserted state or longing for the returning mercies of the Lord.

It is observed that the darkest moment in all the night is the moment which precedes the first break of day. Blessed be God, we are now to contemplate the glories of that bright day created by the presence of him who is "the brightness of his [Father's] glory, and the express image of his person" (Heb. 1:3).

But there is something in the progress of this light which demands our attention. We find some wonderful stirrings of conscience (and it is well when God sets conscience at work) under the preaching of John the Baptist. Plain was his appearance, but powerful was his word: his business was to "prepare ... the way of the Lord." If, however, his words seemed to have but a transient effect upon the minds of his hearers, one could not but suppose that when the Son of God commenced a preacher, wonders indeed would be wrought and that not a hearer could resist when the incarnate Jehovah delivered his own word. But what was accomplished by the preaching of our Lord? His word was indeed with authority and his astonished hearers were constrained to acknowledge "Never man spake like this man" (John 7:46). Notwithstanding all this, and though he was obliged to take the mountains for his pulpit, though he went about from village to village and from city to city to preach the gospel of the kingdom, we find no more after the crucifixion than a hundred and twenty souls, collected together in an upper room for fear of the Jews. Where were the thousands that attended the ministry of the Baptist? Where were the multitudes that attended our Lord and were fed by his miracles? The glorious power was not yet revealed that effectually does the work. "The Holy Ghost was not yet given; because that Jesus was not yet glorified" (John 7:39). He must first "put away sin by the sacrifice of himself" (Heb. 9:26). It was not right that the blessing should be granted till the curse was removed, but when once the great work was finished, when Jesus had ascended into his heavenly kingdom, according to the glorious word, "Lift up your heads O ye gates; and be ye lift up, ye everlasting doors; and the King of glory shall come in" (Ps. 24:7); when he had finished his conquests and had "ascended up on high, he led captivity captive," then came the blessed time when he "gave his gifts unto men" (Eph. 4:8), even the rebellious, and come and dwell among them. Thus, having prepared the mansions for his people, he next sends down his Spirit to prepare his people for those mansions. oh the glories of that sacred day! "Behold, the tabernacle of God is with men!" (Rev. 21:3). According to our Lord's direction, the disciples waited at Jerusalem for the fulfillment of his promise, and lo! he comes, their understandings are enlightened, to understand the Scriptures. Their hearts are inflamed, and they preach the word with faithfulness and power. Before, neither the thunders of John preaching in the wilderness, nor yet the words of grace that dropped from the lips of Jesus Christ himself, could effectually impress the minds almost of any. But how the preaching of a poor set of illiterate fishermen melts the adamantine hearts of the murderers of Christ and brings them by the thousands to submit to his righteous and merciful scepter. On the very first day after the Day of Pentecost was fully come, we hear of three thousand; at another time, we hear the numbers increased to five thousand; then again, that "believers were the more added to the Lord, multitudes both of men and women" (Acts 5:14); and further, "the number of the disciples multiplied . . . greatly;" and, what was the greatest wonder of all wonders, that "a great company of the priests were obedient to the faith" (Acts 6:7). Yes, we hear of whole villages, towns, cities, countries, which at once were subjugated to the Lord Jesus, "so mightily grew the word of God and prevailed" (Acts 19:20). Now was the time that "a nation be born at once, for as soon as Zion travailed, she brought forth her children" (Isa. 66:8). Oh the power that then went with the word! Those that heard were at once pricked to the heart. Their cry directly was, "What must I do to be saved?" and the answer, as directly given, was "Believe on the Lord Jesus Christ, and thou shalt be saved" (Acts 16:30–31). How must the decency, as we suppose, of religious worship have been interrupted thereby, but oh blessed interruption, when God himself wrought so gloriously and so many souls were brought into divine subjection to the cross of

Christ! May God send us such blessed interruptions in all our con-gregations! Oh, they are glorious!

It may be asked what became of the multitudes that attended the ministry of our Lord and his harbinger John? It strikes me that many of those now had their convictions revived, and were found among the happy thousands who received the gospel dispensation. The seed was first sown by John, and by our glorious Lord, and after being watered by the descent of the Holy Ghost, sprang up to the glory of God. What encouragement this is to every sincere minister to be dili-gent in his work! Secret convictions may a long time abide in the heart before a thorough conversion to God is effected. "Cast thy bread upon the waters: for thou shalt find it after many days" (Eccl. 11:1). We shall reap if we faint not.

Oftentimes, when I have been engaged in preaching, and perhaps in the contemptible work of street preaching too, when I have thought that the whole town was dead in trespasses and sins, some few secret ones have been found, allow the plain expression, and I left them like nest eggs. I visited them again, and the numbers soon increased till the little ones became a thousand.

What remarkable evidence is given by all these revivals that the work in which we are engaged is, indeed, the work of God: "Not by might, nor by power, but by my spirit, saith the Lord" (Zech. 4:6). For what was the doctrine especially in the great revival on the Day of Pentecost? The plain simple preaching of the cross of Christ. And who were the instruments? A set of plain, illiterate fishermen. Better a thousand times to have the simplicity of a Peter than the eloquence of a Longinus, if we are but made useful to the souls of our fellow creatures. That preaching is always the best that best answers the end of preaching. Let us, therefore, go forth preaching, as it is worded in the text, "the gospel of the kingdom," and that too with simplicity and godly sincerity, and not with fleshly wisdom, and what has been done shall be done. God will ever stand by his own truth, and if he be for us, who can be against us? Preaching the gospel of the kingdom does all the work. I hate the pride of those who attempt to set aside this glorious dispensation and are ever attempting to establish what they call the powers of reason in its stead and are ever boasting of the mighty things that it can effect. Had they, however, a little more of the same faculty they pretend so plentifully to possess, they would not expose themselves by such assertions, for what can reason do while under the influence of corrupted nature? No, say they, it is passion and appetite, not reason, that then govern the man. But if passion and appetite prevail over the human understanding, so that good is avoided as an evil and evil sought after as a good, and these furnish our reasoning powers with their materials, we may easily conclude what will be the conduct and the choice; no, say they, shall it be said that a drunkard acts according to reason? Certainly not; but he acts according to his reason; and does a man in a violent passion act according to reason? According to that which he at that instant of time calls reason, he certainly does. And both the drunkard and the passionate man will give you a thousand reasons, as they call them, for their conduct; and, however badly they reason, it is reason to them. However wrongly they may be guided, yet their reason was their guide; and it is not likely that a wrong guide will lead a man right. In short, every man's reason directs him to seek after happiness. While the carnal mind supposes there is happiness to be had in the indulgence of lust and passion, reason will lead that road. In short, sound reason can never be engrafted but upon real religion.

The fact proves itself. Where are the converts of these boasted rational preachers? A fig for all their pretensions to wisdom if they cannot produce one single sample of a precious soul being converted from sin to God thereby.

I bring forward the character of the great Mr. Whitefield on this occasion. I hope you do not blush for me that I mention his name on this subject, for verily I shall not blush for myself. God gave him a most enlarged mind, liberating him from all the wretched trammels of education. He knew no party, his glory was to preach the gospel to every creature; bigotry his soul abhorred; and like a second Samson, he has so made her main supporting pillars to totter that you and I, my brethren, rejoice that she trembles to the very foundation, and live in daily hopes that her complete destruction shall complete our joy.

Now I will not say, I thank the devil for anything; but I will say, I thank God for that permissive providence whereby that great man, being turned out of the churches, esteemed it his duty to preach at large. His first attempt was among the poor Kingswood colliers. I defy any missionary upon earth to find a darker spot or to visit a more benighted people. These he called out of the holes and dens of the earth and to these he preached "repentance toward God, and faith toward our Lord Jesus Christ" (Acts 20:21). And oh, it was a lovely sight to behold the glorious effect. Eyes unaccustomed to weep before now began to flow with the tears of repentance unto life, white streaks appearing on their black faces, now turned up towards heaven, praying for mercy and forgiveness; knees unaccustomed to prayer before are now bended down in fervent devotion before God; and their lives well and wisely regulated by the power of that grace which had done such wonders in their hearts. Now mind what these fastidious sons of pride and self-conceit had to say on this occasion: To be sure, Whitefield has done good among these low sort of people. Now we cannot thank them for their compliment, as it is given with such a wretched ill grace; but a higher panegyric cannot be framed. We generally suppose he is the best physician that cures the most desperate diseases. And we should also suppose that he is the best minister, notwithstanding the convenient terms of methodist and enthusiast, that cures the diseases of the mind in its most desperate state.

Let us try how some of these rationalists in religion (as they *humbly* wish to be thought) would be likely to succeed on a similar occasion. Let them seek for some other colliery of the like description; there take one of their nicely composed paper-popguns and read it among the multitude. I would willingly and gladly carry the stools behind them to see what sort of figures they would cut in their attempts to reform. I hate such silly pride, and it is best corrected by the lash of ridicule and contempt.

But a part of our plan is yet to be considered. To trace what has been done since the apostles, days time would by no means allow; and successes of a later date have already been well presented before you. We have now to encourage ourselves from the promises and prophecies of the word of God, of the glory that shall be revealed. The text itself gives blessed encouragement to our expectations, the "gospel of the kingdom shall be preached in all the world for a witness unto all nations; and then shall the end come" (Matt. 24:14). And what may we not yet hope for, when the Lord himself has said to his well-beloved Son, "Ask of me, and I shall give thee the heathen for thine inheritance, and the uttermost parts of the earth for thy possession" (Ps. 2:8).

Our design is all the same: no matter the name of the boat that ferries over the poor, benighted sinner into the land of gospel light and liberty, provided the blessed work be accomplished. I hate bigotry with my soul, and while so many gospel ministers of different denominations assemble together for the same purpose I still hope to live to see it subsist no more, to divide the Christian from the Christian. While each of us serves God in his own line, why cannot we love as brethren?

> Let names and sects and parties fall,
> And Jesus Christ be all in all.

I confess, in the simplicity of my heart, that some expressions have dropped from my lips which I never designed on this very solemn occasion. I am sure your patience and candor will instruct you to forgive, but we must be serious, serious indeed, while we conclude with some remarks on what ought to be the character of the missionaries themselves.

And what manner of persons should these indeed be, in all holy conversation and godliness! How full of that heavenly-mindedness and spiritual-mindedness which shall raise them so far above the world as though they had scarce an existence in it! What a holy, burning zeal for the salvation of souls! And what wisdom from above to conduct that zeal! What purity of knowledge to deal with those whose deep-rooted fondness for their ancient superstitions will make them watch with a jealous eye over every attempt to declare among them the truth as it is in Jesus!

Nor should their patience, meekness, and childlike simplicity be less eminent than their zeal. They must win by love and conquer by holy perseverance. They must not be like some sort of missionaries who suppose they are to be sent on a pleasant voyage at the public expense: but they must be men that count not their lives dear unto themselves, so that they may finish their course with joy, and the ministry which they have received of the Lord"(see Acts 20:24), men that can be contented out of pure love to Christ "to stand in jeopardy every hour." They must not only live like martyrs, but perhaps die like martyrs; we know not but the ancient proverb of the primitive Christians is again to be revived, "The blood of the martyrs is the seed of the church." They must be as dead to themselves as if they had no being. They must be completely crucified with Christ. In short, ere they embark upon the work, they must learn to "leave themselves behind them." With holy triumph, they must be taught to say: "Farewell, my dear, native land, farewell to all the ease and happiness and earthly indulgences I have enjoyed there. Welcome affliction, necessities, distresses of every kind; labors, watchings, fastings, I now dread no more. Welcome a life now to be spent in journeying often, in perils of waters, in perils of robbers, in perils by the heathen, in perils in the city, in perils in the wilderness, in perils by the sea: yea, welcome weariness and painfulness, hunger and thirst, cold and nakedness; yea, welcome death itself, whenever the blessed Lord himself, who died for me, demands that costly sacrifice at my hands." These are the men that shall be made more than conquerors over all the difficulties that human prudence or unbelief would present before us to impede the way.

Human wisdom we well know would soon puzzle herself in the undertaking; while her little taper is brought to find the way through the darkness of the night, she only appears to add blackness and obscurity to all things beyond the little region her rays can reach. But when the sun shines forth, he spreads his light upon the most distant objects, and every path is plain before us.

Some may have apprehensions that little can be done because miracles are wanting and the gift of tongues is withdrawn. Doubtless, Peter had a notable proof at hand of the doctrine he preached while the lame man was leaping in the temple who had been healed by the name of the Lord Jesus just before. But miracles never cease while souls are converted to God; nor will tongues be ever wanting while the wonderful change wrought by the grace of God so loudly bespeaks the praises of his wonder-working power. Let the heathens see what grace can do for a real convert; and we need not any further be discouraged for want of miracles and tongues. And that spirit of unanimity and zeal which has hitherto attended the work is a happy sign that good shall be done, while the torrent runs with such rapidity, for the accomplishment of so good a design. I would not for the world but appear on the Lord's side, on this occasion. "Curse ye Meroz, said the angel of the Lord, curse ye bitterly the inhabitants thereof; because they came not to the help of the Lord, to the help of the Lord against the mighty" (Judg. 5:23) No, my brethren, the providence of God commands that we exert ourselves for his glory. Difficulties there doubtless are; and an abundance of prayer, prudence, and holy zeal will be necessary to conduct the work. But God can provide all that is necessary to carry on his own work in his own way; and we have nothing to do but to follow as he condescends to lead. Thanks be to God for the unanimity and goodwill that have hitherto subsisted among us. May we still be found steadfast, unmoveable, always abounding in the work of the Lord, forasmuch as we are assured that our labors shall not be in vain in the Lord.

Robert Hall: *The Christian Missionary*

ROBERT HALL WAS BORN at Arnsby, England, May 2, 1764, and died at Bristol, February 21, 1831. He was educated at King's College, Aberdeen, where his intimate companion was James Mackintosh, afterwards the celebrated philosopher. Mackintosh lamented that by Hall's choosing the pulpit, speculative thought had lost one of its master minds. He preached for fifteen years in the Baptist church at Cambridge, and afterwards at Bristol. Through his active life he was a great sufferer from an affection of the spine, and much of his writing had to be done when lying on the floor. His noble intellect, too, suffered eclipse on several occasions, requiring his stay in an asylum. During one of these periods of mental aberration, a visitor came to the asylum and, seeing Hall, addressed himself to him, saying in a pompous tone, "And what, my dear sir, brought you here?" "Something," responded Hall, pointing to his forehead, "which will never bring you here!"

Hall was an intellectual preacher of the highest order. His voice and pulpit manner were weak, but the order and sweep of his ideas held vast congregations spellbound. Dugald Stewart, the Scottish philosopher, described Hall as one who "combines the beauties of Johnson, Addison, and Burke." His few printed sermons were written out after their delivery, but the grace and elegance of the sermons as delivered are said to have surpassed even the written sermons. The one which follows was a charge delivered to Eustace Carey when he went out to India as a missionary. It is a grand declaration of the work of the Christian church in the world.

The Christian Missionary

A S it has been usual in the designation of a missionary, after solemnly commending him to God by prayer, to deliver a short address; in compliance with a custom, not perhaps improper or illaudable, I shall request your attention to a few hints of advice, without attempting a regular charge, which I neither judge myself equal to, nor deem necessary, since on your arrival in India you will receive from your venerable relative, Dr. Carey, instruction more ample and appropriate than it is in my power to communicate.

When the first missionaries who visited these western parts were sent out, their designation was accompanied with prayer and fasting; whence we may infer that fervent supplication ought to form the distinguishing feature in the exercises appropriated to these occasions.

An effusion of the spirit of prayer on the church of Christ is a surer pledge of success in the establishment of missions, than the most splendid exhibitions of talent. As there is no engagement more entirely spiritual in its nature, nor whose success is more immediately dependent on God than that on which you are entering, to none is that spiritual aid more indispensably necessary, which is chiefly awarded to the prayers of the faithful.

"Separate to me," said the Holy Ghost to the disciples assembled at Antioch, "separate to me Barnabas and Saul, for the work whereunto I have called them" (Acts 13:2). When the omniscient searcher of hearts separates a Christian minister from his brethren and assigns him a distinct work, it implies the previous perception of certain qualifications for its successful discharge not generally possessed. For though none can give the increase but God, much of his wisdom is to be traced in the selection of instruments fitted to his purpose. The first and most essential qualification for a missionary is a decided predilection for the office; not the effect of sudden impulse, but of serious, deep consideration; a predilection strengthened and matured by deliberately counting the cost. Every man has his proper calling; and while the greater part of Christian teachers are perfectly satisfied with attempting to do all the good in their power in their native land, there are others of a more enterprising character, inflamed with the holy ambition of carrying the glad tidings beyond the bounds of Christendom; like the great apostle of the Gentiles, who was determined not to build on another man's foundation, but if possible to preach Christ in regions where his name was not known. The circumstances which contribute to such a resolution are various, often too subtle and complicated to admit of a distinct analysis: a constitutional ardor of mind, a natural neglect of difficulties and dangers, an impatience of being confined within the trammels of ordinary duties, together with many accidental associations and impressions, may combine to form a missionary spirit; nor is it so necessary minutely to investigate the causes which have led to a given determination, as the legitimacy of the object, and the purity of the motive.

We adore the prolific Source of all good in the variety and discrimination of his gifts, by which he imparts a separate character and allots a distinct sphere of operation to the general and essential principles which form the Christian and the minister. "He gave some apostles: and some, evangelists; and some, pastors and teachers; for the perfecting of the saints, for the work of the ministry, for the edifying of the body of Christ" (Eph. 4:11–12).

The next qualification of whose necessity I must be allowed to remind you, is singular *self-devotement*, without a degree of which it is not possible to be a Christian, still less to any useful purpose a minister, least of all a missionary. In resolving to quit your native country, and to relinquish your nearest connections with little expectation of beholding them again in the flesh, you have given decisive indications of this spirit; nor to a mind like yours, exquisitely alive to the sensibilities of nature and friendship, can the sacrifice you have already made be deemed inconsiderable. But as it is still impossible for you to conjecture the extent of the privations and trials to which, in the pursuit of your object, you may be exposed, your situation is not unlike that of Abraham, who, being commanded to leave his own country and his father's house, went out not knowing whither he went. As you are entering on an untried scene where difficulties may arise to exercise your patience and fortitude, of which you can form but a very inadequate conception, you will do well to contemplate the example and meditate the words of St. Paul in circumstances not very dissimilar: "And now, behold, I go bound in the spirit unto Jerusalem, not knowing the things that shall befall me there: save that the Holy Ghost witnesseth in every city that bonds and afflictions abide me. But none of these things move me, neither count I my life dear unto myself, so that I might finish my course with joy, and the ministry, which I have received of the Lord to Jesus" (Acts 20:22–24).

The next qualification necessary for a teacher of Christianity among the heathen, is the *spirit of faith*, by which I intend, not merely that cordial belief of the truth which is essential to a Christian, but that unshaken persuasion of the promises of God respecting the triumph and enlargement of his kingdom, which is sufficient to denominate its possessor strong in faith. It is impossible that the mind of a missionary should be too much impressed with the beauty, glory, and grandeur of the kingdom of Christ as it is unfolded in the oracles of the Old and New Testament; or with the certainty of the final accomplishment of those oracles, founded on the faithfulness and omnipotence of their Author. To those parts of Scripture his attention should be especially directed, in which the Holy Ghost employs and exhausts the whole force and splendor of inspiration in depicting the future reign of the Messiah, together with that astonishing spectacle of dignity, purity, and peace which his church will exhibit, when, having the glory of God, her bounds shall be commensurate with those of the habitable globe; when every object on which the eye shall rest, shall remind the spectator of the commencement of a new age, in which the tabernacle of God is with men, and he dwells amongst them. His spirit should be imbued with that sweet and tender awe which such anticipations will infallibly produce, whence will spring a generous contempt of the world, and an ardor bordering on impatience to be employed, though in the humblest sphere, as the instrument of accelerating such a period. Compared to this destiny in reserve for the children of men, compared to this glory, invisible at present, and hid behind the clouds which envelop this dark and troubled scene, the brightest day that has hitherto shone upon the world, is midnight, and the highest splendors that have invested it, the shadow of death.

Independent of these assurances, the idea of converting pagan nations to the Christian faith must appear chimerical. The attempt to persuade them to relinquish their ancient mode of thinking, corroborated by habit, by example, by interest, and to adopt a new system of opinions and feelings, and enter on a new course of life, will ever be deemed by the worldly-wise, impracticable and visionary. "Pass over the isles of Chittim, and see;" said the Lord, by the mouth of Jeremiah, "and send unto Kedar, and consider diligently, and see if there be such a thing. Hath a nation changed their gods?" (Jer. 2:10). For a nation to change its gods is represented by the highest authority as an event almost unparalleled: and if it be so difficult to induce them to change the mode of their idolatry, how much more to persuade them to abandon it altogether! Idolatry is not to be looked upon as a mere speculative error respecting the object of worship, of little or no practical efficacy. Its hold upon the mind of a fallen creature is most tenacious, its operation most extensive. It is a corrupt, practical institution, involving a whole system of sentiments and manners which perfectly molds and transforms its votaries. It modifies human nature in every aspect under which it can be contemplated, being intimately blended and incorporated with all its perceptions of good and evil, with all its infirmities, passions, and fears.

As it is easy to descend from an elevation which it is difficult to climb, to fall from the adoration of the Supreme Being to the worship of idols, demands no effort. Idolatry is strongly entrenched in the corruptions, and fortified by the weakness of human nature. Hence, we find all nations have sunk into it in succession, frequently in opposition to the strongest remonstrances of inspired prophets. We have no example in the history of the world of a single city, family, or individual who has renounced it through the mere operation of unassisted reason; such is the fatal propensity of mankind to that enormity. It is the vail of the covering, cast over all flesh, which nothing but the effulgence of revelation has pierced. The true religion satisfies and enlarges the reason, but militates against the inclinations of men. Resting on a few sublime truths, addressed to the understanding and conscience, affording few distinct images to the fancy, and no indulgences to the passions, it can only be planted and preserved by a continual efflux from its Divine Author, of whose spirituality and elevation it so largely partakes.

Allow me to remind you of the absolute necessity of cultivating a mild, conciliating, affectionate temper in the discharge of your office. If an uninterested spectator, after a careful perusal of the New Testament, were asked what he conceived to be its distinguishing characteristic, he would reply without hesitation, that wonderful spirit of philanthropy. It is a perpetual commentary on that sublime aphorism, "God is love." As the Christian religion is an exhibition of the incomprehensible mercy of God to a guilty race, so it is dispensed in a manner perfectly congenial with its nature; and the book which contains it is replete with such unaffected strokes of tenderness and goodness, as are to be found in no other volume. The benign spirit of the gospel infused itself into the breast of its first missionaries. In St. Paul, for example, we behold the most heroic resolution, the most lofty superiority to all the modes of intimidation and danger, a spirit which rose with its difficulties, and exulted in the midst of the most dismaying objects. Yet when we look more narrowly into his character and investigate his motives, we perceive it was his attachment to mankind that inspired him with this intrepidity, and urged him to conflicts more painful and arduous than the votaries of glory have ever sustained. Who would have supposed it possible for the same breast to be the seat of so much energy and so much softness? That he who changed the face of the world by his preaching, and while a prisoner made his judge tremble on the tribunal, could stoop to embrace a fugitive slave, and to employ the most exquisite address to effect his reconciliation with his master? The conversion of Onesimus afforded him a joy like "the joy in harvest, and as men rejoice when they divide the spoil" (Isa. 9:3). When the spiritual interests of mankind were concerned, no difficulties were so formidable as to shake his resolution, no details so insignificant as to escape his notice. To the utmost inflexibility of principle, he joined the gentlest condescension to human infirmity, becoming all things to all men, that he might win some: to the Jews he became a Jew, that he might gain the Jews, to them that were without law, as without law" (see 1 Cor. 9:20), adapting on all occasions his modes of address to the character and disposition of those with whom he conversed. It was the love of Christ and of souls that produced and harmonized those apparent discordances.

The affectionate and conciliatory disposition we have been enforcing must be combined with prudence, and the diligent study of human nature, which you will find absolutely necessary to conduct you through intricate and unbeaten paths. St. Paul frequently reminds the Thessalonians of the manner of his entrance among them. In the first introduction of the gospel amongst a people, it is of great importance that every step be well weighed, that nothing be done which is rash, offensive, or indecorous; but every precaution employed, consistent with godly simplicity, to disarm prejudice, and conciliate respect. There is nothing in the conduct of the first ministers of the gospel more to be admired than the exquisite propriety with which they conducted themselves in the most delicate situations. Their zeal was exempt from indecorum, their caution from timidity or art. In the commencement of every great and hazardous undertaking, the first measures are usually decisive, at least in those instances in which success is dependent, under God, on the voluntary cooperation of mankind. A single act of imprudence is sufficient to blast the undertaking of a missionary, which, in the situation of an ordinary minister, would scarcely be felt. The best method of securing yourself from errors in this quarter, is to endeavor to acquire as large a measure as possible of the graces of the Spirit, to be deeply imbued with the wisdom which is from above. Nothing subtle or refined should enter into the views of a Christian missionary. Let him be continually elevating his principles, and purifying his motives. Let him be clothed with humility, and actuated on all occasions with love to God and the souls of men, and his character cannot fail of being marked with a propriety and beauty which will ultimately command universal esteem. These were the only arts which a Schwartz in the east, and a Brainerd in the west, condescended to cultivate.

There is much in the situation of a missionary calculated to keep him awake and attentive to his duties. He is required to explore new paths, and, leaving the footsteps of the flock, to go in quest of the lost sheep, on whatever mountain it may have wandered, or in whatever valley it may be hid. He must be prepared to encounter prejudice and error in strange and unwonted shapes, to trace the aberrations of reason, and the deviations from rectitude, through all the diversified mazes of superstition and idolatry. He is engaged in a series of offensive operations; he is in the field of battle, wielding "weapons . . . [which] are not carnal, but mighty through God to the pulling down of strong holds" (2 Cor. 10:4). When not in action, he is yet encamped in an enemy's country where nothing can secure his acquisitions or preserve him from surprise, but incessant vigilance. The voluntary exile from his native country to which he submits is sufficient to remind him continually of his important embassy, and to induce a solicitude that so many sacrifices may not be made, so many privations undergone, in vain. He holds the lamp of instruction to those who sit in darkness and in the shadow of death; and while there remains a particle of ignorance not expelled, a single prejudice not vanquished, a sinful or idolatrous custom not relinquished, his task is left unfinished. It is not enough for him, on a stated day, to address an audience on the concerns of eternity. He must teach from house to house, and be instant in season and out of season, embracing every opportunity which offers of inculcating the principles of a new religion, as well as "confirming the souls of the disciples." He must consider himself as the mouth and interpreter of that wisdom which "crieth without; she uttereth her voice in the streets: she crieth in the chief place of concourse" (Prov. 1:20–21).

Be *strong* in the grace that is in the Lord Jesus. Among the nations which will be the scene of your future labors, you will witness a state of things essentially different from that which prevails here, where the name of Christ is held in reverence, the principal doctrines of his religion speculatively acknowledged, and the institutes of worship widely extended and diffused. The leaven of Christian piety has spread itself in innumerable directions, modified public opinion, improved the state of society, and given birth to many admirable institutions unknown to pagan countries. The authority of the Savior is recognized, his injunctions in some instances obeyed, and the outrages of impiety restrained by law, by custom, and above all, by the silent counteraction of piety in its sincere professors.

In India, Satan maintains an almost undisputed empire, and the powers of darkness, secure of their dominion, riot and revel at their pleasure, sporting themselves with the misery of their vassals, whom they incessantly agitate with delusive hopes and fantastic terrors, leading them captive at their will, while few efforts have been made to despoil them of their usurped authority. Partial invasions have been attempted, and a few captives disenthralled; but the strength and sinews of empire remain entire, and that dense and palpable darkness which invests it has scarcely felt the impression of a few feeble and scattered rays. In India you will witness the predominance of a system which provides for the worship of gods many, and of lords many, while it excludes the adoration of the Supreme Being, legitimates cruelty, polygamy, and lust, debases the standard of morals, oppresses with ceremonies those whom it deprives of instruction, and suggests no solid hope of happiness beyond the grave.

You will witness with indignation that monstrous alliance between impurity and devotion, obscenity and religion, which characterizes the popular idolatry of all nations, and which, in opposition to the palliating sophistry of infidels, sufficiently evinces it to be what the Scriptures assert—the worship of devils, not of God.

When we consider that moral causes operate on free agents, we shall not be surprised to find their effects are less uniform than those which result from the action of material and physical powers, and that human minds are susceptible of opposite impressions from the same objects.

On such as have neither been established in the evidences, nor felt the efficacy, of revealed religion, a residence in a pagan country has usually a most pernicious effect, and matures latent irreligion into open impiety. The absence of Christian institutions and Christian examples leaves them at liberty to gratify their sensual inclinations without control, and the familiar contemplating of pagan manners and customs gradually wears out every trace and vestige of the religion in which they were educated, and emboldens them to consider it in the light of a local superstition. They are no further converts to the brahminical faith than to prefer it to their own; that is, they prefer the religion they can despise with impunity, to one that afflicts their consciences, that which leaves them free, to that which restrains them. As the secret language of their heart had always been, "Cause the Holy One of Israel to cease from amongst us," in the absence of God, of his institutes and his worship, they find a congenial element, nor are they at all displeased at perceiving the void filled with innumerable fantastic shapes and chimeras; for they contemplate religion with great composure, providing it be sufficiently ridiculous.

You, I am persuaded, will view the condition of millions who are involved in the shades of idolatry, originally formed in the image of God, now totally estranged from their great Parent and reposing their trust on things which cannot profit, with different emotions, and will be anxious to recall them to the Bishop and Shepherd of their souls. Instead of considering the most detestable species of idolatry as so many different modes of worshipping the One Supreme, agreeable to the jargon of infidels, you will not hesitate to regard them as an impious attempt to share his incommunicable honors; as composing that image of jealousy which he is engaged to smite, confound, and destroy.

When you compare the incoherence, extravagance, and absurdity which pervade the systems of polytheism with the simple and sublime truths of the gospel, the result will be an increased attachment to that mystery of godliness. When you observe the anxiety of the Hindu devotee to obtain the pardon of sin, and the incredible labors and sufferings which he cheerfully undergoes to quiet the perturbations of conscience, the doctrine of the cross will rise, if possible, still higher in your esteem, and you will long for an opportunity of crying in his ears, "Behold the Lamb of God, which taketh away the sin of the world" (John 1:29). When you witness the immolation of females on the funeral piles of their husbands and the barbarous treatment of aged parents left by their children to perish on the banks of the Ganges, you will recognize the footsteps of him who was a murderer from the beginning, and will be impatient to communicate the mild and benevolent maxims of the gospel. When you behold an immense population held in chains by that detestable institution the caste, as well as bowed down under an intolerable weight of brahminical superstitions, you will long to impart the liberty which Christ confers, "where there is neither Greek nor Jew, . . . Barbarian, Scythian, bond nor free: but Christ is all, and in all" (Colossians 3:11).

In recommending the principles of Christianity to a pagan nation, let your instruction be in the form of a *testimony*. Let it, with respect to the mode of exhibiting it, though not to the spirit of the teacher, be *dogmatic*. *Testify repentance* towards God, and faith in our Lord Jesus Christ. It might become a Socrates, who was left to the light of nature, to express himself with diffidence, and to affirm that he had spared no pains in acting up to the character of a philosopher, in other words, a diligent inquirer after truth; but whether he had philosophized aright, or attained the object of his inquiries, he knew not, but left it to be ascertained in that world on which he was entering. In him, such indications of modest distrust were graceful and affecting but would little become the disciple of revelation or the Christian minister, who is entitled to say with St. John, "we know that the whole world lieth in wickedness. And we know that the Son of God is come, and hath given us an understanding, that we may know him that is true, and we are in him that is true, even in his Son Jesus Christ" (1 John 5:19–20).

After reminding them of their state as guilty and polluted creatures, which the ceremonies of their religion teach them to confess, exhibit to the inhabitants of Hindustan the cross of Christ as their only refuge. Acquaint them with his incarnation, his character as the Son of God and the Son of man, his offices, and the design of his appearance; not with the air of a disputer of this world, but of him who is conscious to himself of his possessing the medicine of life, the treasure of immortality, which he is anxious to impart to guilty men. Insist fearlessly on the futility and vanity of all human methods of expiation, on the impotence of idols, and the command of God to "all men every where to repent: because as he hath appointed a day, in the which he will judge the world in righteousness" (Acts 17:30–31). Display the sufferings of Christ like one who was an eye witness of those sufferings, and hold up the blood, the precious blood of atonement, as issuing warm from the cross. It is a peculiar excellence of the gospel, that in its wonderful adaptation to the state and condition of mankind as fallen creatures, it bears intrinsic marks of its divinity, and is supported not less by internal than by external evidence. By a powerful appeal to the conscience, by a faithful delineation of man in his grandeur and in his weakness, in his original capacity for happiness and his present misery and guilt, present this branch of its evidence in all its force. On every occasion, seize features of Christianity which render it interesting; and by awakening the fears and exciting the hopes of your hearers, endeavor to annihilate every other object, and make it appear what it really is, the pearl of great price, the sovereign balm, the cure of every ill, the antidote of death, the precursor of immortality. In such a ministry, fear not to give loose to all the ardor of your soul, to call into action every emotion and every faculty which can exalt or adorn it. You will find ample scope for all its force and tenderness; and should you be called to pour your life as a libation on the offering of the Gentiles, you will only have the more occasion to exult and rejoice.

In order to qualify yourself for the performance of these duties, it is above all things necessary for you to acquaint yourself with the general doctrines of Christianity in their full extent; but it will be neither necessary nor expedient to initiate your converts into those controversies which, through a long course of time, have grown up amongst Christians. Endeavor to acquire as extensive and perfect a knowledge as possible of the dictates of inspiration, and by establishing your hearers in these, preclude the entrance of error, rather than confute it. Be always prepared to answer every modest inquiry into the grounds of your faith and practice; and that you may be more capable of entering into their difficulties, and anticipating their objections, place yourself as much as possible in the situation of those whom you are called to instruct. When we consider the permanent consequences likely to result from first impressions on the minds of pagans, the few advantages they possess for religious discussion, and the extreme confidence they are likely to repose in their spiritual guides, you must be conscious how important it is to *plant wholly a right seed.* Your defective representations of truth will not soon be supplied, nor the errors you plant extirpated, since we find societies of Christians in these parts of the world, where discussion and controversy abound, retain from generation to generation the distinguishing tenets of their leaders. In forming the plan, and laying the foundation of an edifice which it is proposed shall last forever, it is desirable that no materials should be admitted but such as are solid and durable, and no ornaments introduced but such as are chaste and noble. As it would be too much to expect you should perfectly succeed in imparting the mind of Christ, might I be permitted to advise, you will lean rather to the side of *defect* than *excess,* and in points of inferior magnitude omit what is true, rather than inculcate what is doubtful. The influence of religion on the heart depends not on the multiplicity, but on the quality of its objects.

The unnecessary multiplication of articles of faith gives a character of littleness to Christianity, and tends in no small degree to impress a similar character on its professors. The grandeur and efficacy of the gospel results not from an immense accumulation of little things, but from its powerful exhibition of a few great ones.

Among the indirect benefits which may be expected to arise from missions, we may be allowed to anticipate a more pure, simple, apostolic mode of presenting the gospel.

The situation of a missionary retired from the scene of debate and controversy, who has continually before his eyes the objects which presented themselves to the attention of the apostles, is favorable to an emancipation from prejudice of every sort, and to the acquisition of just and enlarged conceptions of Christianity. It will be your lot to walk the same wards in this great hospital, and to prescribe to the same class of patients that first experienced the salutary and renovating power of the gospel. The gods which are worshiped at this time in India are supposed by Sir William Jones to be the very same, under different names, with those who shared the adoration of Italy and Greece when the gospel was first published in those regions; so that you will be an eyewitness of the very evils and enormities which then prevailed in the Western hemisphere, and which the sword of the Spirit so effectually subdued. You will be under great advantages for ascending to first principles, for tracing the stream to its head and spring, by having incessantly to contemplate that state of things in a moral view, of which every page of Scripture assumes the existence, but of which the inhabitants of Europe have no living experience. It is with great satisfaction accordingly I have observed the harmony of doctrine, the identity of instruction, which has pervaded the ministry of Protestant missionaries who have been employed under the auspices of different denominations of Christians.

Few things more powerfully tend to enlarge the mind than conversing with great objects, and engaging in great pursuits. That the object you are pursuing is entitled to that appellation, will not be questioned by him who reflects on the infinite advantages derived from Christianity, to every nation and clime where it has prevailed in its purity, and that the prodigious superiority which Europe possesses over Asia and Africa is chiefly to be ascribed to this cause. It is the possession of a religion which comprehends the seeds of endless improvement, which maintains an incessant struggle with whatever is barbarous, selfish, or inhuman, which, by unveiling futurity, clothes morality with the sanction of a divine law, and harmonizes utility and virtue in every combination of events, and in every stage of existence; a religion which, by affording the most just and sublime conceptions of the Deity and of the moral relations of man, has given birth at once to the loftiest speculation and the most childlike humility, uniting the inhabitants of the globe into one family, and in the bonds of a common salvation. It is this religion which, rising upon us like a finer sun, has quickened moral vegetation, and replenished Europe with talents, virtues, and exploits, which, in spite of its physical disadvantages, have rendered it a paradise, the delight and wonder of the world. An attempt to propagate this religion among the natives of Hindustan may perhaps be stigmatized as visionary and romantic; but to enter the lists of controversy with those who would deny it to be great and noble, would be a degradation to reason.

In the views of the most enlightened statesmen, compared to those of a Christian minister, there is a littleness and limitation, which is not to be imputed in one case as a moral imperfection, nor in the other as a personal merit; the difference arising purely from the disparity in the subjects upon which they respectively speculate. Should you be asked on your arrival in India, as it is very probable you will, what there is in Christianity which renders it so inestimable in your eyes, that you judged it fit to undertake so long, dangerous, and expensive a voyage, for the purpose of imparting it—you will answer without hesitation, it is the power of God to salvation; nor will any view of it short of this, or the inculcation of it for any inferior purpose, enable it to produce even those moralizing and civilizing effects it is so powerfully adapted to accomplish. Christianity will civilize, it is true, but it is only when it is allowed to develop the energies by which it sanctifies. Christianity will inconceivably ameliorate the present condition of being—who doubts it? Its universal prevalence, not in the name but in reality, will convert this world into a semiparadisaical state; but it is only while it is permitted to prepare its inhabitants for a better. Let her be urged to forget her celestial origin and destiny, to forget that "she came from God, and returns to God"; and whether she is employed by the artful and enterprising, as the instrument of establishing a spiritual empire and dominion over mankind, or by the philanthropist, as the means of promoting their civilization and improvement, she resents the foul indignity, claps her wings, and takes her flight, leaving nothing but a base and sanctimonious hypocrisy in her room.

Preach it then, my dear brother, with a constant recollection that such is its character and aim. Preach it with a perpetual view to eternity, and with the simplicity and affection with which you would address your dearest friends, were they assembled round your dying bed. While others are ambitious to form the citizen of earth, be it yours to train him for heaven; to raise up the temple of God from among the ancient desolations; to contribute your part towards the formation and perfection of that eternal society, which will flourish in inviolable purity and order when all human association shall be dissolved and the princes of this world shall come to naught. In the pursuit of these objects, let it be your ambition to tread in the footsteps of a Brainerd and a Schwartz; I may add, of your excellent relative, with whom we are happy in perceiving you to possess a congeniality of character, not less than an affinity of blood.

But should you succeed beyond your utmost hope, expect not to escape the ridicule of the ungodly, or the censure of the world: but be content to sustain that sort of reputation, and run that sort of career, invariably allotted to the Christian missionary; where, agreeable to the experience of St. Paul, obscurity and notoriety, admiration and scorn, sorrows and consolations, attachments the most tender and opposition the most violent, are interchangeably mingled.

But whatever be the sentiments of the world, respecting which you will indulge no excessive solicitude, your name will be precious in India, your memory dear to multitudes, who will reverence in you the instrument of their eternal salvation. And how much more satisfaction will accrue from the consciousness of this than from the loudest human applause, your own reflections will determine. At that awful moment when you are called to bid a final adieu to the world, and to look into eternity; when the hopes, fears, and agitations which sublunary objects shall have occasioned will subside like a feverish dream, or a vision of the night, the certainty of belonging to the number of the saved will be the only consolation; and when to this is joined the conviction of having contributed to enlarge that number, your joy will be full. You will be conscious of having conferred a benefit on your fellow creatures, you know not precisely what, but of such a nature that it will require all the illumination of eternity to measure its dimensions, and ascertain its value. Having followed Christ in the *regeneration,* in the preparatory labors accompanying the renovation of mankind, you will rise to an elevated station in a world where the scantiest portion is a "far more exceeding and eternal weight of glory" (2 Cor. 4:7) and a conspicuous place will be assigned you in that unchanging firmament, where "they that turn many to righteousness [shall shine] as the stars for ever and ever" (Dan. 12:3).

Christmas Evans: *The Triumph of Calvary*

Christmas Evans was born at Ysgarwen, South Wales, on the 25th of December, 1766. The date of his birth accounts for his unusual Christian name. His parents were very poor, and he was brought up in an environment of vice, ignorance, and unkind treatment, and did not learn to read until he was eighteen years of age. At eighteen he experienced a spiritual awakening and became a member of the Arminian Presbyterians. His desire to know the Bible was the stimulus which moved him to learn to read. He now began to exercise his gifts in prayer and testimony, but had made little headway in his Christian life when, at the age of twenty-two, he was immersed in the River Duar and became a preacher of the Calvinistic Baptists. The first years of his preaching were marked by periods of doubt, gloom, and spiritual dryness. But at length the day came when he received "an unction from on high," and henceforth he preached with great joy and assurance. At the age of forty-six, he settled in the Isle of Anglesea, where he remained for twenty years on the salary of seventeen pounds a year. He had several other pastorates in different parts of Wales and in nearly every church had some difficulty or unhappiness. This is reflected in one of the petitions of the quaint covenant he made with God: "Suffer me not to be trodden under the proud feet of members or deacons for the sake of thy goodness." He died at Swansea in 1838, the seventy-third year of his age.

Christmas Evans was one of the great natural preachers. Some think that if he had been better educated, his power and influence as a preacher would have been much greater than it was. But this is doubtful, for a more formal education might have toned down his imagination and stripped him of that garment of allegory which he wore with such splendid effect. After he once found his stride his popularity never waned, and his wonderful descriptive and pictorial powers were as marked in his old age as in his youth. Evans was six feet tall and had a noble appearance in the pulpit. On one of his early trips to England he was beaten by a mob of ruffians and lost the sight of an eye. But this injury seemed to add to, rather than detract from, the power of his presence, and he was known throughout Wales as "the one-eyed man of Anglesea." Sermons lose greatly in power when they are transferred from the pulpit to the printed page, and still more when, as is the case with the sermons of Evans, which were delivered in Welsh, they must be read in a translation. But, notwithstanding this handicap, the printed sermons of Evans clearly show the extraordinary power of his preaching.

Reports of the sermon on the demoniac of Gadara, preached at one of the meetings of the Baptist Association, describe the alternate waves of laughter and weeping which swept like waves over the vast throng, and how the sermon ended with the congregation falling on their knees and calling upon God for mercy. The sermon selected for this volume, "The Triumph of Calvary," shows Evans at his best. It first appeared in the celebrated *Specimens of Welsh Preaching*.

The Triumph of Calvary

"Who is this that cometh from Edom, with dyed garments from Bozrah? this that is glorious in his apparel, travelling in the greatness of his strength? I that speak in righteousness, mighty to save. Wherefore art thou red in thine apparel, and thy garments like him that treadeth in the winefat? I have trodden the winepress alone; and of the people there was none with me: for I will tread them in mine anger, and trample them in my fury; and their blood shall be sprinkled upon my garments, and I will stain all my raiment. For the day of vengeance is in mine heart, and the year of my redeemed is come. And I looked, and there was none to help; and I wondered that there was none to uphold: therefore mine own arm brought salvation unto me; and my fury, it upheld me. And I will tread down the people in mine anger, and make them drunk in my fury, and I will bring down their strength to the earth" (Isaiah 63:1-6).

 HIS passage is one of the sublimest in the Bible. Not more majestic and overwhelming is the voice of God issuing from the burning bush. It represents the Captain of our salvation, left alone in the heat of battle, marching victoriously through the broken columns of the foe, bursting the bars asunder, bearing away the brazen gates, and delivering by conquest the captives of sin and death. Let us first determine the events to which our text relates, and then briefly explain the questions and answers which it contains.

I. We have here a wonderful victory, obtained by Christ, in the city of Bozrah, in the land of Edom. Our first inquiry concerns the time and the place of that achievement.

Some of the prophecies are literal, and others are figurative. Some of them are already fulfilled, and others in daily process of fulfillment. Respecting this prophecy, divines disagree. Some think it is a description of Christ's conflict and victory without the gates of

Jerusalem, eighteen centuries ago; and others understand it as referring to the great Battle of Armageddon predicted in the Apocalypse and yet to be consummated before the end of the world.

I am not willing to pass by Mount Calvary and Joseph's new tomb on my way to the field of Armageddon; nor am I willing to pause at the scene of the crucifixion and the ascension without going farther on to the final conquest of the foe. I believe divine inspiration has included both events in the text: the victory already won on Calvary, and the victory yet to be accomplished in Armageddon; the finished victory of Messiah's passion, and the progressive victory of his gospel and his grace.

The chief difficulty in understanding some parts of the word of God arises from untranslated words, many of which are found in our own version, as well as in that of our English neighbors. For instance, it is said, "He came and dwelt in a city called Nazareth: that it might be fulfilled which was spoken by the prophets, He shall be called a Nazarene" (Matt. 2:23). Where in the prophets is it predicted that Christ shall be called a Nazarene? Nowhere. When the proper names are translated, the difficulty vanishes. "He came and dwelt in a city called *Plantation:* that it might be fulfilled which was spoken by the prophets, He shall be called *the Branch.*" This name is given him by Isaiah, Jeremiah, and Zechariah. Now this is precisely the difficulty that occurs in our text, and the translation of the terms unties the knot: "Who is this that cometh from Edom [*red earth*] with dyed garments from Bozrah [*tribulation*]?"

The former part of the text has reference to the victory of Calvary; the latter part anticipates the battle and triumph of Armageddon, mentioned in Revelation. The victory of Calvary is consummated on the morning of the third day after the crucifixion. The Conqueror comes up from the earth, exclaiming, "I have trodden the winepress alone on Calvary; and I will tread them in mine anger, and make them drunk in my fury at the battle of Armageddon. I will overtake and destroy the beast, and the false prophet, and that old serpent the devil, with all their hosts."

When the tide of battle turned on the field of Waterloo, the Duke of Wellington mounted his horse and pursued the vanquished foe. So Isaiah's Conqueror, having routed the powers of hell on Calvary, pursues and destroys them on the field of Armageddon. Here he is represented as a hero on foot, a prince without an army; but John, the revelator, saw him riding on a white horse, followed by the armies of heaven, all on white horses, and not a footman among them.

The victory of Calvary is like the blood of atonement in the sanctuary. The cherubim were some of them looking one way, and some the other, but all were looking on the atoning blood. Thus, all the great events of time—all the trials and triumphs of God's people—those which happened before, those which have happened since, and those which are yet to happen, are all looking toward the wrestling of Gethsemane, the conflict of Golgotha, and the triumph of Olivet. The escape from Egypt, and the return from Babylon looked forward to the cross of Christ; and the faith of the perfect man of Uz hung on a risen Redeemer. The Christian martyrs overcame by the blood of the Lamb, and all their victories were in virtue of one great achievement. The tomb of Jesus is the birthplace of his people's immortality, and the power which raised him from the dead shall open the sepulchers of all his saints. "Thy dead men shall live, together with my dead body shall they arise. Awake and sing, ye that dwell in dust: for thy dew is as the dew of herbs, and the earth shall cast out the dead" (Isa. 26:19).

Christ offered himself a sacrifice for us, and drank the cup of God's righteous indignation in our stead. He was trodden by almighty justice as a cluster of grapes in the winepress of the Law, till the vessels of mercy overflowed with the wine of peace and pardon, which has made thousands of contrite and humble spirits "rejoice with joy unspeakable and full of glory" (1 Pet. 1:8). He suffered for us that we might triumph with him. But our text describes him as a king and a conqueror. He was, at once, the dying victim and the immortal victor. In "the power of an endless life," he was standing by the altar when the sacrifice was burning. He was alive in his sacerdotal vestments, with his golden censer in his hand. He was alive in his kingly glory, with his sword and scepter in his hand. He was alive in his conquering prowess, and had made an end of sin, and bruised the head of the serpent, and spoiled the principalities and powers of hell, and turned the vanquished hosts of the prince of darkness down to the winepress of the wrath of Almighty God. Then on the morning of the third day, when he arose from the dead, and made a show of them openly—then began the year of jubilee with power!

After the prophets of ancient times had long gazed through the mists of futurity at the sufferings of Christ and the glory that should follow, a company of them were gathered together on the summit of Calvary. They saw a host of enemies ascending the hill, arrayed for battle and most terrific in their aspect. In the middle of the line was the Law of God, fiery, exceeding broad, and working wrath. On the right wing was Beelzebub with his troops of infernals, and on the left Caiaphas with his Jewish priests and Pilate with his Roman soldiers. The rear was brought up by Death, the last enemy. When the holy seers saw this army and perceived that it was drawing near, they started back and prepared for flight. As they looked round, they saw the Son of God advancing with intrepid step, having his face fixed on the hostile band. "Seest thou the danger that is before thee?" asked one of the men of God. "I will tread them in mine anger," he replied, "and trample them in my fury." "Who art thou?" said the prophet. He answered: "I that speak in righteousness, mighty to save." "Wilt thou venture to the battle alone?" asked the seer. The Son of God replied:

"I looked, and there was none to help; and I wondered that there was none to uphold; therefore mine own arm shall bring salvation unto me; and my fury, it shall uphold me." "At what point wilt thou commence thy attack?" inquired the anxious prophet. "I will first meet the Law," he replied, "and pass under its curse: for lo! I come to do thy will, oh God. When I shall have succeeded at the center of the line, the colors will turn in my favor." So saying, he moved forward. Instantly, the thunderings of Sinai were heard, and the whole band of prophets quaked with terror. But he advanced, undaunted, amidst the gleaming lightnings. For a moment he was concealed from view; and the banner of wrath waved about in triumph. Suddenly, the scene was changed. A stream of blood poured forth from his wounded side, and put out all the fires of Sinai. The flag of peace was now seen unfurled, and consternation filled the ranks of his foes. He then crushed, with his bruised heel, the old serpent's head; and put all the infernal powers to flight. With his iron rod he dashed to pieces the enemies on the left wing, like a potter's vessel. Death still remained, who thought himself invincible, having hitherto triumphed over all. He came forward, brandishing his sting, which he had whetted on Sinai's tables of stone. He darted it at the Conqueror, but it turned down and hung like the flexible lash of a whip. Dismayed, he retreated to the grave, his palace, into which the Conqueror pursued. In a dark corner of his den, he sat on his throne of moldering skulls and called upon the worms, his hitherto faithful allies, to aid him in the conflict; but they replied, "His flesh shall see no corruption!" The scepter fell from his hand. The Conqueror seized him, bound him, and condemned him to the lake of fire. The Conqueror then rose from the grave, followed by a band of released captives who came forth after his resurrection to be witnesses of the victory which he had won.

John in the Apocalypse did not look so far back as the treading of this winepress; but John saw him on his white horse, decked with his many crowns, his eyes like flames of fire, a two-edged sword in his hand, in the van of the armies of heaven, going forth conquering and to conquer. This is the fulfillment of his declaration in our text: "For I will tread them in mine anger, and trample them in my fury." This is the beginning of the jubilee, the Battle of Armageddon, wherein all heathen idolatry and superstition shall be overthrown, the beast and the false prophet shall be discomfited, and the devil and his legions shall be taken prisoners by Emmanuel, and shut up in the bottomless pit. He who hath conquered principalities and powers on Calvary, will not leave the field till he make all his enemies his footstool, and sway his scepter over a subject universe. Having sent forth the gospel from Jerusalem, he accompanies it with the grace of his Holy Spirit; and it shall not return unto him void, but shall accomplish that which he pleaseth, and prosper in the thing whereto he hath sent it.

The victory of Armageddon is obtained by virtue of the victory of Calvary. It is but the consummation of the same glorious campaign; and the first decisive blow dealt on the prince of darkness is a sure precursor of the final conquest. "I will meet thee again at Philippi!" said the ghost of Julius Caesar to Brutus. "I will meet thee again at Armageddon!" saith the Son of God to Satan on Calvary. "I will meet thee in the engagement between good and evil, grace and depravity, in every believer's heart; in the contest of divine truth with human errors, of the religion of God with the superstitions of men; in every sermon, every revival, every missionary enterprise; in the spread and glory of the gospel in the latter day, I will meet thee; and the heel which thou hast now bruised, shall crush thy head forever!"

Man's deliverance is of God. Man had neither the inclination nor the power. His salvation originated in the divine love, and burst forth like an ocean from the fountains of eternity. Satan, as a ravenous lion, had taken the prey, and was running to his den with the bleeding sheep in his mouth; but the Shepherd of Israel pursues him, overtakes him, and rends him as if he were a kid. The declaration of war was made in Eden: "I will put enmity between thee and the woman, and between thy seed and her seed; it shall bruise thy head, and thou shalt bruise his heel" (Gen. 3:15). It shall be fulfilled. The league with hell and the covenant with death shall not stand. The rebellion shall be quelled, the conspiracy shall be broken, and the strong man armed shall yield the citadel to a stronger. The works of the devil shall be destroyed, and the prey shall be taken from the teeth of the terrible. The house of David shall grow stronger and stronger, and the house of Saul shall grow weaker and weaker, till the kingdoms of this world shall become the kingdom of our God and of his Christ; Satan shall be bound in chains of darkness and cast into the lake of fire. All the enemies of Zion shall be vanquished, the forfeited favor of God shall be recovered, and the lost territory of peace, holiness and immortality shall be restored to man.

This campaign is carried on at the expense of the government of heaven. The treasury is inexhaustible; the arms are irresistible; therefore, the victory is sure. The almighty King has descended; he has taken the city of Bozrah; he has swayed his scepter over Edom; he has risen victoriously, and gone up with a shout, as the leader of all the army. This is but the pledge and the earnest of his future achievements. In the Battle of Armageddon, he shall go forth as a mighty man; he shall stir up jealousy as a man of war; and he shall prevail against his enemies. They shall be turned back; they shall be greatly ashamed that trust in graven images; that say unto molten images, "Ye are our gods!" Then he will open the blind eyes and bring the prisoners from the prison, and them that sit in darkness out of the prison house. He will make bare his holy arm; he will show the sword in that hand which was hidden under the scarlet robe; he will manifest his power in the destruction of his enemies and the salvation of his people. As certainly as he hath shed his blood on Calvary, he shall stain all his raiment with the blood of his foes on the field of Armageddon. As certainly as he hath drained the cup of wrath and received the baptism of suffering on Calvary, shall he wield the iron rod of justice and sway the golden scepter of mercy on the field of Armageddon. Already the sword is drawn, the decisive blow is struck, the helmet of Apollyon is cleft, and the bonds of iniquity are cut asunder. Already the fire is kindled, and all the powers of hell cannot quench it. It has fallen from heaven; it is consuming the camp of the foe; it is inflaming the hearts of men; it is renovating the earth, and purging away the curse. "The bright and Morning Star" has risen on Calvary; and soon "the Sun of Righteousness" shall shine on the field of Armageddon. The darkness that covers the earth, and the gross darkness that covers the people, shall melt away; and Mohammedism, and paganism, and popery, with their prince, the devil, shall seek shelter in the bottomless pit!

After a battle, we are anxious to learn who is dead, who is wounded, and who is missing from the ranks. In the engagement of Messiah with Satan and his allies on Calvary, Messiah's heel was bruised, but Satan and his allies received a mortal wound in the head. The head denotes wisdom, cunning, power, government. The devil, sin, and death have lost their dominion over the believer in Christ, since the achievement of Calvary. There is no condemnation, no fear of hell. But the serpent, though his head is bruised, may be able to move his tail and alarm those of little faith. Yet it cannot last long. The wound is mortal, and the triumph sure. On Calvary the dragon's head was crushed by the Captain of our salvation; after the battle of Armageddon, his tail shall shake no more!

There is no discharge in this war. He that enlisteth under the banner of the cross must endure faithful until death; must not lay aside his arms till death is swallowed up in victory. Then shall every conqueror bear the image of the heavenly, and wear the crown instead of the cross, and carry the palm instead of the spear. Let us be strong in the Lord and in the power of his might, that we may be able to stand in the evil day; and after all the war is over, to stand accepted in the Beloved, that we may reign with him forever and ever.

II. It remains for us to explain, very briefly, the glorious colloquy in the text; the interrogatives of the church, and the answers of Messiah.

How great was the wonder and joy of Mary when she met the Master at the tomb, clothed in immortality, where she thought to find him shrouded in death! How unspeakable was the astonishment and rapture of the disciples when their Lord, whom they had so recently buried, came into the house where they were assembled and said, "Peace be unto you!" Such are the feelings which the church is represented as expressing in this sublime colloquy with the Captain of her salvation. He has traveled into the land of tribulation; he has gone down to the dust of death; but lo, he returns a conqueror, the golden scepter of love in his left hand, the iron rod of justice in his right, and on his head a crown of many stars. The church beholds him with great amazement and delight. She lately followed him, weeping, to the cross, and mourned over his body in the tomb; but now she beholds him risen indeed, having destroyed death, and him that had the power of death—that is, the devil. She goes forth to meet him with songs of rejoicing, as the daughters of Israel went out to welcome David, when he returned from the valley, with the head of the giant in his hand, and the blood running down his clothes. The choir of the church is divided into two bands which chant to each other in alternate strains. The right hand division begins the glorious colloquy, "Who is this that cometh from Edom?" and the left takes up the interrogative, and repeats it with a variation: "with dyed garments from Bozrah?" "This that is glorious in his apparel," resumes the right-hand company, "glorious notwithstanding the tribulations he hath endured?" "Traveling in the greatness of his strength?" responds the left, "strength sufficient to unbar the gates of the grave, and liberate the captives of corruption?" The celestial Conqueror pauses, and casts upon the company of the daughters of Zion a look of infinite benignity; and with a voice of angel melody, and more than angel majesty, he replies, "I that speak in righteousness, mighty to save!" Now bursts the song again, like the sound of many waters, from the right, "Wherefore art thou red in thine apparel?" and the response rolls back in melodized thunder from the left, "And thy garments like him that treadeth in the winefat?" The divine hero answers, "I have trodden the winepress alone; and of the people there was none with me. Even Peter has left me, with all his courage and affection; and as for John, to talk of love is all that he can do. I have triumphed over principalities and powers. I am wounded, but they are vanquished. Behold the blood which I have lost! Behold the spoils which I have won! Now will I mount my white horse, pursue after Satan, demolish his kingdom, and send him back to the land of darkness in everlasting chains, and all his allies shall be exiles with him forever. My own arm, which has gained the victory on Calvary and brought salvation to all my people from the sepulcher, is still strong enough to wield the golden scepter of love and break my foes on the field of Armageddon. I will destroy the works of the devil, and demolish all his hosts; I will dash them in pieces like a potter's vessel. For the day of vengeance is in my heart, and the year of my redeemed is come. My compassion is stirred for the captives of sin and death; my fury is kindled against the tyrants that oppress them. It is time for me to open the prisons and break off the fetters. I must gather my people to myself. I must seek that which was lost, and bring again that which was driven away. I must bind up that which was broken, and strengthen that which was weak. But I will destroy the fat and the strong, I will feed them with judgment; I will tread them in mine anger, trample them in my fury, bring down their strength to the earth, and stain all my raiment with their blood!"

Let us flee from the wrath to come! Behold, the sun is risen high on the day of vengeance. Let us not be found among the enemies of Messiah, lest we fall a sacrifice to his righteous indignation on the field of Armageddon! Let us escape for our lives, for the firestorm of his anger will burn to the lowest hell! Let us pray for grace to lay hold on the salvation of his redeemed. It is a free, full, perfect, glorious, and eternal salvation. Return, ye ransomed exiles from happiness, return to your forfeited inheritance! Now is the year of jubilee. Come to Jesus, that your debts may be canceled, your sins forgiven, and your persons justified! Come, for the Conqueror of your foes is on the throne! Come, for the trumpets of mercy are sounding! Come, for all things are now ready!

Thomas Chalmers:
The Expulsive Power of a New Affection

THOMAS CHALMERS WAS BORN at Anstruther, Scotland, in 1780, and died at Edinburgh in 1847. His first charge was at Kilmany, in Fifeshire, where he seems to have been more interested in mathematics than in preaching the gospel. A severe and prolonged illness worked a complete change in his pulpit method. His able, ethical discourses were now followed by a burning proclamation of Jesus Christ and him crucified as the true inspirer of conduct and the only way of eternal life. His near approach to death through a prolonged illness left him with the oil of a new consecration upon his mighty brow. As Lord Roseberry phrased it in his address at the celebration of the one hundredth anniversary of Chalmers' settlement in Glasgow: "An illness lifted him into a higher sphere, and he soared aloft. There he remained to the end in communion with the Divine."

In 1815, Chalmers was called to the Tron Church in Glasgow, where, and afterwards at St. John's, he had a notable ministry and became a national character. He was famous not only for his preaching, but for his experiments in Christian philanthropy. In 1823, he took the chair of moral philosophy in St. Andrew's University, and in 1828 the chair of theology at Edinburgh. In the movements which led to the Disruption of 1843, Chalmers was one of the leaders of the evangelical party.

Chalmers was a great topical preacher. He never wearies with textual explanations or references, but drives relentlessly forward the chariot of his proposition from the very beginning of his sermon. He read closely the same sermons over and over again, and with a broad Fifeshire accent; yet contemporaries describe the effect of his preaching as tremendous. When a friend of Chalmers expressed his surprise to a country woman of Fife that she who hated reading so much should yet be so fond of Chalmers, the woman responded: "Nae doubt! But it's fell readin' thon!"

His sermon on the "Expulsive Power of a New Affection" is a noble utterance, worthy of the fame which it has secured. It is celebrated, not only for the truth which it unfolds, but also for its beautiful and imaginative climax.

The Expulsive Power of a New Affection

Love not the world, neither the things that are in the world. If any man love the world, the love of the Father is not in him (1 John 2:15).

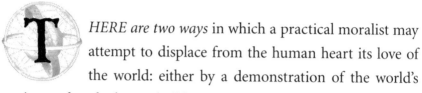*HERE are two ways* in which a practical moralist may attempt to displace from the human heart its love of the world: either by a demonstration of the world's vanity, so that the heart shall be prevailed upon simply to withdraw its regards from an object that is not worthy of it; or by setting forth another object, even God, as more worthy of its attachment, so as that the heart shall be prevailed upon not to resign an old affection, which shall have nothing to succeed it, but to exchange an old affection for a new one. My purpose is to show that from the constitution of our nature, the former method is altogether incompetent and ineffectual; and that the latter method will alone suffice for the rescue and recovery of the heart from the wrong affection that domineers over it. After having accomplished this purpose, I shall attempt a few practical observations.

The ascendant power of a second affection will do what no exposition, however forcible, of the folly and worthlessness of the first, ever could effectuate. And it is the same in the great world. You never will be able to arrest any of its leading pursuits by a naked demonstration of their vanity. It is quite in vain to think of stopping one of these pursuits in any way else, but by stimulating to another. In attempting to bring a worldly man, intent and busied with the prosecution of his objects, to a dead stand, you have not merely to encounter the charm which he annexes to these objects—but you have to encounter the pleasure which he feels in the very prosecution of them. It is not enough, then, that you dissipate the charm by your moral, eloquent, and affecting exposure of its elusiveness. You must address to the eye of his mind another object with a charm powerful enough to dispossess the first of its influence, and to engage him in some other prosecution as full of interest, hope, and congenial activity,as the former. It is this which stamps an impotency on all moral and pathetic declamation about the insignificance of the world. A man will no more consent to the misery of being without an object, because that object is a trifle, or of being without a pursuit, because that pursuit terminates in some frivolous or fugitive acquirement, than he will voluntarily submit himself to torture, because that torture is to be of short duration. If to be without desire and without exertion altogether is a state of violence and discomfort, then the present desire, with its correspondent train of exertion, is not to be got rid of simply by destroying it. It must be by substituting another desire and another line or habit of exertion in its place; and the most effectual way of withdrawing the mind from one subject, is not by turning it away upon desolate and unpeopled vacancy, but by presenting to its regards another object still more alluring.

These remarks apply not merely to love considered in its state of desire for an object not yet obtained. They apply also to love considered in its state of indulgence or placid gratification, with an object already in possession. It is seldom that any of our tastes are made to disappear by a mere process of natural extinction. At least, it is very seldom that this is done through the instrumentality of reasoning. It may be done by excessive pampering, but it is almost never done by the mere force of mental determination. But what cannot be thus destroyed may be dispossessed; and one taste may be made to give way to another, and to lose its power entirely as the reigning affection of the mind. It is thus that the boy ceases, at length, to be the slave of his appetite, but it is because a manlier taste has now brought it into subordination. The youth ceases to idolize pleasure, but it is because the idol of wealth has become stronger and gotten the ascendancy. Even the love of money ceases to have the mastery over the heart of many a thriving citizen, but it is because, drawn into the whirl of city politics, another affection has been wrought into his moral system, and he is now forded over by the love of power. There is not one of these transformations in which the heart is left without an object. Its desire for one particular object may be conquered; but as to its desire for having some one object or other, this is unconquerable. Its adhesion to that on which it has fastened the preference of its regards cannot willingly be overcome by the rending away of a simple separation. It can be done only by the application of something else, to which it may feel the adhesion of a still stronger and more powerful preference. Such is the grasping tendency of the human heart, that it must have something to lay hold of—and which, if wrested away without the substitution of another something in its place, would leave a void and a vacancy as painful to the mind as hunger is to the natural system. It may be dispossessed of one object, or of any, but it cannot be desolated of all. Let there be a breathing and a sensitive heart, but without a liking and without affinity to any of the things that are around it, and in a state of cheerless abandonment, it would have to be alive to nothing but the burden of its own consciousness, and feel it to be intolerable. It would make no difference to its owner whether he dwelt in the midst of a gay and goodly world or placed afar beyond the outskirts of creation, if he dwelt as a solitary unit in dark and unpeopled nothingness. The heart must have something to cling to—and never, by its own voluntary consent, will it so denude itself of all its attachments that there shall not be one remaining object that can draw or solicit it.

The misery of a heart thus bereft of all relish for that which used to minister enjoyment is strikingly exemplified in those, who, satiated with indulgence, have been so belabored with the variety and the poignancy of the pleasurable sensations that they have experienced,

that they are at length fatigued out of all capacity for sensation whatever. The disease of ennui is more frequent in the French metropolis,
where amusement is more exclusively the occupation of higher classes, than it is in the British metropolis, where the longings of the heart
are more diversified by the resources of business and politics. There
are the votaries of fashion, who, in this way, have at length become
the victims of fashionable excess —in whom the very multitude of
their enjoyments has at last extinguished their power of enjoyment—who, with the gratifications of art and nature at command,
now look upon all that is around them with an eye of tastelessness;
who, plied with the delights of sense and of splendor even to weariness, and incapable of higher delights, have come to the end of all
their perfection, and like Solomon of old, found it to be vanity and
vexation. The man whose heart has thus been turned into a desert
can vouch for the insupportable languor which must ensue, when
one affection is thus plucked away from the bosom, without another
to replace it. It is not necessary that a man receive pain from anything
in order to become miserable. It is barely enough that he looks with
distaste on everything—and in that asylum which is the repository
of minds out of joint, and where the organ of feeling as well as the
organ of intellect has been impaired, it is not in the cell of loud and
frantic outcries where you will meet with the acme of mental suffering. But that is the individual who outpeers in wretchedness all his
fellows, who throughout the whole expanse of nature and society,
meets not an object that has at all the power to detain or to interest
him; who neither in earth beneath, nor in heaven above, knows of a
single charm to which his heart can send forth one desirous or
responding movement; to whom the world, in his eye a vast and empty
desolation, has left him nothing but his own consciousness to feed
upon—dead to all that is without him, and alive to nothing but to the
load of his own torpid and useless existence.

It will now be seen, perhaps, why it is that the heart keeps by its present affections with so much tenacity, when the attempt is to do them away by a mere process of extirpation. It will not consent to be so desolated. The strong man, whose dwelling place is there, may be compelled to give way to another occupier; but unless another stronger than he has power to dispossess and to succeed him, he will keep his present lodgment inviolable. The heart would revolt against its own emptiness. It could not bear to be so left in a state of waste and cheerless insipidity. The moralist who tries such a process of dispossession as this upon the heart is thwarted at every step by the recoil of its own mechanism. You have all heard that nature abhors a vacuum. Such at least is the nature of the heart, that though the room which is in it may change one inmate for another, it cannot be left void without the pain of most intolerable suffering. It is not enough then to argue the folly of an existing affection. It is not enough, in the terms of a forcible or an affecting demonstration, to make good the evanescence of its object. It may not even be enough to associate the threats and terrors of some coming vengeance with the indulgence of it. The heart may still resist the every application, by obedience to which it would finally be conducted to a state so much at war with all its appetites as that of downright inanition. So to tear away an affection from the heart, as to leave it bare of all its regards and of all its preferences, were a hard and hopeless undertaking; and it would appear as if the alone powerful engine of dispossession were to bring the mastery of another affection to bear upon it.

We know not a more sweeping interdict upon the affections of nature than that which is delivered by the apostle in the verse before us. To bid a man into whom there is not yet entered the great and ascendant influence of the principle of regeneration, to bid him withdraw his love from all the things that are in the world, is to bid him give up all the affections that are in his heart. The world is the all of a natural man. He has not a taste, nor a desire, that points not to a something placed within the confines of its visible horizon. He loves nothing above it, and he cares for nothing beyond it; and to bid him love not the world is to pass a sentence of expulsion on all the inmates of his bosom. To estimate the magnitude and the difficulty of such a surrender, let us only think that it were just as arduous to prevail on him not to love wealth, which is but one of the things in the world, as to prevail on him to set willful fire to his own property. This he might do with sore and painful reluctance, if he saw that the salvation of his life hung upon it. But this he would do willingly, if he saw that a new property of tenfold value was instantly to emerge from the wreck of the old one. In this case there is something more than the mere displacement of an affection. There is the overbearing of one affection by another. But to desolate his heart of all love for the things of the world, without the substitution of any love in its place, were to him a process of as unnatural violence, as to destroy all the things he has in the world, and give him nothing in their room. So that, if to love not the world be indispensable to one's Christianity, then the crucifixion of the old man is not too strong a term to mark that transition in his history when all old things are done away, and all things are become new.

We hope that by this time, you understand the impotency of a mere demonstration of this world's insignificance. Its sole practical effect, if it had any, would be to leave the heart in a state which to every heart is insupportable, and that is a mere state of nakedness and negation. You may remember the fond and unbroken tenacity with which your heart has often recurred to pursuits, over the utter frivolity of which it sighed and wept but yesterday. The arithmetic of your short-lived days may on Sabbath make the clearest impression upon your understanding—and from his fancied bed of death, may the preacher cause a voice to descend in rebuke and mockery on all the pursuits of earthliness. And as he pictures before you the fleeting generations of men, with the absorbing grave, whither all the joys and interests of the world hasten to their sure and speedy oblivion, may you, touched and solemnized by his argument, feel for a moment as if on the eve of a practical and permanent emancipation from a scene of so much vanity. But the morrow comes, and the business of the world, the objects of the world, and the moving forces of the world come along with it—and the machinery of the heart, in virtue of which it must have something to grasp or something to adhere to, brings it under a kind of moral necessity to be actuated just as before. In utter repulsion towards a state so unkindly as that of being frozen out both of delight and desire, does it feel all the warmth and the urgency of its wonted solicitations—nor in the habit and history of the whole man can we detect so much as one symptom of the new creature—so that the church, instead of being to him a school of obedience, has been a mere sauntering place for the luxury of a passing and theatrical emotion. The preaching, which is mighty to compel the attendance of multitudes, which is mighty to still and to solemnize the hearers into a kind of tragic sensibility, which is mighty in the play of variety and vigor that it can keep up around the imagination, is not mighty to the pulling down of strongholds.

The love of the world cannot be expurgated by a mere demonstration of the world's worthlessness. But may it not be supplanted by the love of that which is more worthy than itself? The heart cannot be prevailed upon to part with the world by a simple act of resignation. But may not the heart be prevailed upon to admit into its preference another, who shall subordinate the world and bring it down from its wanted ascendancy? If the throne which is placed there must have an occupier, and the tyrant that now reigns has occupied it wrongfully, he may not leave a bosom which would rather detain him than be left in desolation. But may he not give way to the lawful sovereign, appearing with every charm that can secure his willing admittance, and taking unto himself his great power to subdue the moral nature of man, and to reign over it? In a word, if the way to disengage the heart from the positive love of one great and ascendant object is to fasten it in positive love to another, then it is not by exposing the worthlessness of the former, but by addressing to the mental eye the worth and excellence of the latter that all old things are to be done away, and all things are to become new.

To obliterate all our present affections by simply expunging them, and so as to leave the seat of them unoccupied, would be to destroy the old character and to substitute no new character in its place. But when they take their departure upon the ingress of other visitors; when they resign their sway to the power and the predominance of new affections; when, abandoning the heart to solitude, they merely give place to a successor who turns it into as busy a residence of desire, and interest, and expectation as before—there is nothing in all this to thwart or to overbear any of the laws of our sentient nature—and we see how, in fullest accordance with the mechanism of the heart, a great moral revolution may be made to take place upon it.

This, we trust, will explain the operation of that charm which accompanies the effectual preaching of the gospel. The love of God and the love of the world are two affections, not merely in a state of rivalship, but in a state of enmity—and that so irreconcilable that they cannot dwell together in the same bosom. We have already affirmed how impossible it were for the heart, by any innate elasticity of its own, to cast the world away from it, and thus reduce itself to a wilderness. The heart is not so constituted, and the only way to dispossess it of an old affection is by the expulsive power of a new one. Nothing can exceed the magnitude of the required change in a man's character when bidden as he is in the New Testament, to love not the

world; no, nor any of the things that are in the world, for this so comprehends all that is dear to him in existence as to be equivalent to a
command of self-annihilation. But the same revelation which dictates so mighty an obedience places within our reach as mighty an
instrument of obedience. It brings for admittance, to the very door of
our heart, an affection which, once seated upon its throne, will either
subordinate every previous inmate, or bid it away. Beside the world,
it places before the eye of the mind him who made the world, and
with this peculiarity, which is all its own: that in the gospel do we so
behold God, as that we may love God. It is there, and there only,
where God stands revealed as an object of confidence to sinners; and
where our desire after him is not chilled into apathy by that barrier of
human guilt which intercepts every approach that is not made to him
through the appointed Mediator. It is the bringing in of this better
hope, whereby we draw nigh unto God—and to live without hope is
to live without God, and if the heart be without God, the world will
then have all the ascendancy. It is God apprehended by the believer
as God in Christ who alone can depose it from this ascendancy. It is
when he stands dismantled of the terrors which belong to him as an
offended lawgiver, and when we are enabled by faith, which is his own
gift, to see his glory in the face of Jesus Christ and to hear his beseech-
ing voice, as it protests good will to men and entreats the return of all
who will to a full pardon, and a gracious acceptance; it is then, that a
love paramount to the love of the world, and at length expulsive of it,
first arises in the regenerating bosom. It is when released from the
spirit of bondage, with which love cannot dwell, and when admitted
into the number of God's children, through the faith that is in Christ
Jesus, the spirit of adoption is poured upon us—it is then that the
heart, brought under the mastery of one great and predominant
affection, is delivered from the tyranny of its former desires, and in
the only way in which deliverance is possible. And that faith which is

revealed to us from heaven as indispensable to a sinner's justification in the sight of God, is also the instrument of the greatest of all moral and spiritual achievements on a nature dead to the influence, and beyond the reach of every other application.

Thus may we come to perceive what it is that makes the most effective kind of preaching. It is not enough to hold out to the world's eye the mirror of its own imperfections. It is not enough to come forth with a demonstration, however pathetic, of the evanescent character of all its enjoyments. It is not enough to travel the walk of experience along with you and speak to your own conscience, your own recollection of the deceitfulness of the heart, and the deceitfulness of all that the heart is set upon. There is many a bearer of the gospel message who has not natural discernment enough, who has not power of characteristic description enough, and who has not the talent of moral delineation enough, to present you with a vivid and faithful sketch of the existing follies of society. But that very corruption which he has not the faculty of representing in its visible details, he may practically be the instrument of eradicating in its principle. Let him be but a faithful expounder of the gospel testimony. Unable as may be to apply a descriptive hand to the character of the present world, let him but report with accuracy the matter which revelation has brought to him from a distant world—unskilled as he is in the work of so anatomizing the heart, as with the power of a novelist to create a graphical or impressive exhibition of the worthlessness of its many affections. Let him only deal in those mysteries of peculiar doctrine, on which the best of novelists have thrown the wantonness of their derision. He may not be able, with the eye of shrewd and satirical observation, to expose to the ready recognition of his hearers the desires of worldliness; but with the tidings of the gospel in commission, he may wield the only engine that can extirpate them. He cannot do what some have done, when, as if by the hand of a magician, they have brought out to view from the hidden recesses of our nature, the foibles and lurking appetites which belong to it. But he has a truth in his possession, which into whatever heart it enters, will, like the rod of Aaron, swallow up them all. Unqualified as he may be to describe the old man in all the nicer shading of his natural and constitutional varieties, with him is deposited that ascendant influence under which the leading tastes and tendencies of the old man are destroyed, and he becomes a new creature in Jesus Christ our Lord.

Let us not cease, then, to ply the only instrument of powerful and positive operation to do away from you the love of the world. Let us try every legitimate method of finding access to your hearts for the love of him who is greater than the world. For this purpose, let us, if possible, clear away that shroud of unbelief which so hides and darkens the face of the Deity. Let us insist on his claims to your affection; and whether in the shape of gratitude or in the shape of esteem, let us never cease to affirm that in the whole of that wondrous economy, the purpose of which is to reclaim a sinful world unto himself, he, the God of love, so sets himself forth in characters of endearment, that naught but faith, and naught but understanding, are wanting, on your part, to call forth the love of your hearts back again.

Now, it is altogether worthy of being remarked of those men who disrelish spiritual Christianity and, in fact, deem it an impracticable acquirement, how much of a piece their incredulity about the demands of Christianity, and their incredulity about the doctrines of Christianity, are with one another. No wonder that they feel the work of the New Testament to be beyond their strength, so long as they hold the words of the New Testament to be beneath their attention. Neither they nor anyone else can dispossess the heart of an old affection but by the impulsive power of a new one. If that new affection be the love of God, neither they nor anyone else can be made to entertain it, but on such a representation of the Deity as shall draw the heart of the sinner towards him. Now it is just their unbelief which screens from the discernment of their minds this representation. They do not see the love of God in sending his Son into the world. They do not see the expression of his tenderness to men in sparing him not, but giving him up unto the death for us all. They do not see the sufficiency of the Atonement or of the sufferings that were endured by him who bore the burden that sinners should have borne. They do not see the blended holiness and compassion of the Godhead in that he passed by the transgressions of his creatures, yet could not pass them by without an expiation. It is a mystery to them how a man should pass to the state of godliness from a state of nature—but had they only a believing view of God manifest in the flesh, this would resolve for them the whole mystery of godliness. As it is, they cannot get quit of their old affections, because they are out of sight from all those truths which have influence to raise a new one. They are like the children of Israel in the land of Egypt, when required to make bricks without straw. They cannot love God, while they want the only food which can aliment this affection in a sinner's bosom. However great their errors may be, both in resisting the demands of the gospel as impractical and in rejecting the doctrines of the gospel as inadmissible, yet there is not a spiritual man (and it is the prerogative of him who is spiritual to judge all men) who will not perceive that there is a consistency in these errors.

But if there be a consistency in the errors, in like manner is there a consistency in the truths which are opposite to them. The man who believes in the peculiar doctrines will readily bow to the peculiar demands of Christianity. When he is told to love God supremely, this may startle another, but it will not startle him to whom God has been revealed in peace, and in pardon, and in all the freeness of an offered reconciliation. When told to shut out the world from his heart, this may be impossible with him who has nothing to replace it—but not impossible with him who has found in God a sure and satisfying portion. When told to withdraw his affections from the things that are beneath, this were laying an order of self-extinction upon the man who knows not another quarter in the whole sphere of his contemplation, to which he could transfer them. But it were not grievous to him whose view has been opened up to the loveliness and glory of the things that are above and can there find, forever feeling of his soul, a most ample and delighted occupation. When told to look not to the things that are seen and temporal, this were blotting out the light of all that is visible from the prospect of him in whose eye there is a wall of partition between guilty nature and the joys of eternity. But he who believes that Christ has broken down this wall, finds a gathering radiance upon his soul as he looks onward in faith to the things that are unseen and eternal.

The object of the gospel is both to pacify the sinner's conscience and to purify his heart; and it is of importance to observe that what mars the one of these objects mars the other also. The best way of casting out an impure affection is to admit a pure one; and by the love of what is good, to expel the love of what is evil. Thus it is, that the freer the gospel, the more sanctifying is the gospel; and the more it is received as a doctrine of grace, the more will it be felt as a doctrine according to godliness. This is one of the secrets of the Christian life, that the more a man holds of God as a pensioner, the greater is the payment of service that he renders back again. On the tenure of "do this and live," a spirit of fearfulness is sure to enter; and the jealousies of a legal bargain chase away all confidence from the intercourse between God and man. The creature striving to be square and even with his Creator is, in fact, pursuing all the while his own selfishness instead of God's glory; and with all the conformities which he labors to accomplish, the soul of obedience is not there, the mind is not subject to the law of God, nor indeed under such an economy ever can be. It is only when, as in the gospel, acceptance is bestowed as a present, without money and without price, that the security which man feels in God is placed beyond the reach of disturbance; or that he can repose in him as one friend reposes in another; or that any liberal and generous understanding can be established between them—the one party rejoicing over the other to do him good—the other finding that the truest gladness of his heart lies in the impulse of a gratitude, by which it is awakened to the charms of a new moral existence. Salvation by grace, salvation by free grace, salvation not of works, but according to the mercy of God—salvation on such a footing is not more indispensable to the deliverance of our persons from the hand of justice, than it is to the deliverance of our hearts from the chill and the weight of ungodliness. Retain a single shred or fragment of legality with the gospel, and you raise a topic of distrust between man and God. You take away from the power of the gospel to melt and to conciliate. For this purpose, the freer it is, the better it is. And never does the sinner find within himself so mighty a moral transformation as when, under the belief that he is saved by grace, he feels constrained thereby to offer his heart a devoted thing, and to deny ungodliness.

To do any work in the best manner, you would make use of the fittest tools for it. And we trust that what has been said may serve in some degree for the practical guidance of those who would like to reach the great moral achievement of our text, but feel that the tendencies and desires of nature are too strong for them. We know of no other way by which to keep the love of the world out of our hearts than to keep in our hearts the love of God; and no other way by which to keep our hearts in the love of God than building ourselves up on our most holy faith. That denial of the world which is not possible to him that dissents from the gospel testimony is possible, even as all things are possible, to him that believeth. To try this without faith is to work without the right tool or the right instrument. But faith worketh by love; and the way of expelling from the heart the love that transgresses the Law is to admit into its receptacles the love which fulfills the Law.

Conceive a man to be standing on the margin of this green world; and that, when he looked towards it, he saw abundance smiling upon every field, and all the blessings which earth can afford scattered in profusion throughout every family, the light of the sun sweetly resting upon all the pleasant habitations, and the joys of human companionship brightening many a happy circle of society—conceive this to be the general character of the scene upon one side of his contemplation; and that on the other, beyond the verge of the goodly planet on which he was situated, he could see nothing but a dark and fathomless unknown. Do you think he would bid a voluntary adieu to all the brightness and all the beauty that were before him upon earth, and commit himself to the frightful solitude away from it? Would he leave its peopled dwelling places, and become a solitary wanderer through the fields of nonentity? If space offered him nothing but a wilderness, would he for it abandon the homebred scenes of life and of cheerfulness that lay so near, and exerted such a power of urgency to detain him? Would not he cling to the regions of sense, of life, and of society? And shrinking away from the desolation that was beyond it, would he not be glad to keep his firm footing on the territory of this world, and to take shelter under the silver canopy that was stretched over it?

But if, during the time of his contemplation, some happy island of the blest had floated by, and there had burst upon his senses the light of its surpassing glories and its sounds of sweeter melody; and he clearly saw that there a purer beauty rested upon every field, and a more heartfelt joy spread itself among all the families; and he could discern there a peace, a piety, and a benevolence which put a moral gladness into every bosom and united the whole society in one rejoicing sympathy with each other, and with the beneficent Father of them all—could he further see that pain and mortality were there unknown and, above all, that signals of welcome were hung out and an avenue of communication was made for him—perceive you not that what was before the wilderness would become the land of invitation, and that now the world would be the wilderness? What unpeopled space could not do, can be done by space teeming with beatific scenes and beatific society. And let the existing tendencies of the heart be what they may to the scene that is near and visible around us. Still, if another stood revealed to the prospect of man, either through the channel of faith or through the channel of his senses, then, without violence done to the constitution of his moral nature, may he die unto the present world, and live to the lovelier world that stands in the distance away from it.

Charles Grandison Finney: *Stewardship*

CHARLES GRANDISON FINNEY WAS BORN in 1792 at Warren, Connecticut, and died at Oberlin, Ohio, in 1875. He studied for the law, but upon his conversion entered the ministry and soon became a power in the pulpit. He conducted great revivals in America and in England. In 1835, he became a professor at Oberlin College, Ohio, and in 1852 was chosen president of the college. His name is associated with the Oberlin School of Theology, which broke with historic Calvinism and taught the perfect free will of man, and the possibility of attaining unto holiness. The sermons of Finney in their clear-cut, matter-of-fact statements show his logical bent and his legal training. The reader of these sermons will wonder that they produced such great effects in the conversion of sinners. Finney, however, said that in his preaching, he threw himself open to the influence of the Holy Spirit and even claimed prophetic power. Be that as it may, he was mightily used of God in the proclamation of the gospel, and thousands found their way into the church through his preaching. His sermon "Stewardship" is a good illustration of his keen, incisive, and logical style, and is a searching and solemn utterance on the subject of man's accountability, especially in the use of money.

That Finney was not so calm and subdued in his preaching as his printed sermons would lead one to suppose is evidenced by contemporary comments on his manner and style. For example, a complaint was brought against a minister in Troy because he had introduced into his pulpit "the notorious Charles G. Finney, whose shocking blasphemies, novel and repulsive sentiments, and theatrical and frantic gesticulations, struck horror into those who entertained any reverence either for religion or decency." One of

Finney's famous sermons was on the text, "One mediator between God and men, the man Christ Jesus" (1 Tim. 2:5). Professor Park of Andover Seminary heard him preach the sermon there in 1831. He tells how the commencement exercises were practically broken up and abandoned because everyone crowded to the church to hear the celebrated Finney. Professor Park describes his discourse as one which could never be printed and not easily forgotten. At the end of a dramatic passage in which Finney described the sorrows of the lost and the music of heaven, Professor Park says that the board stretched across the aisle on which he and five or six men were sitting actually shook beneath them because of the vibrations of emotions produced by the preacher.

Stewardship

"Give an account of thy stewardship" (Luke 16:2).

 STEWARD *is one* who is employed to transact the business of another as his agent or representative in the business in which he is employed.

His duty is to promote, in the best possible manner, the interest of his employer. He is liable at any time to be called to an account for the manner in which he has transacted his business, and to be removed from his office at the pleasure of his employer.

One important design of the parable of which the text is a part is to teach that all men are God's stewards. The Bible declares that the silver and the gold are his, and that he is, in the highest possible sense, the proprietor of the universe. Men are mere stewards, employed by him for the transaction of his business, and required to do all they do for his glory. Even their eating and drinking are to be done for his glory, *i. e.,* that they be strengthened for the best performance of his business.

That men *are* God's stewards is evident from the fact that God treats them as such, removes them at his pleasure, and disposes of the property in their hands, which he could not do did he not consider them merely his agents and not the owners of the property.

1. If men are God's stewards, they are bound to account to him for their *time*. God has created them and keeps them alive, and their time is his. Hearer, should you employ a steward and pay him for his time, would you not expect him to employ that time in your service? Would you not consider it fraud and dishonesty for him, while in your pay, to spend his time in idleness, or in promoting his private interests? Suppose he were often idle, that would be bad enough; but suppose that he *wholly* neglected your business, and that when called to an account, and censured for not doing his duty, he should say,

"Why, what have I done?" Would you not suppose that for him to have done *nothing* and let your business suffer was great wickedness, for which he deserved to be punished?

Now, you are God's steward, and if you are an impenitent sinner, you have wholly neglected God's business and have remained idle in his vineyard, or have been only attending to your own private interest; and now are you ready to ask what you have done? Are you not a knave thus to neglect the business of your great employer, and go about your own private business to the neglect of all that justice and duty and God require of you?

But suppose *your* steward should employ his time in *opposing* your interest, using your capital and time in driving at speculations directly opposed to the business for which he was employed. Would you not consider this great dishonesty? Would you not think it very ridiculous for him to account himself an honest man? Would you not suppose yourself *obliged* to call him to an account? And would you not account anyone a villain who should approve such conduct? Would you not think yourself *bound* to publish him abroad, that the world might know his character, and that you might clear yourself from the charge of upholding such a person?

How, then, shall God dispose of you, if you employ your time in *opposing* his interest and use his capital in your hands, to drive at speculation directly opposed to the business for which he has employed you? Are you not ashamed, then, to account yourself an honest man, and will not God consider himself under an *obligation* to call you to an account? Should he not do this, would not the omission be an evidence on his part of an approval of your abominable wickedness? Must he not feel himself constrained to make you a public example, that the universe may know how much he abhors your crimes?

2. Stewards are bound to give an account of their *talents*. By talents, I mean here the powers of their minds. Suppose you should

educate a man to be your steward, should support him during the time that he was engaged in study, and be at all the expense of his education, and then he should either neglect to employ his mind in your service, or should use the powers of his cultivated intellect for the promotion of his own interests. Would you not consider this as fraud and villainy? Now, God created your minds, and has been at the expense of your education, and has trained you for his service. Do you either let your mind remain in idleness, or pervert the powers of your cultivated intellect to the promotion of your own private interest, and then ask what you have done to deserve the wrath of God?

But suppose your steward should use his education in *opposition* to your interest, and use all the powers of his mind to destroy the very interest for which he was educated and which he is employed to sustain. Would you not look upon his conduct as marked with horrid guilt? And do *you*, sinner, employ the powers of your mind, and whatever education God may have given you, in *opposing* his interest, perverting his truth, scattering "fire-brands, arrows and death" all around you, and think to escape his curse? Shall not the Almighty be avenged upon such a wretch?

3. A steward is bound to give an account for the *influence he exerts* upon mankind around him.

Suppose you should employ a steward, should educate him until he possessed great talents, should put a large capital into his hands, should exalt him high in society, and place him in circumstances to exert an immense influence in the commercial community, and then he should refuse or neglect to exert this influence in promoting your interest. Would you not consider this default a perpetual fraud practiced upon you?

But suppose he should exert all this influence against you, and array himself with all his weight of character, talent and influence, and even employ the capital with which he was entrusted, in *opposing* your interest. What language in your estimation could then express your sense of his guilt?

Hearer, whatever influence God has given you, if you are an impenitent sinner, you are not only neglecting to use it for God, to build up his kingdom, but you are employing it in *opposition* to his interest and glory; and for this, do you not deserve the damnation of hell? Perhaps you are rich or learned, or have, on other accounts, great influence in society, and are refusing to use it to save the souls of men but are bringing all your weight of character and talents as an influence and example, to drag all who are within the sphere of your influence down to the gates of hell.

4. You must give an account for the manner in which you use *the property in your possession*. Suppose your steward should refuse to employ the capital with which you entrusted him for the promotion of your interest, or suppose he were to account it his own and to use it for his own private interest, or apply it to the gratification of his lusts or the aggrandizement of his family; bestowing large portions upon his daughters, or ministering to the lusts and pride of his sons; while at the same time your business was suffering for the want of this very capital. Suppose that this steward held the purse-strings of your wealth, and that you had multitudes of other servants, whose necessities were to be supplied out of the means in his hands, and that their welfare, even their lives, depended on these supplies. Yet this steward should minister to his own lusts and those of his family, and suffer those, your other servants, to perish. What would you think of such wickedness? You entrusted him with your money, and enjoined him to take care of your other servants, and, through his neglect, they were all dead men.

Now, you have God's money in your hands, and are surrounded by God's children, whom he commands you to love as you do yourself. God might, with perfect justice, have given his property to them instead of you. The world is full of poverty, desolation, and death; hundreds and millions are perishing, body and soul; God calls on you to exert yourself as his steward, for their salvation; to use all the property in your possession, so as to promote the greatest possible amount of happiness among your fellow creatures. The Macedonian cry comes from the four winds of heaven, "Come over and help us"; and yet you refuse to help; you hoard up the wealth in your possession, live in luxury, and let your fellow men go down to hell. What language can describe your guilt?

But suppose your servant, when you called him to account, should say, "Have I not acquired this property by my own industry?" would you not answer, "You have employed my capital to do it, and my time, for which I have paid you; and the money you have gained is mine." So when God calls upon you to use the property in your possession for him, do you say it is yours, that you have obtained it by your own industry? Pray, whose time have you used, and whose talents and means? Did not God create you? Has he not sustained you? Has he not prospered you and given you all his success? Yes, your time is his; your all is his. You have no right to say the wealth you have is yours; it is his, and you are bound to use it for his glory. You are a traitor to your trust if you do not so employ it.

If your clerk takes only a little of your money, his character is gone, and he is branded as a villain. But sinners take not only a dollar or so, but all they can get, and use it for themselves. Don't you see that God would do wrong not to call you to account and punish you for filling both your pockets with his money and calling it your own? Professor of religion, if you are doing so, don't call yourself a Christian.

5. You must give an account of your *soul*. You have no right to go to hell. God has a right to your soul; your going to hell would injure the whole universe. It would injure hell, because it would increase its

torments. It would injure heaven, because it would wrong it out of your services. Who shall take the harp in your place in singing praises to God? Who shall contribute your share to the happiness of heaven?

Suppose you had a steward to whom you had given life, and educated him at a great expense, and then he should willfully throw that life away. Has he a right thus to dispose of a life of so much value to you? Is it not as just as to rob you of the same amount of property in anything else? God has made your soul, sustained, and educated you, till you are now able to render him important services and to glorify him forever. Have you a right to go to hell, throw away your soul, and thus rob God of your service? Have you a right to render hell more miserable, and heaven less happy, and thus injure God and all the universe?

Do you still say, "What if I do lose my soul, it is nobody's business but my own"? That is false; it is everybody's business. Just as well might a man bring a contagious disease into a city, and spread dismay and death all around, and say it was nobody's business but his own.

6. You must give an account for the *souls of others*. God commands you to be a co-worker with him in converting the world. He needs your services, for he saves souls only through the agency of men. If souls are lost or the gospel is not spread over the world, sinners charge all the blame upon Christians, as if they only were bound to be active in the cause of Christ, to exercise benevolence, to pray for a lost world, to pull sinners out of the fire. I wonder who has absolved you from these duties? Instead of doing your duty, you lie as a stumbling-block in the way of other sinners. Thus, instead of helping to save a world, all your actions help to send souls to hell.

7. You are bound to give an account of the *sentiments you entertain and propagate*. God's kingdom is to be built up by truth and not

by error. Your sentiments will have an important bearing upon the influence you exert over those around you.

Suppose the business in which your steward was employed required that he should entertain right notions concerning the manner of doing it, and the principle involved in it, of your will and of his duty. And suppose you had given him, in writing, a set of rules for the government of his conduct in relation to all the affairs with which he was entrusted. Then if he should neglect to examine those rules, or should pervert their plain meaning, and should thus pervert his own conduct, and be instrumental in deceiving others, leading them in the way of disobedience, would you not look upon this as criminal and deserving the severest reprobation?

God has given you rules for the government of your conduct. In the Bible you have a plain revelation of his will in relation to all your actions. And now, do you either neglect or pervert it, go astray yourself, and lead others with you in the way of disobedience and death, then call yourself an honest man? For shame!

8. You must give an account of your *opportunities of doing good*.

If you employ a steward to transact your business, you expect him to take advantage of the state of the market and of things in general to improve every opportunity to promote your interest. Suppose at the busy seasons of the year, he should spend his time in idleness or in his own private affairs, and not have an eye at all to the most favorable opportunities of promoting your interest, would you not soon say to him, "Give an account of thy stewardship; for thou mayest be no longer steward?" Now, sinner, you have always neglected opportunities of serving God, of warning your fellow sinners, of promoting revivals of religion, and advancing the interests of truth. You have been diligent merely to promote your own private interests, and have entirely neglected the interests of your great employer. Are you not a wretch, and do you not deserve to be put out of the stewardship as a dishonest man and to be sent to the state prison of the universe? How can you escape the damnation of hell?

Remarks. 1. From this subject, you can see why the business of this world is a snare that drowns men's souls in destruction and perdition.

Sinners transact business to promote their own private interests, not as God's stewards; and thus act dishonestly, defraud God, grieve the Spirit, and promote their own sensuality, pride, and death. If men considered themselves as God's clerks, they would not lie, overreach, and work on the Sabbath to make money for *him;* they would be sure that such conduct would not please him. God never created this world to be a snare to men; it is abused. He designed it to be a delightful abode for them—but how perverted!

Should all men's business be done as for God, they would not find it such a temptation to fraud and dishonesty as to ensnare and ruin their souls. It would have no tendency to wean the soul from him or to banish him from their thoughts. When holy Adam dressed God's garden and kept it, had he a tendency to banish God from his mind? If your gardener should all day be busy in your presence, dressing your plants, consulting your views, and doing your pleasure continually, asking how shall this be done and how shall that be done, would this have a tendency to banish you from his thoughts? So, if you were busy all the day, seeking God's glory, and transacting all your business for him, acting as his steward, sensible that his eyes were upon you; and were this your constant inquiry, how will this please him and how will that please him?—your being busy in such employment would have no tendency to distract your mind and turn your thoughts from God.

Suppose a mother, whose son was in a distant land, was busy all day in putting up clothes, books, and necessities for him, continually questioning, "How will this please him?" and "How will that please him?" Would that employment have a tendency to divert her mind from her absent son? Now if you consider yourself as God's steward, doing his business; if you are in all things consulting his interests and his glory, and consider all your possessions as his, all your time and your talents; the more busily you are engaged in his service, the more God will be present in all your thoughts.

Again. You see why idleness is a snare to the soul. A man that is idle is dishonest, forgets his responsibility, refuses to serve God, and gives himself up to the temptations of the devil. No, the idle man tempts the devil to tempt him.

Again. You see the error of the maxim that men cannot attend to business and religion at the same time. A man's business ought to be a part of his religion. He cannot be religious in idleness. He must have some business to be religious at all, and if it is performed from a right motive, his lawful and necessary business is as much a necessary part of religion as prayer, going to church, or reading his Bible. Anyone who pleads this maxim is a knave by his own confession, for no man can believe that an honest employment pursued for God's glory is inconsistent with religion. The objection supposes in the face of it that he considers his business either as unlawful in itself, or that he pursues it in a dishonest manner. If this be true, he cannot be religious while thus pursuing his business. If his employment be wicked, he must relinquish it; or if honest and pursued in an unlawful manner, he must pursue it lawfully; or in either case he will lose his soul. But if his business is lawful, let him pursue it honestly and from right motives, and he will find no difficulty in attending to his business and being religious at the same time. A life of business is best for Christians, as it exercises their graces and makes them strong.

4. That most men do not account themselves as God's stewards is evident from the fact that they consider the losses they sustain in

business as their own losses. Suppose that some of your debtors should fail and your clerks should speak of it as their loss and say they had met with great losses. Would you not look upon it as ridiculous in the extreme? And is it not quite as ridiculous for you if any of your Lord's debtors fail to make yourself uneasy and unhappy about it? Is it your loss or his? If you have done your duty and taken suitable care of his property, and a loss is sustained, it is not your loss, but his. You should look at your sins and your duty and not be frightened lest God should become bankrupt. If you acted as God's steward or as his clerk, you would not think of speaking of the loss as your own loss. But if you have considered the property in your possession as your own, no wonder that God has taken it out of your hands.

Again. You see that in the popular acceptation of the term, it is ridiculous to call institutions for the extension of the Redeemer's kingdom in the world, *charitable institutions.* In one sense, indeed, they may be called such. Should you give your steward orders to appropriate a certain amount of funds for the benefit of the poor in a certain parish, this would be charity in *you,* but not in *him;* it would be ridiculous in *him* to pretend that the charity was *his.* So, institutions for the promotion of religion are the charities of God, and not of man. The funds are God's, and it is his requirement that they be expended according to his directions to relieve the misery or advance the happiness of our fellow men. God, then, is the giver, not *men,* and to consider the charities as the gift of *men* is to maintain that the funds belong to *men* and not to God. To call them charitable institutions, in the sense in which they are usually spoken of, is to say that men confer a favor upon God that they give him *their* money and consider *him* as an object of charity.

Suppose that a company of merchants in the city should employ a number of agents to transact their business in India, with an immense capital. Suppose these agents should claim the funds as their property, and whenever a draft was made upon them, should consider it *begging,* and asking *charity* at their hands, and should call the servant by whom the order was sent a *beggar.* Furthermore, suppose they should get together and form a *charitable society* to pay these drafts, of which they should become "life members" by each paying a few dollars of their employers' money into a common fund, and then hold themselves exonerated from all farther calls. When an agent was sent with drafts, they might direct the treasurer of their society to let him have a little as a matter of almsgiving. Would not this be vastly ridiculous? What then do you think of yourself when you talk of supporting these *charitable institutions,* as if God, the owner of the universe, was to be considered as soliciting charity and his servants as the agents of an infinite *beggar?* How wonderful it is that God does not take such presumptuous men and put them in hell in a moment, and then with the money in their hands, execute his plans for converting the world.

It is no less ridiculous for them to suppose that by paying over the funds in their hands for this purpose, *they* confer a charity upon *men:* for it should be borne in mind that the money is not *theirs.* They are God's stewards and only pay it over to his order. In doing this, therefore, *they* neither confer a charity upon the servants who are sent with the orders nor upon those for whose benefit the money is expended.

Again. When the servants of the Lord come with a draft upon you to pay over some of the money in your possession into his treasury, to defray the expenses of his government and kingdom, why do you call it your own and say you can't spare it? What do you mean by calling the agents beggars and saying you are sick of seeing so many beggars—disgusted with those agents of *charitable* institutions? Suppose your steward under such circumstances should call your agents beggars and say he was sick of so many beggars. Would you not call him to an account, and let him see that the property in his possession was yours and not his?

Again. You see the great wickedness of men's hoarding up property as long as they live, and at death leaving a part of it to the church. What a will! To leave God half of his own property. Suppose a clerk should do so, and make a will, leaving his employer part of his own property! Yet this is called *piety.* Do you think that Christ will always be a beggar? And yet the church is greatly puffed up with their great charitable donations and legacies to Jesus Christ.

Again. You see the wickedness of laying up money for your children, and why money so laid up is a *curse* to them. Suppose your steward should lay up your money for his children, would you not consider him a knave? How then dare you take God's money and lay it up for your children, while the world is sinking down to hell? But will you say, Is it not my duty to provide for my "own household"? Yes, it is your duty *suitably* to provide for them, but what is a suitable provision? Give them the best education you can for the service of God. Make all *necessary* provision for the supply of their *real* wants, until they become of sufficient age to provide for themselves. Then if *you see them disposed to do good in serving God and their generation,* give them all the advantages for *doing this* in your power. But to make them rich, to gratify their pride, to enable them to live in luxury or ease, to provide that they may become rich, to give your daughters what is called a genteel education, to allow them to spend their time in dress, idleness, gossiping, and effeminacy, you have no right. It is defrauding God, ruining your own soul, and greatly endangering theirs.

Again. Impenitent sinners will be finally and eternally disgraced. Do you not account it a disgrace to a man, to be detected in fraud and every species of knavery in transacting the business of his employer? Is not such a man deservedly thrown out of business; is he not a disgrace to himself and his family; can anybody trust him? How then will you appear before an injured God and an injured universe—a

God whose laws and rights you have despised—a universe with whose interests you have been at war? How will you, in the solemn judgment, be disgraced, your name execrated, and you become the hissing and contempt of hell for the numberless frauds and villainies you have practiced upon God and upon his creatures! But perhaps you are a professor of religion: Will your profession cover up your selfishness and vile hypocrisy while you have defrauded God, spent his money upon your lusts, and accounted those as beggars who came with drafts upon you to pay over into his treasury? How will you hold up your head in the face of heaven? How dare you now pray; how dare you sit at the communion table; how dare you profess the religion of Jesus Christ if you have set up a private interest and do not consider all that you have as his, and use it all for his glory?

Again. We have here a true test of Christian character. True Christians *consider themselves* as God's stewards. They act for him, live for him, transact business for him, eat and drink for his glory, live and die to please him. But sinners and hypocrites live for themselves. They account their time, their talents, their influence as their own and dispose of them all for their own private interests and thus drown themselves in destruction and perdition.

At the judgment, we are informed that Christ will say to those who are accepted, "Well done, good and faithful servants." Hearer! could he truly say this of you, "Well done, good and faithful servant: thou hast been faithful over a few things" (Matt. 25:21), *i. e.* over the things committed to your charge. He will pronounce no false judgment, put no false estimate upon things; and if he cannot say this truly, "Well done, good and faithful servant," you will not be accepted, but will be thrust down to hell. Now, what is your character, and what has been your conduct? God will soon call you to give an account of your stewardship. Have you been faithful to God, faithful to your own soul, and the souls of others? Are you ready to have your accounts examined, your conduct scrutinized, and your life weighed in the balance of the sanctuary? Are you interested in the blood of Jesus Christ? If not, repent, *repent now*, of all your wickedness, and lay hold upon the hope that is set before you; for, hark! a voice cries in your ears, "Give an account of thy stewardship; for thou mayest be no longer steward."

Thomas Guthrie: *Sins and Sorrows of the City*

THOMAS GUTHRIE WAS BORN at Brechin, Scotland, on July 12, 1803, and died at St. Leonards on February 24, 1873. His first charge was at Arbilot, where for seven years he was minister of the Established Church. It was during these years that he adopted the pictorial method of preaching, for which he was shortly to become famous. He had an afternoon service for the young people at which he catechized them on the morning sermon. He very soon discovered that the portions of the sermons which they remembered were the illustrations. This determined him to cultivate an illustrative style. Almost every printed sermon by Guthrie opens with some kind of illustration or anecdote. He spoke of the three chief homiletic rules as the "Three P's"—Painting, Proving, and Persuading. But with him the chief thing was the painting. In 1837, Guthrie became minister of Old Greyfriars, Edinburgh, and in 1840 of St. John's Church, Edinburgh. He at once attracted attention, and for a period of thirty-five years his vast popularity never waned. He had nothing of the Scottish taste for metaphysics, nor was he a dreamer or a mystic. His themes are commonplace, and his arrangement ordinary and mechanical. Yet, in the annals of the Scottish pulpit none has surpassed him in the ability to draw and hold great throngs, year after year. It is impossible to define the secret of any preacher's power. But in the case of Guthrie his (at that time) novel, dramatic and pictorial power undoubtedly played a large part in his extraordinary popularity. Guthrie was not only a great preacher, but a great humanitarian. The fine statue to Guthrie on Princes Street, Edinburgh, shows him with two street Arabs taking refuge under his arms. This is in commemoration of the Ragged Schools which Guthrie founded for the protection and instruction of the homeless and destitute children of Edinburgh. Dr. James McCosh, afterward president of Princeton College, was a neighbor to Guthrie when he was at Arbilot. Commenting on his preaching, Dr. McCosh says: "Some hard men thought of him that his discourses were not very logical; some finical men and women regarded his illustrations rather vivid; but they all went to hear him because they got their hearts warmed."

The sermon selected for this volume, "Sins and Sorrows of the City," in its noble introduction reveals Guthrie's fine gift of description. The sermon is one that is still terribly appropriate in Scotland.

Sins and Sorrows of the City

"He beheld the city, and wept over it" (Luke 19:41).

HERE is a remarkable phenomenon to be seen on certain parts of our own coast. Strange to say, it proves, notwithstanding such expressions as the stable and solid land, that it is not the land but the sea which is the stable element. On some summer day when there is not a wave to rock her nor breath of wind to fill her sail or fan a cheek, you launch your boat upon the waters. Pulling out beyond lowest tide mark, you idly lie upon her bow to catch the silvery glance of a passing fish, or watch the movements of the many curious creatures that travel the sea's sandy bed, or, creeping out of their rocky homes, wander its tangled mazes. If the traveler is surprised to find a deep-sea shell embedded in the marbles of a mountain peak, how great is your surprise to see beneath you a vegetation foreign to the deep! Below your boat, submerged many feet beneath the surface of the lowest tide, away down in these green crystal depths, you see no rusting anchor, no moldering remains of some shipwrecked one, but in the standing stumps of trees you discover the moldering vestiges of a forest, where once the wild cat prowled, and the birds of heaven, singing their loves, had nestled and nursed their young. In counterpart to those portions of our coast where sea-hollowed caves, with sides the waves have polished, and floors still strewed with shells and sand, now stand high above the level of the strongest stream tides, there stand these dead decaying trees entombed in the deep. A strange phenomenon, which admits of no other explanation than this, that there the coastline has sunk beneath its ancient level.

Many of our cities present a phenomenon as melancholy to the eye of a philanthropist, as the other is interesting to a philosopher or geologist. In their economical, educational, moral, and religious aspects, certain parts of this city bear palpable evidence of a corresponding subsidence. Not a single house, nor a block of houses, but whole streets, once from end to end the abodes of decency, industry, wealth, rank, and piety have been engulfed. A flood of ignorance, misery, and sin now breaks and roars above the top of their highest tenements. Nor do the old stumps of a forest, still standing up erect beneath the sea wave, indicate a greater change, a deeper subsidence, than the relics of ancient grandeur and the touching memorials of piety which yet linger about these wretched dwellings like evening twilight on the hills—like some traces of beauty on a corpse. The unfurnished floor, the begrimed and naked walls, the stifling, sickening atmosphere, the patched and dusty window through which a sunbeam, like hope, is faintly stealing, the ragged, hunger-bitten, sad-faced children, the ruffian man, the heap of straw where some wretched mother, in muttering dreams, sleeps off last night's debauch, or lies unshrouded and uncoffined in the ghastliness of a hopeless death, are sad scenes. We have often looked on them. And they appear all the sadder for the restless play of fancy. Excited by some vestiges of a fresco painting that still looks out from the foul and broken plaster, the massive marble rising over the cold and cracked hearthstone, an elaborately carved cornice too high for shivering cold to pull it down for fuel, some stucco flowers or fruit yet pendant on the crumbling ceiling, fancy, kindled by these, calls up the scenes and actors of other days—when beauty, elegance and fashion graced these lonely halls, plenty smoked on groaning tables, and where these few cinders, gathered from the city dust heap, are feebly smoldering, hospitable fires roared up the chimney.

But there is that in and about these houses which bears witness of a deeper subsidence, a yet sadder change. Bent on some mission of mercy, you stand at the foot of a dank and filthy stair. It conducts you to the crowded rooms of a tenement, where—with the exception of some old decent widow who has seen better days, when her family are all dead, and her friends are all gone, still clings to God and her faith in the dark hour of adversity—amid the wreck of fortune from the cellardens below to the garrets beneath the roof-tops, you shall find none either reading their Bibles, or even with Bibles to read. Alas! Of prayer, of morning and evening psalms, of earthly or heavenly peace, it may be said that the place that once knew them, knows them no more. But before you enter the doorway, raise your eyes to the stone above it. Mute, it speaks of other and better times. Carved in Greek or Latin, or our own mother tongue, you decipher such texts as these: "Peace be to this house." "Except the Lord build the house, they labour in vain that build it" (Ps. 127:1). "We have a building of God, a house not made with hands, eternal in the heavens" (2 Cor. 5:1). "Fear God;" or this, "Love your neighbor." Like the moldering remnants of a forest that once resounded with the melody of birds, but hears nothing now save the angry dash or melancholy moan of breaking waves, these vestiges of piety furnish a gauge which enables us to measure how low in these dark localities the whole stratum of society has sunk.

Now there are forces in nature which, heaving up the crust of our earth, may convert the sea bed again into forest or corn land. At this moment these forces are in active operation. Working slowly, yet with prodigious power, they are now raising the coasts of Sweden in the old world and of Chile in the new. And who knows but these subterranean agencies, elevating our own coasts, may yet restore verdure to those deep sea sands, giving back to the plow its soil, to waving pines their forest land. And thus on our shores, redeemed from the grasp of the ocean in some future era, golden harvests may fall to the reaper's song, and tall forests to the woodsman's ax. We know not whether this shall happen. But I do know that there is a force at work in this world—gentle, yet powerful—commonly slow in action, but always sure in its results, which, mightier than volcanic fires, pent-up vapor, or rocking earthquake, is adequate to raise the most sunken masses of society, and restore the lowest and longest neglected districts of our cities to their old level, to set them on the platform even of a higher Christianity.

We cannot despair, so long as we do not forget, that the power of God, the wisdom of God, and the grace of God, have nothing to do within our shores which they have not done already. Are our lapsed classes rude and uncultivated, ignorant and vicious? So were our forefathers when Christianity landed on this island. She took possession of it in Jesus' name and conquered bold savages, whom the Romans could never subdue, by the mild yet mighty power of the gospel. God's "hand is not shortened, that it cannot save; nor his ear heavy, that it cannot hear" (Isa. 59:1). Therefore, whatever length of time may be required to evangelize our city masses, however long we may be living before the period when a "nation shall be born in a day," whatever trials of patience we may have to endure, whatever tears we may have to shed over our cities, our tears are not such as Jesus wept when he beheld Jerusalem.

No. Jerusalem was sealed to ruin, doomed beyond redemption. Our brethren, our cities are not so. We have not to mourn as those who have no hope. As on a summer day I have seen the sky at once so shine and shower that every raindrop was changed by sunbeams into a falling diamond, so hopes mingle here with fears, and the promises of the gospel shed sunlight on pious sorrows. Weep we may; weep we should—weep and work, weep and pray. But ever let our tears be such as Jesus shed beside the tomb of Lazarus, when, while weeping, groaning, he bade the bystanders roll away the stone, anticipating the moment when the grave at his command would give up its dead and Lazarus be folded, a living brother, in the arms that four days ago had swathed his corpse. Be such our tears and anticipations. Sustained by them, we shall work all the better; and all the sooner shall our heavenly Father embrace the most wretched of these wretched outcasts.

We have turned your attention to the extent of intemperance; let us now secondly, attend to the effects of this vice.

The Spartans, a brave and, although heathen, in many respects a virtuous people, held intemperance in the deepest abhorrence. When Christian parents initiate their children in drinking habits, and—as we have seen and wondered at—teach them to carry their glass to infant lips, copy whom they may, the wise old Spartans are not their model. They were not more careful to train the youth of their country to athletic exercises, and from their boyhood and almost their mother's breasts to "endure hardship as good soldiers" of Sparta, than to rear them up in habits of strictest, sternest temperance. It formed a regular branch of their national education. Why should it not of ours? It would be an incalculable blessing to the community. It would do incalculably more to promote domestic comfort, to guard the welfare of families, and secure the public good, than other branches that, while they improve the taste and polish the mind, put no real pith or power into the man. Well, once a year these Greeks assembled their slaves, and having compelled them to drink to intoxication, they turned them out—all reeling, staggering, besotted, brutalized— into a great arena, that the youths who filled its benches might go home from this spectacle of degradation to shun the wine cup, and cultivate the virtues of sobriety. Happy country! Thrice happy land where drunkenness was to be seen but once a year, and formed but an annual spectacle. Alas! we have no need to employ such unjustifiable means even for so good an end! We do not require to get up any annual show, from the pulpit to tell, or on the stage of a theater to represent, its accursed, direful, and disgusting effects. The lion is daily ravaging on our streets. He goes about "seeking whom he may devour."

Once a year, indeed, when church courts meet, our city may present a spectacle which fools regard with indifference, but wise men with compassion and fear. A pale and haggard man, bearing the title of "Reverend," stands at the bar of his church. Not daring to look up, he bends there with his head buried in his hands, blushes on his face, his lips quivering, and a hell raging, burning within him, as he thinks of home, a brokenhearted wife, and the little ones so soon to leave that dear, sweet home to shelter their innocent heads where best, all beggared and disgraced, they may. "Ah, my brother" there! And ah, my brethren here, learn to "watch and pray, that ye enter not into temptation" (Matt. 26:41). See there the issue of all a mother's anxieties, and a father's self-denying and parsimonious toil, to educate their promising, studious boy. In this deep darkness has set forever a brilliant college career. Alas, what an end to the solemn day of ordination, the bright day of marriage, and all those Sabbaths when an affectionate people hung on his eloquent lips! Oh! If this sacred office, if the constant handling of things divine, if hours of study spent over the word of God, if frequent scenes of death with their most awful and sobering solemnities, if the irredeemable ruin into which degradation from the holy office plunges a man and his house along with him, if the unspeakable heinousness of this sin in one who held the post of a sentinel, and was charged with the care of souls—if these do not fortify and fence us against excess, then, in the name of God, "let him that thinketh he standeth take heed lest he fall" (1 Cor. 10:12).

On leaving a church court, where he has seen so strange and dreadful a spectacle as a man of cultivated mind, a man of literary habits, a man of honorable position, a man of sacred character, sacrifice all—the cause of religion, the bread of his family, the interests of his children, the happiness of his wife, his character, his soul—all, to this base indulgence, no man, after such a terrible proof of the might and mastery of this tyrant vice, will be astonished at anything he may encounter in our streets. Yet if the soul of Paul was "stirred within him," stirred to its deepest depths when he saw the idolatry of Athens, I think that he who can walk from this neighboring castle to yonder palace, nor groan in spirit, must have a heart about as hard as the pavement that he walks on. The degradation of humanity, the ragged poverty, the squalid misery, the suffering childhood, the pining, dying infancy, oh, how do these obliterate all the romance of the scene, and make the most picturesque street in Christendom one of the most painful to travel. They call the street in Jerusalem, along which tradition says that a bleeding Savior bore his cross, the *Via Dolorosa;* and I have thought that our own street was baptized in the sorrows of as mournful a name. With so many countenances that have misery stamped on them as plain as if it were burned in with a red-hot iron—hunger staring at us out of these hollow eyes, drink-palsied men, drink-blotched and bloated women; sad and sallow infants who pine away into slow death with their weary heads lying so pitifully on the shoulders of some half dehumanized woman—this poor little child who never smiles, without shoe or stocking on his ulcered feet, shivering, creeping, limping along with the bottle in his emaciated hand to buy a parent drink with the few pence that, poor hungry creature, he would wish to spend on a loaf of bread, but dare not—the whole scene is like the roll of the prophet, "written within and without, lamentations, mourning, and woe." How has it wrung our hearts to see a poor, ragged boy looking greedily in at a window on the food he has no one to give him and dare not touch, to watch him as he alternately lifted his naked feet lest they should freeze to the icy pavement. He starves in the midst of abundance. Neglected among a people who would take more pity on an ill-used horse or a dying dog, he is a castaway upon the land. Of the throngs that pass heedlessly by him to homes of comfort, intent on business or on pleasure, there is no one cares for him. Poor wretch! Oh if he knew a Bible which none has taught him, how might he plant himself before us and bar our way to church or prayer meeting, saying as he fixed on us an imploring eye, "'Pure religion and undefiled before God' is to feed me, is to clothe these naked limbs, is to fill up these hollow cheeks, is to pour the light of knowledge into this darkened soul, is to save me, is not to go to the house of God or place of prayer, but first coming with me to our miserable home, 'to visit the fatherless and widows in their affliction, and keep himself unspotted from the world.'" (James 1:27).

You can test the truth of these statements. You have only to walk along the street to verify them. Look there! In that corpse you see the cold, dead body of one of the best and godliest mothers it was ever our privilege to know. She had a son. He was the stay of her widowhood—so kind, so affectionate, so loving. Some are taken away from the "evil to come"; laid in the lap of mother earth, safe beneath the grave's green sod; they hear not and heed not the storm that rages above. Such was not her happy fortune. She lived to see that son a disgrace, and all the promises of his youth blighted and gone. He was drawn into habits of intemperance. On her knees, she pleaded with him. On her knees, she prayed for him. How mysterious are the ways of Providence! She did not live to see him changed; and with such thorns in her pillow, such daggers, planted by such a hand, in her heart, she could not live. She sank under these griefs, and died of a broken heart. We told him so. With bitter, burning tears, he owned it, charging himself with his mother's death—confessing himself a mother's murderer. Crushed with sorrow, and all alone, he went to see the body. Alone, beside that cold, dead, unreproaching mother, he knelt down and wept out his terrible remorse. After a while, he rose. Unfortunately—how unfortunate that a spirit bottle should have been left there—his eye fell on the old tempter. You have seen the iron approach the magnet. Call it spell, call it fascination, call it anything bad, demoniacal, but as the iron is drawn to the magnet, or as a fluttering bird, fascinated by the burning eye and glittering skin of the serpent, walks into its envenomed, expanded jaws, so was he drawn to the bottle. Wondering at his delay, they entered the room—and now the bed holds two bodies—a dead mother, and her dead-drunk son. What a sight! What a humbling, horrible spectacle! And what a change from those happy times when night drew her peaceful curtains around the same son and mother—he, a sweet babe, sleeping, angel-like, within her loving arms! "How is the gold become dim, the most fine gold changed!"

Or look there. The bed beside which you have at other visits conversed and prayed with one who, in the very bloom and flower of youth, was withering away under a slow decline—is empty. The living need it; and so its long, spent, and weary tenant lies now, stretched out in death, on the top of two rude chests beside the window. And as you stand by the body, contemplating it in that pallid face lighted up by a passing sun-gleam you see, along with lingering traces of no common beauty, the calmness and peace which were her latter end. But in this hot, sultry, summer weather, why lies she there uncoffined? Drink has left us to do that last office for the dead. Her father—how unworthy the name of father—when his daughter pled with him for his soul, pled with him for her mother, pled with him for her little sister, had stood by her dying pillow to damn her, fiercely damning her to her face. He has left his poor, dead child to the care of others. With the wages he retains for drink, he refuses to buy that lifeless form a coffin and a grave!

But what emotions do the cases I have told you of awaken? To be matched by many and surpassed by some that I could tell, samples of the stock, what passion can they, what passion ought they to move, but the deepest indignation? Nor would I, however fiercely it may run, seek to stem the flood. The deeper it flows, the higher it rises, the stronger it swells, so much the better. I would not seek to stem, but to direct it—directing it not against the victims, but against the vice.

I pray you, do not hate the drunkard; he hates himself. Do not despise him; oh, he cannot sink so low in your opinion as he is sunk in his own. Your hatred and contempt may rivet, but will never rend his chains. Lend a kind hand to pluck him from the mire. With a strong hand, shatter that bowl—remove the temptations which, while he hates, he cannot resist. Hate, abhor, tremble at his sin. And for pity's sake, for God's sake, for Christ's sake, for humanity's sake, rouse yourselves to the question, What can be done? Without heeding others, whether they follow or whether they stay, rush down to the beach, throw yourself into the boat, push away, and bend on the oar, like a man, to the wreck. Say, I will not stand by and see my fellow creatures perish. They are perishing. To save them I will do anything. What luxury will I not give up? What indulgence will I not abstain from? What customs, what shackles of old habits will I not break, that these hands may be freer to pluck the drowning from the deep? God my help, his word my law, the love of his Son my ruling motive, I shall never balance a poor, personal indulgence against the good of my country and the welfare of mankind. Brethren, such resolutions, such high, holy, sustained, and self-denying efforts, the height of this evil demands.

Before God and man, before the church and the world, I impeach intemperance. I charge it with the murder of innumerable souls. In this country, blessed with freedom, plenty, the word of God, and the liberties of true religion, I charge it as the cause—whatever be their source elsewhere—of almost all the poverty, almost all the crime, almost all the misery, and almost all the ignorance, and almost all the irreligion that disgrace and afflict the land. "I am not mad, most noble Festus; but speak I the words of truth and soberness" (Acts 26:5). I do in my conscience believe that these intoxicating stimulants have sunk into perdition more men and women than found a grave in that deluge which swept over the highest hilltops, engulfing a world, of which but eight were saved. As compared with other vices, it may be said of this, "Saul has slain his thousands, and David his ten thousands" (1 Sam. 18:7).

Lastly, consider what cure we should apply to this evil. The grand and only sovereign remedy for the evils of this world is the gospel of our Lord Jesus Christ. I believe that. There is no man more convinced of that than I am. But he rather hinders than helps the cause of religion who shuts his eyes to the fact that, in curing souls as in curing bodies, many things may be important as auxiliaries to the remedy which cannot properly be considered as remedies. In the day of his resurrection, Lazarus owed his life to Christ; but they who rolled away the stone that day did good service. They were allies and auxiliaries. And to such in the battle which the gospel has to wage with this monster vice, allow me in closing this discourse to direct your attention. And I remark:

First, That the legislature may render essential service in this cause.

This is an alliance between church and state which no man could quarrel with. Happy for our country, if by such help, the state would thus fulfill to the church—the woman of prophecy—this apocalyptic vision: "And the serpent cast out of his mouth water as a flood after the woman, that he might cause her to be carried away of the flood. And the earth helped the woman, and the earth opened her mouth, and swallowed up the flood which the dragon cast out of his mouth" (Rev. 12:15–16).

Many people feel no sympathy with the sufferings of the lowest class. They are not hard-hearted, but engrossed with their own affairs or, raised far above them in social position, they are ignorant of their temptations and trials. Therefore, they talk ignorantly about them and seldom more so than when they repudiate all attempts of the legislature by restrictive acts of Parliament to abate, if not abolish, this evil. They have their remedies. Some plead for better lodgings and sanitary measures, which we also regard as highly valuable. Some put their faith in education—an agent, the importance of which, to the rising generation, it is impossible to overestimate. Some seem to have no confidence in anything but the preaching of the gospel. To one or other of these or the combined influence of them all, they trust for the cure of drunkenness, repudiating and deprecating all legislative interference. Now, I should like as much as they to see the very lowest of our people so elevated in their tastes, with minds so cultivated, and hearts so sanctified that they could resist the temptations which on every hand beset them. But thousands, tens of thousands, are unable to do so. They must be helped with crutches till they have acquired the power to walk. They must be fenced round with every possible protection until they are "rooted and grounded in the love of God." In the country, I have often seen a little child with her sun-browned face and long golden locks, sweet as any flower she pressed beneath her naked foot, merry as any bird that sung from bush or brake, driving the cattle home. With fearless hand, she controls the sulky leader of the herd, as with armed forehead and colossal strength he quailed before that slight image of God. Some days ago, I saw a different sight—such a child, with hanging head, no music in his voice, nor blush but that of shame upon his cheek, leading home a drunken father along the public street. The man required to be led, guided, guarded. And into a condition hardly less helpless, large masses of our people have sunk. I don't wonder that they drink.

Look at their unhappy and most trying circumstances. Many of them are born with a propensity to this vice. They suck it in with a mother's milk, for it is a well-ascertained fact that other things are hereditary besides cancer, consumption, and insanity. The drunken parent transmits to his children a proneness to his fatal indulgence. The foul atmosphere which many of them breathe, the hard labor by which many of them earn their bread, produce a prostration which seeks in stimulants something to rally the system, nor will be debarred from their use by any prospect of danger or experience of a corresponding reaction. With our improved tastes, our books, our recreations, our domestic comforts, we have no adequate idea of the temptations to which the poor are exposed and from which it is the truest kindness to protect them. They are cold, and the glass is warmth. They are hungry, and drink is food. They are miserable, and there is laughter in the flowing cup. They are sunk in their own esteem, and the bowl or the bottle surrounds the drunkard with a bright-colored halo of self-respect, and, so long as the fumes are in his brain, he feels himself a man. "Let him drink, and forget his poverty, and remember his misery no more" (Prov. 31:7).

The removal of the temptation may not always cure the drunkard. But it will certainly check the growth of his class and prevent many others from learning his habits until sanguine men might entertain the blessed hope that, like the monsters of a former epoch which now lie entombed in the rocks, drunkards may be numbered among the extinct races, classified with the winged serpents and gigantic sloths that were once inhabitants of our globe.

The subject before us is eminently calculated to illustrate the profound remark of one who was well-acquainted with the temptations and circumstances of the poor. He said, "It is justice, not charity, that the poor most need." And all we ask is that you be as kind to them as to the rich; that you guard the one class as carefully as you guard the other from the temptations peculiar to their lot. I am sorry to say— but truth and the interests of those who, however sunk and degraded, are bone of our bone and flesh of our flesh, require that I should say—that this is not done. The poor, says Amos, are sold for a pair of shoes, and with us they are sold to save the wealth of the rich. In this I make no charge which I am not prepared to prove. For example: certain measures were proposed in Parliament with the view of promoting the comforts and improving the moral habits of the common people. It was admitted that these, by introducing weak French and Rhenish wines instead of ardent spirits and strongly intoxicating liquors, would be attended with the most happy and desirable result. Yet they were rejected. And rejected because their adoption, although it saved the people, would damage the revenue. As if there was not money enough in the pockets of the wealthy through means of other taxes to meet the debts of the nation and sustain the honor of the Crown. How different the tone of morals even in China! The ministers of that country proved to their sovereign that he would avert all danger of war with Britain, and also add immensely to his revenue, if he would consent to legalize the trade in opium. He refused, firmly refused, nobly refused. And it was a glorious day for Britain, a happy day for ten thousand miserable homes—a day for bonfires, jubilant cannon, merry bells, bannered processions, and holy thanksgivings, which saw our beloved Queen rise from her throne, and in the name of this great nation address to her Lords and Commons the memorable speech of that pagan monarch: "I will never consent to raise my revenue out of the ruin and vices of my people." With such a spirit may God imbue our land! "Even so come, Lord Jesus. Come quickly."

Secondly, That the example of abstaining from all intoxicating liquors would greatly aid in the cure of this evil.

No principle is more clearly inculcated in the word of God and none carried out into action makes a man more Christ-like than self-denial. "If meat make my brother to offend, I will eat no flesh while the world standeth, lest I make my brother to offend" (1 Cor.

8:13). That is the principle of temperance, as I hold it. I cannot agree with those, who, in their anxiety for good, attempt to prove too much, and condemn as positively sinful the moderate use of stimulants. But still less sympathy have I with those who dare to call in Jesus Christ to lend his holy countenance to their luxurious boards. It is shocking to hear men attempt to prove by the word of God that it is a duty to drink—to fill the winecup and drain off the glass.

I was able to use without abusing. But seeing to what monstrous abuse the thing had grown, seeing in what a multitude of cases the use was followed by the abuse, and seeing how the example of the upper classes, the practices of ministers, and the habits of church members were used to shield and sanction indulgences so often carried to excess, I saw the case to be one for the apostle's warning: "Take heed lest by any means this liberty of yours become a stumbling-block to them that are weak" (1 Cor. 8:9).

This moral revolution in our national habits, this greatest of all reforms, everyone can engage in. Women and children, as well as men, can help it onwards to the goal. It is attainable, if we would only attempt it. It is hopeful, if we would but give the subject a fair consideration. Why should not the power of Christianity, by its mighty arguments of love and self denial, lead to the disuse of intoxicating stimulants, and so achieve that which Mohammedanism and Hinduism have done? Must the cross pale before the crescent? Must the divine religion of Jesus, with that God-man upon the tree for its invincible ensign, blush before such rivals, and own itself unable to accomplish what false faiths have done? Tell us not that it cannot be done. It can be done. It has been done—done by the enemies of the cross of Christ, done by the followers of an impostor, done by worshippers of stocks and stones. "And their rock is not as our Rock" (Deut. 32:31). If that is true, and it cannot be gainsaid, I may surely claim from every man who has faith in God, and loves Jesus, and is willing to live for the benefit of mankind, a candid, a full, and a prayerful consideration of this subject. But, whatever be the means, whatever the weapons you will judge it best to employ, when trumpets are blowing in Zion and the alarm is sounding and echoing in God's holy mountain, come, come to the help of the Lord against the mighty, crowd to the standard, throw yourself into the thick of battle, and die in harness fighting for the cause of Jesus. So "to live is Christ, and to die is gain" (Phil. 1:21).

Frederick W. Robertson:
Selfishness, as Shown in Balaam's Character

Frederick W. ROBERTSON, KNOWN AS "Robertson of Brighton," was born in London in 1816, and died at Brighton in 1853. His father was an officer in the British Army, and the son at first was ambitious for a military career. But after preliminary studies for the army, he was ordained at Winchester in 1840. In 1847, after passing through a period of doubt and perplexity, Robertson entered upon his famous ministry at Brighton.

Robertson is often spoken of as "the preachers' preacher," and his sermons are probably more widely read by thoughtful ministers than those of any other preacher. The printed sermons are often little more than outlines, yet sufficient to show the searching mind and fine spirit of the preacher. Many of his most striking sermons are on the characters of the Bible, and most notable of these are the two sermons on the character of Balaam. Balaam is a subject which has attracted preachers of all generations. For all students of the Scriptures and of human nature, there is a certain fascination in this strange prophet, now rising to the sublimest heights in his magnificent predictions of the future of Israel, and praying that he may die the death of the righteous, but finally perishing in a despicable conspiracy against the life and honor of Israel. Always there will be a degree of mystery about Balaam, yet he deserves the terrible denunciations of Peter, Jude and John. Robertson's treatment of his character is perhaps as satisfactory as any in homiletical literature. It is difficult to choose between the two sermons by Robertson on Balaam, but after some hesitation I have selected the sermon, "Selfishness, as Shown in the Character of Balaam." This sermon is memorable for the sentences, "He would not transgress a rule, but he would violate a principle. He would not say white was black, but he would sully it till it looked black."

Selfishness, as Shown in Balaam's Character

"Who can count the dust of Jacob, and the number of the fourth part of Israel? Let me die the death of the righteous, and let my last end be like his!" (Num. 23:10).

W E *acquainted ourselves* with the earlier part of Balaam's history last Sunday. We saw how great gifts in him were perverted by ambition and avarice—ambition making them subservient to the admiration of himself, avarice transforming them into mere instruments for accumulating wealth. And we saw how his conscience was gradually perverted by insincerity till his mind became the place of hideous contradictions, and even God himself had become to him a lie. With his heart disordered, until the bitterness of all going wrong within vented itself on innocent circumstances, he found himself so entangled in a false course that to go back was impossible.

Now we come to the second stage. He has been with Balak; he has built his altars, offered his sacrifices and tried his enchantments to ascertain whether Jehovah will permit him to curse Israel. And the voice in his heart through all says "Israel is blessed." He looks down from the hilltop, and sees the fair camp of Israel afar off in beautiful array, their white tents gleaming "as the trees of lign aloes which the Lord hath planted" (Num. 24:6). He feels the solitary grandeur of a nation unlike all other nations—people which "shall dwell alone, and shall not be reckoned among the nations" (Num. 23:9). A nation too numberless to give Balak any hope of success in the coming war. "Who can count the dust of Jacob, and the number of the fourth part of Israel?" A nation too strong in righteousness for idolaters and enchanters to cope with. "Surely there is no enchantment against

Jacob, neither is there any divination against Israel" (Num. 23:23). Then follows a personal ejaculation: "Let me die the death of the righteous, and let my last end be like his!" (v. 10).

Now, to prevent the possibility of misconception, or any supposition that Balaam was expressing words whose full significance he did not understand—that when he was speaking of righteousness, he had only a heathen notion of it—we refer to the sixth chapter of Micah, from the fifth verse. We will next refer to Numbers 31:8, and Joshua 13 :22, from whence it appears that he who desired to die the death of the righteous, died the death of the ungodly, and fell, not on the side of the Lord, but fighting against the Lord's cause. The first thing we find in this history of Balaam is an attempt to change the will of God.

Let us clearly understand what was the meaning of all those reiterated sacrifices.

1. Balaam wanted to please himself without displeasing God. The problem was how to go to Balak, and yet not offend God. He would have given worlds to get rid of his duties, and he sacrificed, not to learn what his duty was, but to get his duty altered. Now see the feeling that lay at the root of all this—that God is mutable. Yet of all men one would have thought that Balaam knew better, for had he not said, "God is not a man, that he should lie; neither the son of man, that he should repent: hath he said, and shall he not do it?" (Num. 23:19). But, when we look upon it, we see Balaam had scarcely any feeling higher than this—God is more inflexible than man. Probably had he expressed the exact shade of feeling, he would have said, more obstinate. He thought that God had set his heart upon Israel, and that it was hard, yet not impossible, to alter this partiality. Hence, he tries sacrifices to bribe and prayers to coax God.

How deeply rooted this feeling is in human nature, this belief in God's mutability, you may see from the Romish doctrine of indulgences and atonements. The Romish church permits crime for certain considerations. For certain considerations, it teaches that God will forgive crimes. Atonements after, and indulgences before sin, are the same. But this Romish doctrine never could have succeeded if the belief in God's mutability and the *desire* that he should be mutable were not in man already.

What Balaam was doing in these parables, enchantments, and sacrifices was simply purchasing an indulgence to sin; in other words, it was an attempt to make the Eternal Mind change. What was wanting for Balaam to feel was this—God *cannot* change. What he did feel was this—God *will* not change. There are many writers who teach that this and that is right because God has willed it. All discussion is cut short by the reply: God has determined it; therefore it is right. Now there is exceeding danger in this mode of thought, for a thing is not right because God has willed it, but God wills it because it is right. It is in this tone the Bible always speaks. Never, except in one obscure passage, does the Bible seem to refer right and wrong to the sovereignty of God, and declare it a matter of will: never does it imply that if he so chose, he could reverse evil and good. It says, "Is not my way equal? are not your ways unequal?" (Ezek. 18:25). "Shall not the Judge of all the earth do right?" (Gen. 18:25) was Abraham's exclamation in a mind of hideous doubt whether the Creator might not be on the eve of doing injustice. So the Bible *justifies* the ways of God to man. But it could not do so unless it admitted eternal laws, with which no will can interfere. Moreover, see what ensues from this mode of thought. If right is right because God wills it, then if God chose, he could make injustice, cruelty, and lying to be right. This is exactly what Balaam thought. If God could but be prevailed on to hate Israel, then for him to curse them would be right. And again, if power and sovereignty makes right, then supposing that the Ruler were a demon, devilish hatred would be as right as now it is wrong.

There is great danger in some of our present modes of thinking. It is a common thought that might makes right, but for us there is no rest, no rock, no sure footing, so long as we feel right and wrong are mere matters of will and decree. There is no safety, then, from these hankering feelings and wishes to alter God's decree. You are unsafe until you feel, "Heaven and earth shall pass away, but my [God's] word shall not pass away" (Matt. 24:35).

2. We notice, secondly, an attempt to blind himself. One of the strangest leaves in the book of the human heart is here turned. We observe perfect veracity with utter want of truth. Balaam was veracious. He will not deceive Balak. Nothing was easier than to get the reward by muttering a spell, knowing all the while that it would not work. Many a European has sold incantations to rich savages for jewels and curiosities, thus enriching himself by deceit. Now Balaam was not supernaturally withheld. That is a baseless assumption. Nothing withheld him but his conscience. No bribe on earth could induce Balaam to say a falsehood, to pretend a curse which was powerless, to get gold, dearly as he loved it, by a presence. "If Balak would give me his house full of silver and gold, I cannot go beyond the commandment of the Lord, either good or bad" (Num. 24:13), was no mere fine saying, but the very truth. You might as soon have turned the sun from his course as induced Balaam to utter falsehood.

And yet, with all this, there was utter truthlessness of heart. Balaam will not utter what is not true; but he will blind himself so that he may not see the truth and so speak a lie, believing it to be the truth.

He will only speak the thing he feels; but he is not careful to feel all that is true. He goes to another place, where the whole truth may not force itself upon his mind—to a hill where he shall not see the whole of Israel, from hill to hill for the chance of getting to a place where the truth may disappear. But there stands the stubborn fact: Israel is blessed, and he will look at the fact in every way to see if he cannot get it into a position where it shall be seen no longer. Ostrich-like!

Such a character is not so uncommon as, perhaps, we think. There is many a lucrative business which involves misery and wrong to those who are employed in it. The man would be too benevolent to put the gold in his purse if he knew of the misery. But he takes care not to know. There is many a dishonorable thing done at an election, and the principal takes care not to inquire. Many an oppression is exercised on a tenantry, and the landlord receives his rent, asking no questions. Or there is some situation which depends upon the holding of certain religious opinions, and the candidate has a suspicion that if he were to examine, he could not conscientiously profess these opinions, and perchance he takes care not to examine.

3. Failing in all these evil designs against Israel, Balaam tries his last expedient to ruin them, and that partially succeeds.

He recommends Balak to use the fascination of the daughters of Moab to entice the Israelites into idolatry. He has tried enchantments and sacrifices in vain to reverse God's will. He has tried in vain to think that will is reversed. It will not do. He feels at last that God has not beheld iniquity in Jacob, neither hath he seen perverseness in Israel. Now, therefore, he tries to reverse the character of these favorites, and so to reverse God's will. God will not curse the good; therefore, Balaam tries to make them wicked; he tries to make the good curse themselves and so exasperate God.

A more diabolical wickedness we can scarcely conceive. Yet Balaam was an honorable, veracious man; a man of delicate conscientiousness and unconquerable scruples, a man of lofty religious professions, highly respectable and respected. The Lord of heaven and earth said there is such a thing as straining at a gnat, and swallowing a camel.

There are men who would not play false and yet would wrongly win. There are men who would not lie and yet who would bribe a poor man to support a cause which he believes in his soul to be false. There are men who would resent at the sword's point the charge of dishonor, who would yet for selfish gratification entice the weak into sin, and damn body and soul in hell. There are men who would be shocked at being called traitors, who in time of war will yet make a fortune by selling arms to their country's foes. There are men respectable and respected, who give liberally, support religious societies, go to church, and would not take God's name in vain, who have made wealth in some trade of opium or spirits out of the wreck of innumerable human lives. Balaam is one of the accursed spirits now, but he did no more than these are doing.

Now see what lay at the root of all this hollowness: Selfishness.

From first to last, one thing appears uppermost in this history: Balaam's self—the honor of Balaam as a true prophet (therefore he will not lie); the wealth of Balaam (therefore, the Israelites must be sacrificed). In his sublimest visions, his egotism breaks out. In the sight of God's Israel, he cries, "Let *me* die the death of the righteous." In anticipation of the glories of the eternal Advent, "*I* shall see him, but not now" (Num. 24:17). He sees the vision of a kingdom, a church, a chosen people, a triumph of righteousness. In such anticipations, the nobler prophets broke out into strains in which their own personality was forgotten. Moses, when he thought that God would destroy His people, prays in agony, "Yet now, if thou wilt, forgive their sin—and if not, blot me, I pray thee, out of thy book" (Exod. 32:32). Paul speaks in impassioned words: "I have . . . continual sorrow in my heart. For I could wish that myself were accursed from Christ for my brethren, my kinsmen according to the flesh: who are Israelites" (Rom. 9:2–3). But Balaam's chief feeling seems to be, "How will all this advance *me?*" And the magnificence of the prophecy is thus marred by a chord of melancholy and diseased egotism. Not for one moment—even in those moments when uninspired men gladly forget themselves, men who have devoted themselves to a monarchy or dreamed of a republic in sublime self-abnegation—can Balaam forget himself in God's cause.

Observe then: Desire for personal salvation is not religion. It *may* go with it, but it is not religion. Anxiety for the state of one's own soul is not the healthiest or best symptom. Of course, everyone wishes, "Let me die the death of the righteous." But it is one thing to wish to be saved, another to wish God's right to triumph; one thing to wish to die safe, another to wish to live holily. Not only is this desire for personal salvation not religion, but if soured, it passes into hatred of the good. Balaam's feeling became spite against the people who are to be blessed when he is not blessed. He indulges a wish that good may not prosper, because personal interests are mixed up with the failure of good.

We see anxiety about human opinion is uppermost. Throughout we find in Balaam's character semblances, not realities. He would not transgress a rule, but he would violate a principle. He would not say white was black, but he would sully it till it looked black.

Now consider the whole.

A bad man prophesies under the fear of God, restrained by conscience, full of poetry and sublime feelings, with a full clear view of death as dwarfing life, and the blessedness of righteousness as compared with wealth. And yet we find him striving to disobey God, hollow and unsound at heart; using for the devil wisdom and gifts bestowed by God; sacrificing all with a gambler's desperation for name and wealth; tempting a nation to sin, crime, and ruin; separated in selfish isolation from all mankind; superior to Balak, and yet feeling that Balak knew him to be a man that had his price; with the bitter anguish of being despised by the men who were inferior to himself; forced to conceive of a grandeur in which he had no share, and a righteousness in which he had no part. Can you not conceive the end of one with a mind so torn and distracted—death in battle; the insane frenzy with which he would rush into the field, and finding all go against him, and that lost for which he had bartered heaven, after having died a thousand worse than deaths, finds death at last upon the spears of the Israelites?

In application, we remark first, the danger of great powers. It is an awful thing, this conscious power to see more, to feel more, to know more than our fellows.

Secondly, let us mark well the difference between feeling and doing.

It is possible to have sublime feelings, great passions, even great sympathies with the race, and yet not to love man. To feel mightily is one thing, to live truly and charitably another. Sin may be felt at the core and yet not be cast out. Brethren, beware. See how a man may be going on uttering fine words, orthodox truths, and yet be rotten at the heart.

Henry Parry Liddon:
The First Five Minutes After Death

HENRY PARRY LIDDON WAS BORN in Hampshire, England, in 1829 and died in London in 1890. In 1870, when prebendary of Salisbury Cathedral, he delivered his Bampton Lectures on the divinity of Christ. These lectures established his fame as a preacher and theologian. In 1870, he became canon of St. Paul's Cathedral, where his preaching attracted such crowds that it became necessary to change the afternoon service from the choir to the nave. There, under the great dome of St. Paul's, Liddon poured forth his noble defense of the great doctrines of the Christian faith. In his preaching he dwelt not on the periphery of the Christian revelation, but upon what Chalmers called its "grand particularities." Against the growing skepticism of the day, Liddon took an uncompromising stand for the integrity of the Scriptures and the truth of the doctrines of Christianity. When he preached on the Resurrection he made it clear that the Christian doctrine of the future was the doctrine of the resurrection of the body and not a mere continuance of spirit existence after death. When he referred to the Second Advent of Christ, it was a real, personal Advent to which he testified, and not the mere triumph of the principles of righteousness. Concerning this doctrine he said, "Then let us turn the key in the west door of this cathedral if Christ is not coming back in glory." No one can read the sermons of Liddon without realizing that here was a preacher who sincerely received the great affirmations of the Christian revelation and believed in his heart of hearts that men are lost sinners, saved only through faith in the eternal Son of God.

He dwelt much on subjects dealing with man's life beyond the grave. His sermon, "The First Five Minutes After Death," although not as doctrinal as most of his sermons, is an intensely interesting and arresting treatment of that solemn theme.

The First Five Minutes After Death

"Then shall I know even as also I am known" (1 Cor. 13:12).

A N *Indian officer,* who in his time had seen a great deal of service and had taken part in more than one of those decisive struggles by which the British authority was finally established in the East Indies, had returned to end his days in this country, and was talking with his friends about the most striking experiences of his professional career. They led him, by their sympathy and their questions, to travel in memory through a long series of years; and as he described skirmishes, battles, sieges, personal encounters, hairbreadth escapes, the outbreak of the mutiny and its suppression, reverses, victories, all the swift alternations of anxiety and hope which a man must know who is entrusted with command and is before the enemy—their interest in his story, as was natural, became keener and more exacting. At last he paused with the observation, "I expect to see something much more remarkable than anything I have been describing." As he was some seventy years of age, and was understood to have retired from active service, his listeners failed to catch his meaning. There was a pause; then he said in an undertone, "I mean in the first five minutes after death."

"The first five minutes after death!" Surely the expression is worth remembering, if only as that of a man to whom the life to come was evidently a great and solemn reality. "The first five minutes." If we may employ for the moment when speaking of eternity standards of measurement which belong to time, it is at least conceivable that, after the lapse of some thousands or tens of thousands of years, we shall have lost all sense of a succession in events; that existence will have come to seem to be only a never-ceasing present; an unbegun and unending now. It is, I say, at least conceivable that this will be so;

but can we suppose that at the moment of our entrance on that new and wonderful world we shall already think and feel as if we had always been there, or had been there, at least, for ages?

There is no doubt, an impression sometimes to be met with that death is followed by a state of unconsciousness.

> If sleep and death be truly one,
>   And every spirit's folded bloom,
>   Through all its intervital gloom,
> In some long trance should slumber on,
>
> Unconscious of the sliding hour,
>   Bare of the body, might it last,
>   And all the traces of the past
> Be all the color of the flower.

But that is a supposition which is less due to the exigencies of reason than to the sensitiveness of imagination. The imagination recoils from the task of anticipating a moment so full of awe and wonder as must be that of the introduction of a conscious spirit to the invisible world. And accordingly, the reason essays to persuade itself, if it can, that life after death will not be conscious life, although it is difficult to recognize a single reason why if life, properly speaking, survives at all, it should forfeit consciousness. Certainly, the life of the souls under the heavenly altar, who intercede perpetually with God for the approach of the Last Judgment, is not an unconscious life. Certainly the paradise which our Lord promised to the dying thief cannot be reasonably imagined to have been a moral and mental slumber, any more than can those unembodied ministers of God who do his pleasure, who are sent forth to minister to them that are the heirs of salvation, be supposed to reach a condition no higher than that which is produced by chloroform. No, this supposition of an unconscious state after death is a discovery, not of revelation, not of reason, but of desire; of a strong desire on the one hand to keep a hold on immortality, and on the other to escape the risks which immortality may involve. It cannot well be doubted that consciousness—if not retained to the last in the act of dying, if suspended by sleep, by physical disease, or by derangement—must be recovered as soon as the act of death is completed, with the removal of the cause which suspended it. Should this be the case, the soul will enter upon another life with the habits of thought which belong to time still clinging to it; they will be unlearned gradually, if at all, in the after stages of existence. And assuredly, the first sense of being in another world must be overwhelming. Imagination can, indeed, form no worthy estimate of it; but we may do well to try to think of it as best we can this afternoon, since it is at least one of the approaches to the great and awful subject which should be before our thoughts at this time of the year, namely, the second coming of Jesus Christ to judgment. And here the apostle comes to our assistance with his anticipation of the future life as a life of enormously enhanced knowledge: "Then shall I know even as also I am known." Let us try to keep it before our minds, reverently and earnestly, for a few minutes; and let us ask ourselves, accordingly, what will be the most startling additions to our existing knowledge at our first entrance on the world to come.

I.

First, then, at our entrance on another state of being, we shall know what it is to exist under entirely new conditions. Here we are bound up—we hardly suspect, perhaps, how intimately—in thought and affection, with the persons and objects around us. They influence us subtly and powerfully in a thousand ways; in some cases, they altogether shape the course of life. In every life, it has been truly said, much more is taken for granted than is ever noticed. The mind is eagerly directed to the few persons and subjects which affection or interest force prominently upon its notice; it gazes inertly at all the rest. As we say, it does not take them in until some incident arises which forces them one by one into view. A boy never knows what his home was worth until he has gone for the first time to school; and then he misses, and as he misses he eagerly recollects and realizes all that he has left behind him.

This may enable us, in a certain sense, to understand what is in store for all of us at our entrance by dying, into the unseen world. I do not, of course, mean that this life is our home, and that the future at all necessarily corresponds to school as being an endless banishment. God forbid! If we only will have it, the exact reverse of this shall be the case. But the parallel will so far hold good that at death we must experience a sense of strangeness to which nothing in this life has even approached. We shall exist, thinking, feeling, and exercising memory, will, and understanding; but without bodies. Think what that means. We are at present at home in the body; we have not yet learned, by losing it, what the body is to us. The various activities of the soul are sorted out and appropriated by the several senses of the body, so that the soul's action from moment to moment is made easy, we may well conceive, by being thus distributed. What will it be to compress all that the senses now achieve separately into a single act; to see, but without these eyes; to hear, but without these ears; to experience something purely supersensuous that shall answer to the grosser senses of taste and smell; and to see, hear, smell, and taste by a single movement of the spirit, combining all these separate modes of apprehension into one? What will it be to find ourselves with the old self, divested of this body which has clothed it since its first moment of existence; able to achieve, it may be so much, it may be so little; living on, but under conditions so totally new? This experience alone will add no little to our existing knowledge; and the addition will have been made in the first five minutes after death.

II.

The entrance on the next world must bring with it a knowledge of God such as is impossible in this life. In this life, many men talk of God, and some men think much and deeply about him. But here men do not attain to that sort of direct knowledge of God which the Bible calls "sight." We do not see a human soul. The soul makes itself felt in conduct, in conversation, in the lines of the countenance; although these often enough mislead us. The soul speaks through the eye, which misleads us less often. That is to say, we know that the soul is there, and we detect something of its character, power, and drift. We do not see it. In the same way, we feel God present in nature, whether in its awe or its beauty; and in human history, whether in its justice or its weird mysteriousness; and in the life of a good man, or the circumstances of a generous or noble act. Most of all, we feel him near when conscience, his inward messenger, speaks plainly and decisively to us. Conscience, that invisible prophet, surely appeals to and implies a law, and a law implies a legislator. But we do not see him. Of the children of men in this mortal state, the rule holds good that no one has seen God at any time.

But after death, there will be a change. It is said of our Lord's glorified manhood, united as it is forever to the Person of the eternal Son, that "every eye shall see him, and they also which pierced him" (Rev. 1:7). Even the lost will then understand much more of what God is to the universe and to themselves, although they are forever excluded from the direct vision of God. He will be there before us. We shall see him as he is. His vast illimitable life will present itself to the apprehension of our spirits as a clearly consistent whole; not as a complex problem to be painfully mastered by the effort of our understandings, but as a present, living, encompassing being, who inflicts himself on the very sight of his adoring creatures.

III.

Once more: At our entrance on another world, we shall know our old selves as never before. The past will lie spread out before us, and we shall take a comprehensive survey of it. Each man's life will be displayed to him as a river, which he traces from its source in a distant mountain till it mingles with the distant ocean. The course of that river lies sometimes through dark forests which hide it from view, sometimes through sands or marshes in which it seems to lose itself. Here it forces a passage angrily between precipitous rocks, there it glides gently through meadows which it makes green and fertile. At one while, it might seem to be turning backwards out of pure caprice; at another to be parting, like a gay spendthrift, with half its volume of waters; while later on it receives contributory streams that restore its strength; and so it passes on, till the ebb and flow of tides upon its bank tells that the end is near. What will not the retrospect be when, after death, we survey for the first time, as with a bird's-eye view, the whole long range—the strange vicissitudes, the loss and gain, as we deem it, the failures and the triumphs of our earthly existence; when we measure it as never before, in its completeness now that it is at last over!

This, indeed, is the characteristic of the survey after death, that it will be complete.

> There no shade can last,
> In that deep dawn behind the tomb,
> But clear from merge to merge shall bloom
> The eternal landscape of the past.

That survey of life which is made by the dying is less than complete; it cannot include the closing scene of all. While there is life, there is room for recovery, and the hours which remain may be very different from those which have preceded.

It may be thought that to review life will take as long a time as to live it; but this notion betrays a very imperfect idea of the resource and capacity of the human soul. Under the pressure of great feeling, the soul lives with a rapidity and intensity which disturbs all its usual relations to time. Witness the reports which those who have nearly lost their lives by drowning have made of their mental experiences. It once happened to me to assist at the recovery of a man who nearly forfeited life while bathing. He had sunk the last time, and there was difficulty in getting him to land, and when he was landed, still greater difficulty in restoring him. Happily there was skilled assistance at hand. And so presently my friend recovered, not without much distress, first one and then another of the sensations and faculties of his bodily life. In describing his experience of what must have been the whole conscious side of the act of dying by drowning, he said that the time had seemed to him of very great duration; he had lost his standard of the worth of time. He had lived his whole past life over again; he had not epitomized it; he had repeated it, as it seemed to him, in detail and with the greatest deliberation. He had difficulty in understanding that he had only been in the water for a few minutes. During these intenser moments of existence, the life of the soul has no sort of relation to what we call time.

Yes, in entering another world, we shall know what we have been in the past as never before; but we shall know also what we are. The soul, divested of the body, will see itself as never before; and it may be that it will see disfigurements and ulcers which the body, like a beautiful robe, had hitherto shrouded from sight, and which are revealed in this life only by the shock of a great sorrow or of a great fall. There is a notion abroad—a notion which is welcomed because, whether true or not, it is very comfortable—that the soul will be so changed by death as to lose the disfigurements which it may have contracted through life; that the death agony is a furnace, by being plunged into which the soul will burn out its stains; or that death involves such a shock as to break the continuity of our moral condition, though not of existence itself; and thus that, in changing worlds, we shall change our characters, and that moral evil will be buried with the body in the grave, while the soul escapes, purified by separation from its grosser companion, to the regions of holiness and peace.

Surely, brethren, this is an illusion which will not stand the test—we need not for the moment say of Christian truth, but of reasonable reflection. It is a contradiction to all that we know about the character and mind of man, in which nothing is more remarkable than the intimate and enduring connection which subsists between its successive states or stages of development. Every one of us here present is now exactly what his past life has made him. Our present thoughts, feelings, mental habits, good and bad, are the effects of what we have done or left undone, of cherished impressions, of passions indulged or repressed, of pursuits vigorously embraced or willingly abandoned. And as our past mental and spiritual history has made us what we are, so we are at this very moment making ourselves what we shall be. I do not forget that intervention of a higher force which we call "grace" and by which the direction of a life may be suddenly changed, as in St. Paul's case at his conversion; although these great changes are often prepared for by a long preceding process, and are not as sudden as they seem. But we are speaking of the rule, and not of the exception. The rule is that men are in each stage of their existence what with or without God's supernatural grace they have made themselves in the preceding stages; and there is no reasonable ground for thinking that at death the influences of a whole lifetime will cease to operate upon character, and that, whatever those influences may have been, the soul will be purified by the shock of death. Why, I ask, should death have any such result? What is there in death to bring it about? Death is the dissolution of the bodily frame, of the limbs and organs through which the soul now acts. These organs are, no doubt, very closely connected with the soul, which strikes its roots into them and acts through them. But, although closely connected with the soul, they are distinct from it: thought, conscience, affection, will are quite independent of the organs which are dissolved by death. And it is impossible to see why the soul should put on a new character simply because it lays aside for awhile the instrument which it has employed during a term of years, any more than why a painter's hand should forget its cunning because he has sold his easel or why a murderer should cease to be a murderer at heart because he has lost his dagger and cannot afford to replace it. True, at death, the ear, the eye, the hands, perish. But when they are destroyed in this life by an accident, does character change with them? The indulgence of the purely animal appetite may depend on the healthy condition of the organ; but the mental condition which permits, if it does not dictate, the indulgence remains unaffected. Principles of right action or their opposites outlive the faculties, as they outlive the opportunities for asserting themselves in act. The habit of thieving is not renounced because the right hand has been cut off; nor are sensual dispositions because the body is prostrate through illness; nor is evil curiosity because the eye is dim and the ear deaf. And when all the instruments through which in this life the soul has expressed itself, and which collectively make up the body, are laid aside by the emphatic act of death, the soul itself and all its characteristic thought and affections, will remain unaffected, since its life is independent of its bodily envelope as is the body's life of the clothes which we wear.

One being there is who knows us now, who knows us perfectly, who has always known us. When we die, we shall for the first time know ourselves, even as also we are known. We shall not have to await the Judge's sentence; we shall read it at a glance, whatever it be, in this new apprehension of what we are.

It may help us, then, this Advent to think from time to time of what will be our condition in the first five minutes after death. Like death itself, the solemnities which follow it must come to all of us. We know not when, or where, or how we shall enter in; this only we know—that come it must. Those first five minutes, that first awakening to a new existence, with its infinite possibilities, will only be tolerable if we have indeed, with the hands of faith and love, laid hold on the hope set before us in the Person of Jesus Christ our Lord and Savior; who for us men and for our salvation took flesh, was crucified, rose from death, ascended into heaven, and has pleaded incessantly at the right hand of the Father for us, the weak and erring children of the Fall. Without him, a knowledge of that new world, of its infinite and awful Master, still more of ourselves as we really are, will indeed be terrifying. With him, we may trust that such knowledge will be more than bearable; we may think calmly even of that tremendous experience, if he, the eternal God, is indeed our Refuge and underneath are the everlasting arms.

Charles Haddon Spurgeon: *Spared!*

CHARLES HADDON SPURGEON WAS BORN at Kelvedon, England, June 19, 1834, and died at Mentone, Switzerland, January 31, 1892. He became celebrated as a "boy preacher," and at twenty-two years of age was the most popular preacher in the world. The Metropolitan Tabernacle, seating six thousand, was built for him, and there he preached for almost two generations. His sermons were taken down in shorthand and scattered by thousands through the English-speaking world. If we take into consideration the number of weekly readers, as well as the congregations which heard him at the Tabernacle, it is safe to say that Spurgeon preached to more people than any preacher in the history of the Christian church. Nearly all those who have recorded their impression of Spurgeon's preaching bear witness to the singular beauty and charm of his voice. His preaching was direct and personal. He once said: "I hope I may never preach before a congregation—I desire always to preach to you." Charles Francis Adams, American minister to England during the Civil War, gives this impression of Spurgeon: "There was no characteristic thought nor novel reasoning. His power consisted in sympathy with the current of human feeling in all ages on that solemn topic of moral responsibility to a higher power, both here and hereafter." No preacher left so many printed sermons behind him as did Spurgeon. From these thousands of sermons, it is difficult to make a choice, for Spurgeon is less interesting to read than almost any of the great preachers. But nearly all his sermons show his manner and his deep desire to save the souls of those to whom he was preaching.

I have chosen the sermon on the striking text, "I was left." In this sermon, the reader will find that, as Adams noted, Spurgeon kept ever in the foreground the "solemn topic of moral responsibility to a higher power, both here and hereafter."

Spared!

"I was left" (Ezek. 9:8).

HE *vision of Ezekiel,* which is recorded in the previous chapter, brought to light the abominations of the house of Judah. The vision which follows in this chapter shows the terrible retribution that the Lord God brought upon the guilty nation, beginning at Jerusalem.

He beheld the slaughtermen come forth with their weapons, he marked them begin the destroying work at the gate of the temple, he saw them proceed through the main streets and not omit a single lane; they slew utterly all those who were not marked with the mark of the writer's inkhorn on their brow. He stood alone, that prophet of the Lord, himself spared in the midst of universal carnage; and as the carcasses fell at his feet, and the bodies stained with gore lay all around him, he said, "I was left." He stood alive amongst the dead because he was found faithful among the faithless. He survived in the midst of universal destruction because he had served his God in the midst of universal depravity.

We shall now take the sentence apart altogether from Ezekiel's vision and appropriate it to ourselves. I think when we read it over and repeat it, "I was left," it very naturally invites us to take a *retrospect* of the past, very readily also it suggests a *prospect* of the future, and, I think, it permits also a terrible *contrast* in reserve for the impenitent.

1. First of all, then, my brethren, we have here a pathetic reflection, which seems to invite us to take a *solemn retrospect*: "I was left." You remember, many of you, times of sickness, when cholera was in your streets. You may forget that season of pestilence, but I never can, when the duties of my pastorate called me continually to walk among

your terror-stricken households and to see the dying and the dead. Impressed upon my young heart must ever remain some of those sad scenes I witnessed when I first came to this metropolis and was rather employed at that time to bury the dead than to bless the living. Some of you have passed through not only one season of cholera but many, and you have been present, too, perhaps, in climates where fever has prostrated its hundreds, and where the plague and other dire diseases have emptied out their quivers, and every arrow has found its mark in the heart of some one of your companions. Yet you have been left. You walked among the graves, but you did not stumble into them. Fierce and fatal maladies lurked in your path, but they were not allowed to devour you. The bullets of death whistled by your ears, and yet you stood alive, for his bullet had no billet for your heart. You can look back, some of you, through fifty, sixty, seventy years. Your bald and gray heads tell the story that you are no more raw recruits in the warfare of life. You have become veterans, if not invalids, in the army. You are ready to retire, to put off your armor, and give place to others. Look back, brethren, I say, you have come into the sere and yellow leaf; remember the many seasons in which you have seen death hailing multitudes about you and think: "I was left." And we, too, who are younger, in whose veins our blood still leaps in vigor, can remember times of peril when thousands fell about us, yet we can say in God's house with great emphasis, "I was left"—preserved, great God, when many others perished; sustained, standing on the rock of life when the waves of death dashed about me, the spray fell heavy upon me, and my body was saturated with disease and pain, yet am I still alive—permitted still to mingle with the busy tribes of men.

Now, then, what does such a retrospect as this suggest? Ought we not each one of us to ask the question, "What was I spared for? Why was I left?" Many of you were at that time, and some of you even now are dead in trespasses and sins. You were not spared because of your faithfulness, for you brought forth nothing but the grapes of Gomorrah. Certainly, God did not stay his sword because of anything good in you. A multitude of clamorous evils in your disposition if not in your conduct might well have demanded your summary execution. You were spared. Let me ask you why. Was it that mercy might yet visit you, that grace might yet renew your soul? Have you found it so? Has sovereign grace overcome you, broken down your prejudices, thawed your icy heart, broken your stony will in pieces? Say, sinner, in looking back upon the times when you have been left, were you spared in order that you might be saved with a great salvation? And if you cannot say yes to that question, let me ask you whether it may not be so yet? Soul, why has God spared you so long, while you are yet his enemy, a stranger to him, and far off from him by wicked works? Or, on the contrary, has he spared you—I tremble at the bare mention of the possibility—has he prolonged your days to develop your propensities that you may grow riper for damnation, that you may fill up your measure of crying iniquity, and then go down to the pit a sinner seared and dry, like wood that is ready for the fire? Can it be so? Shall these spared moments be spoiled by misdemeanors, or shall they be given up to repentance and to prayer? Will you now, ere the last of your suns shall set in everlasting darkness, will you now look unto him? If so, you will have reason to bless God through all eternity that you were left, because you were left that you might yet seek and might yet find him who is the Savior of sinners.

Do I speak to many of you who are Christians and you, too, have been left? When better saints than you were snatched away from earthly ties and creature kindred, when brighter stars than you were enclouded in night, were you permitted still to shine with your poor, flickering ray? Why was it, great God? Why am I now left? Let me ask myself that question. In sparing me so long, my Lord, have you not something more for me to do? Is there not some purpose as yet unconceived in my soul which thou wilt yet suggest to me, to carry out which thou wilt yet give me grace and strength, and spare me again a little while? Am I yet immortal, or shielded at least from every arrow of death, because my work is incomplete? Is the tale of my years prolonged because the full tale of the bricks hath not been made up? Then show me what thou would have me do. Since I have been left, help me to feel myself a specially consecrated man, left for a purpose, reserved for some end, else I had been worms, meat years ago, and my body had crumbled back to its mother earth. Christian, I say, always be asking yourself this question; but especially be asking it when you are preserved in times of more than ordinary sickness and mortality. If I am left, why am I left? Why am I not taken home to heaven? Why do I not enter into my rest? Great God and Master, show me what thou would have me do, and give me grace and strength to do it.

Let us change the retrospect for a moment and look upon the sparing mercy of God in another light. "I was left." Some of you now present, whose history I well know, can say, "I was left" and say it with peculiar emphasis. You were born of ungodly parents; the earliest words you can recollect were base and blasphemous, too bad to repeat. You can remember how the first breath your infant lungs received was tainted air—the air of vice, sin, and iniquity. You grew up, you and your brothers and your sisters, side by side; you filled the home with sin, you went on together in your youthful crimes, and encouraged each other in evil habits. Thus, you grew up to manhood, and then you were banded together in ties of obliquity as well as in ties of consanguinity. You added to your number; you took in fresh associates. As your family circle increased, so did the flagrancy of your conduct. You all conspired to break the Sabbath; you devised the same scheme and perpetrated the same improprieties. Perhaps you can recollect the time when Sunday invitations used always to be sent, a sneer at godliness was couched in the invitations. You recollect how one and another of your old comrades died; you followed them to their graves, and your merriment was checked a little while, but it soon broke out again. Then a sister died, steeped to the mouth in infidelity; after that a brother was taken; he had no hope in his death; all was darkness and despair before him. And so, sinner, you have outlived all your comrades. If you are inclined to go to hell, you must go there along a beaten track: a path which, as you look back upon the way you have trodden, is stained with blood. You can remember how all that have been before you have gone to the long home in dismal gloom, without a glimpse or ray of joy. And now you are left, sinner; and, blessed be God, it may be you can say, "Yes, and I am not only left, but I am here in the house of prayer; and if I know my own heart, there is nothing I should hate so much as to live my old life over again. Here I am, and I never believed I should ever be here. I look back with mournfulness indeed upon those who have departed; but though mourning them, I express my gratitude to God that I am not in torments—not in hell—but still here; yes, not only here, but having a hope that I shall one day see the face of Christ, and stand amidst blazing worlds robed in his righteousness and preserved by his love." You have been left, then, and what ought you to say? Ought you to boast? Oh, no; be doubly humble. Should you take the honor to yourself? No; put the crown upon the head of free, rich, undeserved grace. And what should you do above all other men? Why, you should be doubly pledged to serve Christ. As you have served the devil through thick and thin, until you came to serve him alone and your company had all departed, so by divine grace may you be pledged to Christ— to follow him, though all the world should despise him, and to hold on to the end, until, if every professor should be an apostate, it might yet be said of you at the last, "He was left. He stood alone in sin while his comrades died, and then he stood alone in Christ when his companions deserted him." Thus of you it should ever be said, "He was left."

This suggests also one more form of the same retrospect. What a special providence has watched over some of us, and guarded our feeble frames! There are some of you, in particular, who have been left to such an age that as you look back upon your youthful days, you revoke far more of kinsfolk in the tomb than remain in the world, more under the earth than above it. In your dreams, you are the associates of the dead. Still you are left. Preserved amidst a thousand dangers of infancy, then kept in youth, steered safely over the shoals and quicksands of an immature age, over the rocks and reefs of manhood, you have been brought past the ordinary period of mortal life, and yet you are still here. Seventy years exposed to perpetual death, and yet preserved till you have come almost, perhaps, to your fourscore years. You have been left, my dear brother, and why are you left? Why is it that brothers and sisters are all gone? Why is it that your old school companions have gradually thinned? You cannot recollect one, now alive, who was your companion in youth. How is that now, you who have lived in a certain quarter so long, see new names there on all the shop doors, new faces in the streets, and everything new to what you once saw in your young days? Why are you spared? Are you an unconverted man? Are you an unconverted woman? To what end are you spared? Is it that you may at the eleventh hour be saved—God grant it may be so—or are you spared till you shall have sinned yourself into the lowest depths of hell that you may go there the most aggravated sinner because of oft-repeated warnings as often neglected—are you spared for this, or is it that you may be saved? But are you a Christian? Then is it not hard for you to answer the question, Why are you spared? I do not believe there is an old woman on earth, living in the most obscure cot in England, and sitting this very night in the dark garret, with her candle gone out, without means to buy another—I do not believe that old woman would be kept out of heaven five minutes unless God had something for her to do on earth; and I do not think that yon grayheaded man now would be preserved here unless there was something for him to do. Tell it out, tell it out, you aged man; tell the story of that preserving grace which has kept you up till now. Tell to your children and to your children's children what a God he is whom you have trusted. Stand up as a hoary patriarch and tell how he delivered you in six troubles, and in seven suffered no evil to touch you. Bear to coming generations your faithful witness that his word is true, and that his promise cannot fail. Lean on your staff, and say before you die in the midst of your family, "Not one thing hath failed of all the good things which the Lord your God spake concerning you" (Josh. 23:14). Let your ripe days bring forth a mellow testimony to his love; and as you have more and more advanced in years, so be more and more advanced in knowledge and in confirmed assurance of the immutability of his counsel, the truthfulness of his oath, the preciousness of his blood, and the sureness of the salvation of all those who put their trust in him. Then shall we know that you are spared for a high and noble purpose, indeed. You shall say it with tears of gratitude, and we will listen with smiles of joy: "I was left."

2. I must rather suggest these retrospects than follow them up, though, did time permit, we might well enlarge abundantly, and therefore I must hurry on to invite you to a *prospect*. "And I was left." You and I shall soon pass out of this world into another. This life is but the ferry boat; we are being carried across, and we shall soon come to the true shore, the real *terra firma*, for here there is nothing that is substantial. When we shall come into the next world, we have to expect by and by a resurrection—a resurrection both of the just and of the unjust; and in that solemn day we are to expect that all that

dwell upon the face of the earth shall be gathered together in one place. And he shall come, who came once to suffer, "he cometh to judge the earth: with righteousness shall he judge the world, and the people with equity" (Ps. 98:9). He who came as an infant shall come as the Infinite. He who lay wrapped in swaddling bands shall come girt about the paps with a golden girdle, with a rainbow wreath, and robes of storm. There shall we all stand a vast innumerable company; earth shall be crowned from her valley's deepest base to the mountain's summit, and the sea's waves shall become the solid standing place of men and women who have slept beneath its torrents. Then shall every eye be fixed on him, every ear shall be open to him, and every heart shall watch with solemn awe and dread suspense for the transactions of that greatest of all days, that day of days, that sealing up of the ages, that completing of the dispensation. In solemn pomp, the Savior comes and his angels with him. You hear his voice as he cries, "Gather ye together first the tares in bundles to burn them" (Matt. 13:30). Behold the reapers, how they come with wings of fire! See how they grasp their sharp sickles which have long been grinding upon the millstone of God's long-suffering but have become sharpened at the last. Do you see them as they approach? And there they are mowing down a nation with their sickles. The vile idolaters have just now fallen, and yonder a family of blasphemers has been crushed beneath the feet of the reapers. See there a bundle of drunkards being carried away upon the reapers' shoulders to the great blazing fire. See again in another place the whoremonger, the adulterer, the unchaste, tied up in vast bundles—bundles the withes of which shall never be rent—and see them cast into the fire, and see how they blaze in the unutterable torments of that pit; and shall I be left? Great God, shall I stand there wrapped in his righteousness alone, the righteousness of him who sits my Judge erect upon the judgment seat? Shall I, when the wicked shall cry, "Rocks, hide us, mountains on us fall," shall this eye look up, shall this face dare to turn itself to the face of him that sits upon the throne? Shall I stand calm and unmoved amid universal terror and dismay? Shall I be numbered with the godly company who, clothed with the white linen which is the righteousness of the saints, shall await the shock, shall see the wicked hurled to destruction, and feel and know themselves secure? Shall it be so, or shall I be bound up in a bundle to burn, and swept away forever by the breath of God's nostrils, like the chaff driven before the wind? It must be one or the other; which shall it be? Can I answer that question? Can I tell? I can tell it—tell it now—for I have in this very chapter that which teaches me how to judge myself. They who are preserved have the mark in their foreheads, and they have a character as well as a mark, and their character is, that they sigh and cry for all the abominations of the wicked. Then, if I hate sin, and if I sigh because others love it—if I cry because I myself through infirmity fall into it—if the sin of myself and the sin of others is a constant source of grief and vexation of spirit to me, then have I that mark and evidence of those who shall neither sigh nor cry in the world to come, for sorrow and sighing shall flee away? Have I the blood mark on my brow today? Say, my soul, hast thou put thy trust in Jesus Christ alone, and as the fruit of the faith, has thy faith learned how to love, not only him that saveth thee, but others, too, who as yet are unsaved? And do I sigh and cry within while I bear the blood mark without? Come, brother, sister, answer this for yourself, I charge you; I charge you do so by the tottering earth and by the ruined pillars of heaven, that shall surely shake. I pray you by the cherubim and seraphim that shall be before the throne of the great Judge; by the blazing lightnings, that shall kindle the thick darkness, make the sun amazed, and turn the moon into blood; by him whose tongue is a flame-like sword of fire; by him who shall judge you, try you, read your heart and declare your ways, and divide unto you your eternal portion. I urge you, by the certainties of death, by the sureness of judgment, by the glories of heaven, by the solemnities of hell—I beseech, implore, command, entreat you—ask yourself now, "Shall I be left? Do I believe in Christ? Have I been born again? Have I a new heart and a right spirit? Or, am I still what I always was—God's enemy, Christ's despiser, cursed by the Law, cast out from the gospel, without God and without hope, a stranger to the commonwealth of Israel?" Oh, I cannot speak to you as earnestly as I would to God I could. I want to thrust this question into your very loins and stir up your heart's deepest thoughts with it. Sinner, what will become of you when God shall winnow the chaff from the wheat, what will be thy portion? You who stand in the aisle yonder, what will be your portion, you who are crowded there, what will be your portion, when he shall come, and nothing shall escape his eye? Say, will you hear him? Say, and will your heart-strings crack while he utters the thundering sound, "Depart, ye cursed"; or shall it be your happy lot—your soul transported all the while with bliss unutterable—to hear him say, "Come, ye blessed of my Father, inherit the kingdom prepared for you from the foundations of the world" (Matt. 25:34)? Our text invites a prospect. I pray you take it, and look across the narrow stream of death, and say, "Shall I be left?"

> When thou, my righteous Judge, shalt come,
> To fetch thy ransomed people home,
>   Shall I among them stand?
> Shall such a worthless worm as I,
> Who sometimes am afraid to die,
>   Be found at thy right hand?

3. But now we come to a terrible *contrast*, which I think is permitted in the text, "I was left." Then there will be some who will not be left in the sense we have been speaking of and yet who will be left after another and more dreadful manner. They will be left by mercy,

forsaken by hope, given up by friends, and become a prey to the implacable fury, to the sudden, infinite, and unmitigated severity and justice of an angry God. But they will not be left or exempted from judgment, for the sword shall find them out, the vials of Jehovah shall reach even to their hearts. And that flame, the pile whereof is wood, and much smoke shall suddenly devour them, and that without remedy. Sinner, you shall be left. I say, you shall be left of all those fond joys that you hug now—left of that pride which now steels your heart; you will be low enough then. You will be left of that iron constitution which now seems to repel the dart of death. You shall be left of those companions of yours that entice you on to sin and harden you in iniquity. You shall be left then of that pleasing fancy of yours, and of that merry wit which can make sport of Bible truths and mock at divine solemnities. You shall be left then of all your buoyant hopes, and of all your imaginary delights. You shalt be left of that sweet angel, Hope, who never forsakes any but those who are condemned to hell. You shall be left of God's Spirit, who sometimes now pleads with you. You shall be left of Jesus Christ, whose gospel has been so often preached in your ear. You shall be left of God the Father; he shall shut his eyes of pity against you, his bowels of compassion shall no more yearn over you; nor shall his heart regard your cries. You shall be left; but oh, I again tell you, you shall not be left as one who has escaped, for when the earth shall open to swallow up the wicked, it shall open at your feet and swallow you up. When the fiery thunderbolt shall pursue the spirit that falls into the pit that is bottomless, it shall pursue you and reach you and find you. When God rends the wicked in pieces, and there shall be none to deliver, he shall rend you in pieces, he shall be unto you as a consuming fire, your conscience shall be full of gall, your heart shall be drunken with bitterness, your teeth shall be broken even with gravel stones, your hopes riven with his hot thunderbolts, and all your joys withered and blasted by his breath. Oh! careless sinner, mad sinner, you who are dashing yourself now downward to destruction, why will you play the fool at this rate? There are cheaper ways of making sport for yourself than this. Dash your head against the wall; go scrabble there, and, like David, let your spittle fall upon your beard, but let not your sin fall upon your conscience, and let not your despite of Christ be like a millstone hanged about your neck, with which you shall be cast into the sea forever. Be wise, I pray you. Oh, Lord, make the sinner wise; hush his madness for awhile; let him be sober and hear the voice of reason; let him be still and hear the voice of conscience; let him be obedient and hear the voice of Scripture. "Thus saith the Lord, because I will do this, consider thy ways." "Prepare to meet thy God" (Amos 4:12). Oh, Israel, "set thine house in order; for thou shalt die, and not live" (2 Kings 20:1). "Believe on the Lord Jesus Christ, and thou shalt be saved" (Acts 16:31). I do feel I have a message for someone tonight. Though there may be some who think the sermon not appropriate to a congregation where there is so large a proportion of converted men and women, yet what a large portion of ungodly ones there are here, too! I know that you come here, many of you, to hear some funny tale or to catch at some strange, extravagant speech of one whom you repute to be an eccentric man. Ah, well, he is eccentric, and hopes to be so till he dies; but it is simply eccentric in being in earnest, and wanting to win souls. Oh, poor sinners, there is no odd tale I would not tell if I thought it would be blessed to you. There is no grotesque language which I would not use, however it might be thrown back at me again, if I thought it might be serviceable to you. I set not my account to be thought a fine speaker; they that use fine language may dwell in the king's palaces. I speak to you as one who knows he is accountable to no man, but only to his God; as one who shall have to render his account at the last great day. And I pray you now go not away to talk of this and that which you have remarked in my language. Think of this one thing, "Shall I be left? Shall I be saved? Shall I be caught up and dwell with Christ in heaven? Or shall I be cast down to hell forever and ever?" Turn over these things. Think seriously of them. Hear that voice which says, "Him that cometh to me I will in no wise cast out" (John 6:37). Give heed to the voice which expostulates: "Come now, let us reason together, saith the Lord: though your sins be as scarlet, they shall be as white as snow; though they be red like crimson, they shall be as wool" (Isa. 1:18). How else shall your life be spared when the wicked are judged? How else shall you find shelter when the tempest of divine wrath rages? How else shall you stand in the lot of the righteous at the end of the days?

Phillips Brooks: *The Candle of the Lord*

PHILLIPS BROOKS WAS BORN in Boston, Massachusetts, on the 13th of December, 1835, and died in Boston, on the 23rd day of January, 1893. He was educated at Harvard and studied for the ministry at the theological seminary of the Protestant Episcopal Church in Alexandria. He then became rector of the Church of the Advent, Philadelphia, and from 1862 to 1869 was rector of Holy Trinity Church, Philadelphia. From 1869 until 1891, he was rector of Trinity Church, Boston. In 1891, he was elected bishop of Massachusetts and served in that capacity until his death.

Phillips Brooks was of a noble and commanding presence, well over six feet in stature. His reputation as a preacher was established when he was rector of Holy Trinity Church, Philadelphia, but his fame and influence reached their climax in Boston. His sermons were carefully written out before their delivery and spoken with an extraordinary speed of utterance. The great collection of sermons which he left behind him do not reveal a mind which grappled with the deeper problems of life and destiny, nor do they ring with the "grand particularities" of the Christian revelation. His sermons deal more with the suburban territory of Christian truth; but in that field they are among the best that have been produced.

One of his best known and most frequently preached sermons was, "The Candle of the Lord." He preached this sermon in Westminster Abbey on the Fourth of July, 1879, and Lady Frances Baillie, Dean Stanley's sister-in-law, relates how after the service she slipped out into the deanery by a private door and reached the drawing room before any of the guests who were to come in from the abbey. There she found the dean in tears, and when he saw her, he exclaimed that never had he been so moved by any sermon that he could remember. He who reads this sermon will have a good understanding of the pulpit range and the method of Phillips Brooks.

The Candle of the Lord

"The spirit of man is the candle of the Lord" (Prov. 20:27).

THE *essential connection* between the life of God and the life of man is the great truth of the world; and that is the truth which Solomon sets forth in the striking words which I have chosen for my text this morning. The picture which the words suggest is very simple. An unlighted candle is standing in the darkness, and someone comes to light it. A blazing bit of paper holds the fire at first, but it is vague and fitful. It flares and wavers and at any moment may go out. But the vague, uncertain, flaring blaze touches the candle, the candle catches fire, and at once you have a steady flame. It burns straight and clear and constant. The candle gives the fire a manifestation point for all the room which is illuminated by it. The candle is glorified by the fire, and the fire is manifested by the candle. The two bear witness that they were made for one another by the way in which they fulfill each other's life. That fulfillment comes by the way in which the inferior substance renders obedience to its superior. The candle obeys the fire. The docile wax acknowledges that the subtle flame is its master, and it yields to his power; and so, like every faithful servant of a noble master, it at once gives its master's nobility the chance to utter itself, and its own substance is clothed with a glory which is not its own. The disobedient granite, if you try to burn it, neither gives the fire a chance to show its brightness nor gathers any splendor to itself. It only glows with sullen resistance, and, as the heat increases, splits and breaks but will not yield. But the candle obeys, and so in it the scattered fire finds a point of permanent and clear expression.

Can we not see, with such a picture clear before us, what must be meant when it is said that one being is the candle of another being?

There is in a community a man of large, rich character, whose influence runs everywhere. You cannot talk with any man in all the city but you get, shown in that man's own way, the thought, the feeling of that central man who teaches all the community to think, to feel. The very boys catch something of his power, and have something about them that would not be there if he were not living in the town. What better description could you give of all that, than to say that that man's life was fire and that all these men's lives were candles which he lighted, which gave to the rich, warm, live, fertile nature that was in him multiplied points of steady exhibition, so that he lighted the town through them? Or, not to look so widely, I pity you if in the circle of your home there is not some warm and living nature which is your fire. Your cold, dark candle-nature, touched by that fire, burns bright and clear. Wherever you are carried, perhaps into regions where that nature cannot go, you carry its fire and set it up in some new place. No, the fire itself may have disappeared, the nature may have vanished from the earth and gone to heaven; and yet still your candle-life, which was lighted at it, keeps that fire still in the world, as the fire of the lightning lives in the tree that it has struck, long after the quick lightning itself has finished its short, hot life and died. So the man in the counting room is the candle of the woman who stays at home, making her soft influence felt in the rough places of trade where her feet never go. So a man who lives like an inspiration in the city for honesty, purity, and charity may be only the candle in whose obedient life burns still the fire of another strong, true man who was his father, and who passed out of men's sight a score of years ago. Men call the father dead, but he is no more dead than the torch has gone out which lighted the beacon that is blazing on the hill.

And now, regarding all this lighting of life from life, two things are evident, the same two which appeared in the story of the candle and its flame: First, there must be a correspondency of nature between the two; and second, there must be a cordial obedience of the less to the greater. The nature which cannot feel the other nature's warmth, even if it is held close to it; and the nature which refuses to be held where the other nature's flame can reach it—both of these must go unlighted, no matter how hotly the fire of the higher life may burn.

I think that we are ready now to turn to Solomon and read his words again and understand them. "The spirit of man is the candle of the Lord," he says. God is the fire of this world, its vital principle, a warm, pervading presence everywhere. What thing of outward nature can so picture to us the mysterious, the subtle, the quick, live, productive, and destructive thought, which has always lifted men's hearts and solemnized their faces when they have said the word "God," as this strange thing, so heavenly, so unearthly, so terrible, and yet so gracious; so full of creativeness, and yet so quick and fierce to sweep whatever opposes it out of its path—this marvel, this beauty, glory, and mystery of fire? Men have always felt the fitness of the figure; and the fire has always crowded, closest of all earthly elements, about the throne on which their conception of Deity was seated. And now of this fire the spirit of man is the candle. What does that mean? If, because man is of a nature which corresponds to the nature of God, and just so far as man is obedient to God, the life of God, which is spread throughout the universe, gathers itself into utterance; and men, aye, and all other things, if such beings there are, capable of watching our humanity, see what God is, in gazing at the man whom he has kindled, then is not the figure plain? It is a wondrous thought, but it is clear enough. Here is the universe, full of the diffused fire of divinity. Men feel it in the air, as they feel an intense heat which has not broken into a blaze. That is the meaning of a great deal of the unexplained, mysterious awfulness of life, of which they who are very much in its power are often only half aware. It is the sense of God, felt but unseen, like an atmosphere burdened with heat that does not burst out into fire. Now in the midst of this solemn, bur-dened world, there stands up a man, pure, God-like, and perfectly obedient to God. In an instant, it is as if the heated room had found some sensitive, inflammable point where it could kindle to a blaze. The vague oppressiveness of God's felt presence becomes clear and definite. The fitfulness of the impression of divinity is steadied into permanence. The mystery changes its character, and is a mystery of light, not of darkness. The fire of the Lord has found the candle of the Lord, and burns clear and steady, guiding and cheering instead of bewildering and frightening us, just so soon as a man who is obedi-ent to God has begun to catch and manifest his nature.

I hope that we shall find that this truth comes very close to our personal, separate lives; but, before we come to that, let me remind you first with what a central dignity it clothes the life of man in the great world. Certain philosophies, which belong to our time, would depreciate the importance of man in the world, and rob him of his centralness. Man's instinct and man's pride rebel against them, but he is puzzled by their speciousness. Is it indeed true, as it seems, that the world is made for man, and that from man, standing in the center, all things besides which the world contains get their true value and receive the verdict of their destiny? That was the old story that the Bible told. The Book of Genesis with its Garden of Eden and its obe-dient beasts waiting until the man should tell them what they should be called, struck firmly, at the beginning of the anthem of the world's history, the great note of the centralness of man. And the Garden of Eden, in this its first idea, repeats itself in every cabin of the western forests or the southern jungles, where a new Adam and a new Eve, a solitary settler and his wife, begin the human history anew. There once again the note of Genesis is struck, and man asserts his central-ness. The forest waits to catch the color of his life. The beasts hesitate in fear or anger till he shall tame them to his service or bid them depart. The earth under his feet holds its fertility at his command and answers the summons of his grain or flower seeds. The very sky over his head regards him, and what he does upon the earth is echoed in the changes of the climate and the haste or slowness of the storms. This is the great impression which all the simplest life of man is ever creating, and with which the philosophies, which would make little of the separateness and centralness of the life of man, must always have to fight. And this is the impression which is taken up, strengthened, made clear, and turned from a petty pride to a lofty dignity and a solemn responsibility, when there comes such a message as this of Solomon's. He says that the true separateness, superiority, and centralness of man is in that likeness of nature to God, and that capacity of spiritual obedience to him, in virtue of which man may be the declaration and manifestation of God to all the world. So long as that truth stands, the centralness of man is sure. "The spirit of man is the candle of the Lord."

This is the truth of which I wish to speak to you today, the perpetual revelation of God by human life. You must ask yourself first what God is. You must see how at the very bottom of his existence, as you conceive of it, lie these two thoughts-purpose and righteousness; how absolutely impossible it is to give God any personality except as the fulfillment of these two qualities the intelligence that plans in love, and the righteousness that lives in duty. Then ask yourself how any knowledge of these qualities, of what they are, of what kind of being they will make in their perfect combination, could exist upon the earth if there were not a human nature here in which they could be uttered, from which they could shine. Only a person can truly utter a person. Only from a character can a character be echoed. You might write it all over the skies that God was just, but it would not burn there. It would be, at best, only a bit of knowledge; never a gospel; never something which it would gladden the hearts of men to know. That comes only when a human life, capable of a justice like God's, made just by God, glows with his justice in the eyes of men, a candle of the Lord.

I have just intimated one thing which we need to observe. Man's utterance of God is purely an utterance of quality. It can tell me nothing of the quantities which make up his perfect life. That God is just, and what it is to be just—those things I can learn from the just lives of the just men about me; but how just God is, to what unconceived perfection, to what unexpected development of itself, that majestic quality of justice may extend in him—of that I can form no judgment that is worth anything, from the justice that I see in fellowman. This seems to me to widen at once the range of the truth which I am stating. If it be the quality of God which man is capable of uttering, then it must be the quality of manhood that is necessary for the utterance; the quality of manhood, but not any specific quantity, not any assignable degree of human greatness. Whoever has in him the human quality, whoever really has the spirit of man, may be a candle of the Lord. A larger measure of the spirit may make a brighter light; but there must be a light wherever any human being, in virtue of his humanness, by obedience becomes luminous with God. There are the men of lofty spiritual genius, the leaders of our race. How they stand out through history! How all men feel as they pass into their presence that they are passing into the light of God! They are puzzled when they try to explain it. There is nothing more instructive and suggestive than the bewilderment which men feel when they try to tell what inspiration is—how men become inspired. The lines which they draw through the continual communication between God and man are always becoming unsteady and confused. But in general, he who comes into the presence of any powerful nature, whose power is at all of a spiritual sort, feels sure that in some way he is coming into the presence of God. But it would be melancholy if only the great men could give us this conviction. The world would be darker than it is if every human spirit, so soon as it became obedient, did not become the Lord's candle. A poor, meager, starved, bruised life, if only it keeps the true human quality and does not become inhuman, and if it is obedient to God in its blind, dull, half-conscious way, becomes a light. Lives yet more dark than it is, become dimly aware of God through it. A mere child, in his pure humanity, and with his easy and instinctive turning of his life toward the God from whom he came—it is one of the commonplaces of your homes how often he may burn with some suggestion of divinity, and cast illumination upon problems and mysteries whose difficulty he himself has never felt. There are great lamps and little lamps burning everywhere. The world is bright with them. You shut your book in which you have been holding communion with one of the great souls of all time; and while you are standing in the light which he has shed about him, your child beside you says some simple, childlike thing, and a new thread of shining wisdom runs through the sweet and subtle thoughts that the great thinker gave you, as the light of a little taper sends its special needle of brightness through the pervasive splendor of a sunlit world. It is not strange. The fire is the same, whatever be the human lamp that gives it its expression. There is no life so humble that, if it be true and genuinely human and obedient to God, it may not hope to shed some of his light. There is no life so meager that the greatest and wisest of us can afford to despise it. We cannot know at all at what sudden moment it may flash forth with the life of God.

And in this truth of ours, we have certainly the key to another mystery which sometimes puzzles us. What shall we make of some man rich in attainments and in generous desires, well-educated, well-behaved, who has trained himself to be a light and help to other men, and who, now that his training is complete, stands in the midst of his fellowmen completely dark and helpless? There are plenty of such men. We have all known them who have seen how men grow up. Their brethren stand around them expecting light from them, but no light comes. They themselves are full of amazement at themselves. They built themselves for influence, but no one feels them. They kindled themselves to give light, but no one shines a grateful answer back to them. Perhaps they blame their fellowmen, who are too dull to see their radiance. Perhaps they only wonder what is the matter, and wait, with a hope that never quite dies out into despair, for the long-delayed recognition and gratitude. At last they die, and the men who stand about their graves feel that the saddest thing about their death is that the world is not perceptibly the darker for their dying. What does it mean? If we let the truth of Solomon's figure play upon it, is not the meaning of the familiar figure simply this: These men are unlighted candles; they are the spirit of man, elaborated, cultivated, finished to its very finest, but lacking the last touch of God. As dark as a row of silver lamps, all chased and wrought with wondrous skill, all filled with rarest oil, but all untouched with fire, so dark in this world is a long row of cultivated men, set up along the corridors of some age of history, around the halls of some wise university, or in the pulpits of some stately church, to whom there has come no fire of devotion, who stand in awe and reverence before no wisdom greater than their own, who are proud and selfish, who do not know what it is to obey. There is the explanation of your wonder when you cling close to some man whom the world calls bright, and find that you get no brightness from him. There is the explanation of yourself, oh puzzled man, who never can make out why the world does not turn to you for help. The poor, blind world cannot tell its need, analyze its instinct, nor say why it seeks one man and leaves another; but through its blind eyes, it knows when the fire of God has fallen on a human life. This is the meaning of the strange helpfulness which comes into a man when he truly is converted. It is not new truth that he knows, not new wonders that he can do, but it is that the unlighted nature, in the utter obedience and self-surrender of that great hour, has been lifted up and lighted at the life of God and now burns with him.

But it is not the worst thing in life for a man to be powerless or uninfluential. There are men enough for whom we would thank God if they did no harm, even if they did no good. I will not stop now to question whether there be such a thing possible as a life totally without influence of any kind, whether perhaps the men of whom I have been speaking do not also belong to the class of whom I want next to speak. However that may be, I am sure you will recognize the fact that there is a multitude of men whose lamps are certainly not dark, and yet who certainly are not the candles of the Lord. A nature furnished richly to the very brim, a man of knowledge, of wit, of skill, of thought, with the very graces of the body perfect, and yet profane, impure, worldly, and scattering skepticism of all good and truth about him wherever he may go. his is no unlighted candle. He burns so bright and lurid that often the purer lights grow dim in the glare. But if it be possible for the human candle, when it is all made, when the subtle components of a human nature are all mingled most carefully, if it be possible that then, instead of being lifted up to heaven and kindled at the pure being of him who is eternally and absolutely good, it should be plunged down into hell and lighted at the yellow flames that burn out of the dreadful brimstone of the pit, then we can understand the sight of a man who is rich in every brilliant human quality, cursing the world with the continual exhibition of the devilish instead of the godlike in his life. When the power of pure love appears as a capacity of brutal lust; when the holy ingenuity with which man may search the character of a fellowman, that he may help him to be his best, is turned into the unholy skill with which the bad man studies his victim, that he may know how to make his damnation most complete; when the almost divine magnetism which is given to a man in order that he may instill his faith and hope into some soul that trusts him, is used to breathe doubt and despair through all the substance of a friend's reliant soul; when wit, which ought to make truth beautiful, is deliberately prostituted to the service of a lie; when earnestness is degraded to be the slave of blasphemy, and the slave's reputation is made the cloak for the master's shame, in all these cases, and how frequent they are no man among us fails to know, you have simply the spirit of man kindled from below, not from above, the candle of the Lord burning with the fire of the devil. Still it will burn; still the native inflammableness of humanity will show itself. There will be light; there will be power; and men who want nothing but light and power will come to it. It is wonderful how mere power, or mere brightness, apart altogether from the work that the power is doing and the story that the brightness has to tell, will win the confidence and admiration of men from whom we might have expected better things. A bright book or a bright play will draw the crowd, although its meaning be detestable. A clever man will make a host of boys and men stand like charmed birds while he draws their principles quietly out of them and leaves them moral idiots. A whole great majority of a community will rush like foolish sheep to the polls and vote for a man whom they know is false and brutal, because they have learned to say that he is strong. All this is true enough; and yet while men do these wild and foolish things, they know the difference between the illumination of a human life that is kindled from above and that which is kindled from below. They know the pure flames of one and the lurid glare of the other; and however they may praise and follow wit and power, as if to be witty or powerful were an end sufficient in itself, they will always keep their sacredest respect and confidence for that poorer wit which is inspired by God, and works for righteousness.

There is still another way, more subtle and sometimes more dangerous than these, in which the spirit of man may fail of its completest function as the candle of the Lord. The lamp may be lighted, and the fire at which it is lighted may be indeed the fire of God, and yet it may not be God alone who shines forth upon the world. I can picture to myself a candle which should in some way mingle a peculiarity of its own substance with the light it shed, giving to that light a hue which did not belong essentially to the fire at which it was lighted. Men who saw it would see not only the brightness of the fire. They would see also the tone and color of the lamp. And so it is, I think, with the way in which some good men manifest God. They have really kindled their lives at him. It is his fire that burns in them. They are obedient, and so he can make them his points of exhibition; but they cannot get rid of themselves. They are mixed with the God they show. They show themselves as well as him. It is as when a mirror mingles its own shape with the reflections of the things that are reflected from it, and gives them curious convexity because it is itself convex. This is the secret of all pious bigotry, of all holy prejudice. It is the candle, putting its own color into the flame which it has borrowed from the fire of God. The violent man makes God seem violent. The speculative man makes God look like a beautiful dream. The legal man makes God look like a hard and steel-like law. Here is where all the harsh and narrow part of sectarianism comes from. The narrow Presbyterian or Methodist, or Episcopalian or Quaker, full of devoutness, really afire with God—what is he but a candle which is always giving the flame its color, and which, by a disposition which many men have to value the little parts of their life more than the greater, makes less of the essential brightness of the flame than of the special color which it lends to it? It seems, perhaps, as if in saying this, I threw some slight or doubt upon that individual and separate element in every man's religion, on which, upon the contrary, I place the very highest value. Every man who is a Christian must live a Christian life that is peculiarly his own. Every candle of the Lord must utter its peculiar light. Only the true individuality of faith is marked by these characteristics which rescue it from bigotry: first, it does not add something to the universal light, but only brings out most strongly some aspect of it which is specially its own. Second, it always cares more about the essential light than about the peculiar way in which it utters it. Third, it easily blends with other special utterances of the universal light, in cordial sympathy and recognition of the value which it finds in them. Let these characteristics be in every man's religion, and then the individuality of faith is an inestimable gain. Then the different candles of the Lord burn in long rows down his great palace halls of the world; and all together, each complementing all the rest, they light the whole vast space with him.

I have tried to depict some of the difficulties which beset the full exhibition in the world of this great truth of Solomon, that "the spirit of man is the candle of the Lord." Man is selfish, disobedient, and will not let his life burn at all. Man is willful, passionate, and kindles his life with ungodly fire. Man is narrow, bigoted, and makes the light of God shine with his own special color. But all these are accidents. All these are distortions of the true idea of man. How can we know that? Here is the perfect man, Christ Jesus! What a man he is! How nobly, beautifully, perfectly human! What hands, what feet, what an eye, what a heart! How genuinely, unmistakably a man! I bring the men of my experience or of my imagination into his presence, and behold, just when the worst or best of them falls short of him, my human consciousness assure me that they fall short also of the best idea of what it is to be a man. Here is the spirit of man in its perfection. And what then? Is it not also the candle of the Lord? "I am come a light into the world" (John 12:46) said Jesus. "He that hath seen me hath seen the Father" (John 14:9). "In him was life; and the life was the light of men" (John 1:4). So wrote the man of all men who knew him best. And in Him where are the difficulties that we saw? Where for one moment is the dimness of selfishness? Oh, it seems to me a wonderful thing that the supremely rich human nature of Jesus never for an instant, turned with self-indulgence in on its own richness, or was beguiled by that besetting danger of all opulent souls, the wish, in the deepest sense, just to enjoy himself. How fascinating that desire is. How it keeps many and many of the most abundant natures in the world from usefulness. Just to handle over and over their hidden treasures, and with a spiritual miserliness to think their thought for the pure joy of thinking, and turn emotion into the soft atmosphere of a life of gardened selfishness. Not one instant of that in Jesus. All the vast richness of his human nature only meant for him more power to utter God to man.

And yet how pure his rich life was. How it abhorred to burn with any fire that was not divine. Such abundant life, and yet such utter incapacity of any living but the holiest; such power of burning, and yet such utter incapacity of being kindled by any torch but God's; such fullness with such purity as was never seen besides upon the earth; and yet we know as we behold it that it is no monster, but only the type of what all men must be, although all men but him as yet have failed to be it.

Yet again there was intense personality in him without a moment's bigotry. A special life, a life that stands distinct and self-defined among all the lives of men, and yet a life making the universal God all the more universally manifest by its distinctness, appealing to all lives just in proportion to the intensity of the individuality that filled his own. Oh, think I need only bid you look at him, and you must see what it is to which our feeble lights are struggling. There is the true spiritual man who is the candle of the Lord, the light that lighteth every man.

It is distinctly a new idea of life, new to the standards of all our ordinary living, which this truth reveals. All our ordinary appeals to men to be up and doing and make themselves shining lights, fade away and become insignificant before this higher message which comes in the words of Solomon and in the life of Jesus. What does this higher message say? "You are a part of God! You have no place or meaning in this world but in relationship to him. The full relationship can only be realized by obedience. Be obedient to him, and you shall shine by his light, not your own. Then you cannot be dark, for he shall kindle you. Then you shall be as incapable of burning with false passion as you shall be quick to answer with the true. Then the devil may hold his torch to you, as he held it to the heart of Jesus in the desert, and your heart shall be as uninflammable as his. But as soon as God touches you, you shall burn with a light so truly your own that you shall reverence your own mysterious life, and yet so truly his that pride shall be impossible." What a philosophy of human life is that. "Oh, to be nothing, nothing!" cries the mystic singer in his revival hymn, desiring to lose himself in God. "No, not that: Oh, to be something, something," remonstrates the unmystical man, longing for work, ardent for personal life and character. Where is the meeting of the two? How shall self-surrender meet that high self-value without which no man can justify his living and honor himself in his humanity? Where can they meet but in this truth? Man must be something that he may be nothing. The something which he must be must consist in simple fitness to utter the divine life which is the only original power in the universe. And then man must be nothing that he may be something. He must submit himself in obedience to God, that so God may use him, in some way in which his special nature only could be used, to illuminate and help the world. Tell me, do not the two cries meet in that one aspiration of the Christian man to find his life by losing it in God, to be himself by being not his own but Christ's?

In certain lands, for certain holy ceremonies, they prepare the candles with most anxious care. The very bees which distill the wax are sacred. They range in gardens planted with sweet flowers for their use alone. The wax is gathered by consecrated hands; and then the shaping of the candles is a holy task, performed in holy places, to the sound of hymns, and in the atmosphere of prayers. All this is done because the candles are to burn in the most lofty ceremonies on most sacred days. With what care must the man be made whose spirit is to be the candle of the Lord! It is his spirit which God is to kindle with himself. Therefore, the spirit must be the precious part of him. The body must be valued only for the protection and the education which the soul may gain by it. And the power by which his spirit shall become a candle is obedience. Therefore, obedience must be the struggle and desire of his life; obedience, not hard and forced, but ready, loving, and spontaneous; the obedience of the child to the father, of the candle to the flame; the doing of duty not merely that the duty may be done, but that the soul in doing it may become capable of receiving and uttering God; the bearing of pain not merely because the pain must be borne, but that the bearing of it may make the soul able to burn with the divine fire which found it in the furnace; the repentance of sin and acceptance of forgiveness, not merely that the soul may be saved from the fire of hell, but that it may be touched with the fire of heaven and shine with the love of God as the stars, forever.

Above all the pictures of life—of what it means, of what may be made out of it—there stands out this picture of a human spirit burning with the light of the God whom it obeys, and showing him to other men. Oh, my young friends, the old men will tell you that the lower pictures of life and its purposes turn out to be cheats and mistakes. But this picture can never cheat the soul that tries to realize it. The man whose life is a struggle after such obedience, when at last his earthly task is over, may look forward from the borders of this life into the other and humbly say, as his history of the life that is ended, and his prayer for the life that is to come, the words that Jesus said: "I have glorified thee on the earth: . . . And now, O Father, glorify thou me with thine own self with the glory which I had with thee before the world was" (John 17:4–5).

Francis L. Patton: *The Letter and the Spirit*

Francis Landey Patton was born on January 22, 1843, at Warwick, Bermuda. He was educated at Knox College, Toronto, and Princeton Theological Seminary. He was ordained as a minister in the Presbyterian Church in 1865, and was pastor of churches in Nyack, New York, Brooklyn, and Chicago. From 1872 to 1881, he was the Cyrus H. McCormick professor in McCormick Theological Seminary and from 1874 to 1888, professor of the relations of philosophy and science to the Christian religion in Princeton Theological Seminary. From 1888 to 1902, he was president of Princeton University and from 1902 to 1913, president of Princeton Theological Seminary. In 1878, he was elected Moderator of the General Assembly of the Presbyterian Church in the United States of America. A great apologete, Dr. Patton is also unique and powerful as a preacher. He makes liberal use of scholastic terms and theological conceptions, but has been able to interest popular audiences in the great themes of philosophy and religion. He is a stalwart defender of the supernatural in the Christian revelation and an ardent proclaimer of the "bleeding Christ as the central fact of the Scriptures." As he leans on his pulpit, turning sharply to the right, his fine intellectual face lighted up with the glow of truth, and his voice in the midst of his climaxes piercing like a trumpet, Dr. Patton leaves an impression upon his hearers never to be forgotten.

The Letter and the Spirit

"For the letter killeth, but the spirit giveth life" (2 Cor. 3:6).

THERE *is no doubt,* I suppose, that when the apostle made use of this familiar antithesis he intended, in the first place, to distinguish between the Law and the gospel: between the written code, with its rigid requirements which can only awaken a sense of helplessness and only intensify the feeling of loss; and the indwelling, grace-bestowing, comfort-giving Spirit. But it can hardly be questioned that the words of this verse may be properly used in a wider sense, and that this wider sense is at least implicitly recognized by the apostle himself. I should only be illustrating the truth of the text understood in this broader sense, were I to insist upon a literalism of interpretation that would tolerate no application of it outside of the sphere within which it was originally employed. I think I can better serve the purpose I have in view today, and can better adapt my discourse to the circumstances of this time and place, by taking advantage of some of the more obvious contrasts which these words are so well fitted to suggest.

1. It is true that the word *pneuma* here has special reference to the Holy Spirit, but it also signifies the human spirit and with the word *gramma* as the other term of the antithesis, I think there is nothing violent or strained in making the suggested contrast between Language and Thought the first topic for consideration.

Thought and not the mode of its expression, mind and not the drapery in which it is enveloped, should be our first concern. It is fatal to elevating work to let energy terminate in the letter. The aim of the true scholar is to go behind the letter to the spirit. The bare suggestion of language as the means of communicating thought presents to us one of the most wonderful facts in life. It is the commonplace after all that is the most mysterious. Thought leaps the chasm of two separate personalities and excites no wonder. We lay bare the secrets of our inner lives to each other and then wonder at *actio in distans* and cavil at the possibility of divine communication. So easy is it to strain at the gnat and swallow the camel.

To think and speak; to have ideas and register them; to make ourselves plain; to find a common measure of thought among the many coins of speech; to converse with our contemporaries in the morning newspaper and hold fellowship with the dead in the books that keep their memories alive—this, if we only stopped to consider it, is the marvel of existence. A mystery, I grant, and one made no easier of solution by the suicidal philosopher who tries through pages of labored excogitation to reduce thought to mechanism and then sends his book with his compliments to the courteous reader, in the hope that he will think that the author is a thinker of uncommon intellect in thus demonstrating with such convincing logic, and such array of physiological testimony, that there is no thought and no thinker at all.

Thought and not the mode of its expression, mind and need no other. Language is thought's portrait, the print of thought's finger. It is easy to see, therefore, why the study of language, as distinguished from literature, should occupy a high place in the academic curriculum. It is of great moment to understand the forms of thought, to follow its curves and watch its subtleties and niceties of distinction as we are able to do after it has been hardened and colored in speech. You may learn a great deal of psychology from the Greek prepositions. The subjunctive mood will often prove a shorter road to the human mind than the psychometric experiments of Fechner and Wundt. We may, however, make too much of philology, and even though we had to be satisfied with less grammar, I would have more literature. Let us read Milton rather than read about him, and read him as we love to read him, rather than at the snail's pace indicated by Ruskin.

Translation is difficult work, as we have been so recently reminded by Mr. Pater and Mr. Lowell. To do it well requires that we should know the letter, but it requires also—what is more difficult to attain—that we should catch the spirit of the author, that we should see with his eyes and rethink his thoughts. It is a pretty conceit of Marion Crawford which leads him, in one of his later works, to represent his hero as taking advantage of the recent advances in electrical science—thereby removing the barriers that separate him from the unseen world—and holding face-to-face fellowship "with the immortals." This is exactly what a liberal education is intended to do. This is what it has done for you, if you have improved your opportunities here, unless our methods are deplorably bad. This is why we learn Latin and Greek and master the difficulties of vocabulary. I do not deny that it is of advantage to know the laws of phonetic change, and that there is intellectual training in the knowledge of word forms. But when classical training is useful only as dumbbells and parallel bars are useful, it is writing a commentary on my text. Master syntax for disciplinary cuds; and master it also, as Richard de Bury says, that we may thereby open royal roads into literature. But remember that the thought is more than the word; that at best the word is but a symbol, a suggestion of the thought, and rarely its equivalent. He who reads literally reads poorly. Even jurisprudence, the science that holds speech to strictest account, admits that there are times when we must not only judge what a man intends to say by what he says, but what he says by what he obviously meant to say. *Hæret in literâ, hæret in cortice.* There is too little classical study of the purely literary kind among us. We either know as specialists and know little else, or we know practically nothing. And it is probably hard to unite the functions of the general and the special scholar. Few men can expend energy on the letter sufficient to write the notes to Mayor's *Juvenal,* and then write an "advertisement" to the volume that quivers in every line with sympathetic interest in the questions of the day.

I say nothing regarding letters which is not true of science also. For the facts which the man of science handles are only the letters with which he is trying to spell out the thought embodied in them. He may amuse himself with the shapes of these letters, put them in bundles, and give them names, but so long as he is simply engaged with facts, he is employed in business no better than playing chess or solving puzzles. It is when he hits upon some key to nature's cipher; it is when he is using his facts in verification of hypothesis that stands for thought that he is doing work worthy of scientific fame. Otherwise, he is only a census taker in the kingdom of nature; a cataloguer in the library of truth, writing titles and reading the backs of books.

Let not the humanist, however, speak to disparage science, for if he is only using language as material for the exercise of his own thought, if the results of his labors are not the basis of generalizations that stand for thought, then he is simply collecting facts, gathering useless knowledge, and printing interminable masses of unreadable material. And indeed this, to a large extent, is the condition of things today. We are overspecializing; and the danger is that our scholars will become simply operatives under a great system of contract labor; full of opinions on subjects of which we have no knowledge, and full of knowledge on subjects that give no basis for opinion. We are overwhelmed with material and in danger of being submerged in the mass of facts which we cannot reduce to system. How often, as we see ambition spurred to new endeavor, are we reminded of these words of the text: The letter killeth; the spirit giveth life.

Ah, Science! You want fact. You proclaim the sovereignty of fact, the reign of law, the almightiness of induction, the empire of sense.

Your votaries have reduced history to science, philosophy to science, religion to science, and language to science; and when you have done all, what have you gained? A mass of unorganized material; a box of Chinese puzzles; a rubbish heap of monographs on Greek adverbs, Coptic manuscripts, Babylonian pottery, the Pythagorean theory of the universe, without order and without plan—or else there is a thought, an idea, a generalization behind it all. The destiny of it all is death and the dunghill, or else there is some informing, quickening idea to give it shape and comeliness. Do your best: the philosopher, the apostle of the idea, is needed to make these dry bones live.

Whose thought then lies behind this language of fact? Is it your subjective state that you have been imposing upon nature as the law of her operations when you have formulated the doctrine of gravitation? Is it your subjectivity that imposes a meaning upon Hamlet and Faust, no thanks to Shakespeare and Goethe? Will you split the difference between the two rival philosophers by an arbitrary decision to be objective in your recognition of the fact, and subjective in your explanation of the fact? Or will you see behind the letter the spirit, behind the fact the idea that gives meaning to the fact and makes you a sharer in the thought of God? I do not wonder that the man of science magnifies his office and feels proud of his high calling. Back of the barriers of speech, indeed, that melt away with our knowledge of a foreign tongue stand "the immortals," and we may converse with them to our heart's content. But back of the syllables of science and waiting only for the spirit of reverence for its enjoyment lies fellowship with God. The literary artist has recalcitrant material to deal with. With the author, thought is too volatile, and with the translator, language is too opaque. So that between the incapacity of the containing vessel and the chance of spilling in our attempts to decant it into another, we run the risk of losing some of the wine of genius. This is true of human thought; how much more true must it be of divine thought. We cannot give too much attention then to the very words in which our Bible is written, and the more fully we believe in its inspiration, the more anxious we shall be to have a correct text and a close translation. But we may have both and miss the spirit of Revelation. We may have a bald literalism of rendering that sacrifices good English to Greek idiom, and saves the letter at the expense of the spirit. We may load our memory with "various readings" and be so microscopic in our study of the text as to be unable to see the full contour of a divine idea. We may carry reverence for the Word to the extent of being undiscriminating worshippers of words, and by our unintelligent literalism miss the meaning that the words convey. When I find men treating metaphor as fact and reading poetry as they would construe an act of Congress, seeking a spiritual sense in every commonplace expression, missing the point of the parable of the prodigal son by asking who was the "elder brother" and invoking the joint assistance of chemistry and the book of Leviticus in the interpretation of the parable of the leaven, I feel that Matthew Arnold, with all his faults, at least deserves credit for reminding us that the Bible is to be treated as literature. But we must go further before we can be said to have passed beyond the letter in our study of Scripture. For though as literature, it may be read with due regard to the historical conditions under which it was produced, with proper attention to differences of style and form of composition, we have not read it as we should when we have mastered its geographical details, studied its archeology, learned to prize the beauties of Isaiah and Job, or appreciate the high moral level of the Sermon on the Mount. To regard the Bible simply as literature provokes in me a feeling akin to that which I have for the system once in vogue of making the Gospel of John an easy introduction to the study of Greek. We degrade the book by teaching it under false pretenses. We dishonor truth when we teach it with a *suppressio veri*. I am in full sympathy with the idea that the Bible—the English Bible if you like that way of describing it better—should have a place in the college curriculum, but I want it understood that it is to be taught with distinct regard to its divine authority and the great doctrines of redemption that it contains.

You have made but a poor use of your facilities here, my friends, if you are not able to make the distinction I have named. This indeed is no small part of education. We have tried to train you so as to bring you under the power of ideas. We have aimed to educate you so that you may become scholars and not pedants; jurists and not pettifoggers; men of science and not the bottle washers of a laboratory; theologians and not textualists; religious men who think again through God's word the thoughts of God, and not dealers in cant phrases or slaves of a stupid literalism.

2. The same antithesis with which we are dealing may serve also to stand for the contrast between the accidental and the essential in matters of literary judgment and of religious opinions. Print does not discriminate. Even punctuation is a modern device, and jurisprudence disdains it to this day. It gives no weight to the commas and semicolons with which we sprinkle our pages, sometimes in default of a clear style or a correct syntax. It allows no vulgar italics to lend artificial emphasis to what is written, but leaves the thought to make its way to the mind with no other presupposition than the intelligence of the reader. This is indeed often a large demand, but there seems to be as yet no sufficient substitute for brains; and to one normally furnished in this regard it is a self-evident proposition that though the printed word does not say so, all thoughts are not of equal value nor worthy of the same emphasis. No obligation rests upon us, for instance, to treat all the poet's verse as of equal beauty and force because he has not seen fit to show any favoritism to the children of his brain. It is not our fault that there are only three lines worth remembering in Wordsworth's "Peter Bell." All that is said is not

worth repeating. All human deeds are not worth recording. Worthless when new, they do not gain importance with the lapse of time. The phonograph that listens today and reproduces the nonsense of conversation a hundred years hence will amuse, but it will not edify. It occurs to me to say this when I consider the prevalent mania for original research. Just now it is affecting historians and men of letters. You may know history—you may have your Gibbon, your Hallam, and your Freeman at your fingers' ends, but you are no historian unless you have studied the sources. If, however, you have discovered a manuscript that will add a new chapter to the life of some tenth-rate Cavalier or Round- head, if you can come forth from your labors with the dust of an old library on your fingers, you have earned the title to fame. But why? Why discriminate thus against the man who knows much in favor of him who produces little? Do I deny that your work is good? By no means. That you have brought something new to light, and so have made a contribution to knowledge? No. Or that your work has given you good training in the use of tools? No. Nor would I deny that it is a useful thing for our young civil engineers to survey the college campus every year, or measure the Brooklyn Bridge. I am only thinking that you lack perspective; that you are mistaking pains, trouble, and a monopoly of useless information for history; that you are in danger of putting all facts upon the same level and of ranking the genealogy of a Mayflower family with the Norman Conquest. You are deceived by the letter and miss the spirit. You have adopted Gradgrind's philosophy. The demand is for fact, and so it comes to pass that in the examination paper Oklahoma counts for as much as Thermopylae, and the date of the last constitutional amendment is thought to have as good a right to a vacant memory cell as A.D. 1453 or 1688.

We read books and study the history of opinion often with the same disregard of proportion—remembering what we ought to forget and forgetting what we ought to remember, making no allowance for circumstances and giving the same value to *obiter dicta* that we accord to reasoned opinions. Find Calvin tripping in a casual remark, then vilify his system: this is what men do. Or because one calls himself a disciple of Augustine, hold him responsible for all that Augustine taught, as though one must believe the virtues of tar-water because he is a Berkleyan.

Uneducated men, perhaps, find it hard to make the distinctions between essence and accident here referred to. All statements appear to them like items on a ledger to be reckoned in the same way. But educated men ought to know better. They ought to know that a man can be a Lutheran without believing all that Luther believed, or accept the Hegelian conception of the universe without sympathizing in detail with Hegel's peculiar views. It ought not to be difficult to understand that a creed statement may be accurate in doctrinal content, though colored by the time in which it was written, and dealing with conditions of thought that no longer exist. And it must also be evident that it would be hard to avoid the appearance of anachronism if we undertook to weave the thoughts of this generation into a document that on its title page purports to have been written two hundred and fifty years ago. A little exercise of judgment, however, a little effort to distinguish between essence and accident, abiding fact and accidental setting, in short, to read the spirit in the letter would save all the trouble. We may as well learn to exercise this power of judgment on the creeds, for we shall have to exercise it on the Scriptures. All Scripture is inspired, but it does not all possess the same religious value. All Scripture is truth, but all Scriptural truth is not of equal importance. Essential to the organic structure of the Bible all of it undoubtedly is, but not equally essential to spiritual life and religious education. When men say they wish the Bible to be taught without doctrine, I reply that the doctrines of the Bible are more important than much of the Bible itself. The sense of Scripture is the Scripture, and rather than miss the sense, we could afford to do without certain forms of Bible knowledge. There is in the Bible as in other literature what may be called the essential and the accidental, and it is an act of intelligence to distinguish between them. I read the Cosmogony and get out of it the doctrine of creation, the ascent of life, the supremacy of man and his primeval purity. I am willing to fill up the great categories of Genesis with the help of science and so make the generalizations that follow the study of one of God's books help in the interpretation of the other. I read in the words of the Savior the generic ideas that should control social existence and the great principles that should guide conduct, but I do not suppose that the illustration of a principle should be construed with literal exactness. I do not expect to handle venomous reptiles with impunity. I do not expect faith to supersede medical treatment or cure organic disease; and I do not find either in the Sermon on the Mount or in the apostolic community of goods an argument for socialism and the denial of the rights of property. I believe that Paul was inculcating an important principle when he discouraged the appearance of Christians as litigants in heathen courts; but I would not on that account conclude that all litigation is sin, and that the legal profession is incompatible with Christianity. To be sure, the distinction between essence and accident involves serious responsibility, for in attempting to make it we may err. I am sure that Arnold erred and that his literary judgment was warped by his prejudices when he made ethics the main thing in Scripture and represented the dogmas of Christianity as the accidents of Pauline teaching. For what is the Bible? What is the evolution of biblical ideas but the growth of a few great, dogmatic conceptions? The essence of Scripture, the core of the Old Testament and the New, is the doctrine that without the shedding of blood there is no remission of sins, and that God was in

Christ reconciling the world unto himself, not imputing unto men their trespasses. It is the divine purpose that brings the Bible into line with the facts of the material world. It is the Incarnation that gives organic character to Scripture. It is human guilt that constitutes the great presupposition of Revelation. It is the doctrine of faith as man's response to the overtures of love that meets the exigencies of man's moral nature and makes the Bible the best and greatest message that man ever had. Why, then, do men tell me that they wish the Bible taught religiously but not doctrinally? Why do educated men who have been taught to distinguish between the letter and the spirit show such proneness to mistake when they touch religious themes? Yet the world is full of men who speak in this way. These are the men who stand in our pulpits and preach on the patience of Job and the moral courage of Daniel; who find material for sentimental sermons on the seasons, entertaining sermons on the social follies of the day, practical sermons on the importance of sleep, or the need of restricting immigration, but who are silent respecting the tremendous fact of sin and the dogmatic significance of atoning blood. I do not see that such men are handling the Word of God deceitfully, for I am willing to have them plead guilty if they prefer to an unscholarly stupidity that prevents them from seeing that the bleeding Christ is the central fact of Scripture. Let me beg you, gentlemen, to heed this lesson of the text. Cultivate a wise discrimination. Read the best books. Seize upon master thoughts. Get hold of the big end of the questions that invite your scrutiny. Distinguish between what is vital and what is of no importance. Garner the wheat; let the chaff go. Rest your opinions on broad and deep rational foundations. Follow this method in religion. A few principles, a few facts, carry the whole fabric of Christianity. Follow the great trend of evidence and do not halt for minor difficulties. Let the great outlying facts of Christianity determine your faith, and do not let trifles feed your doubt. You are sticking in the bark, you may be sure, when you let a textual difficulty, a historical discrepancy, a hard question in ethics, or a dogmatic mystery hinder your acceptance of the historic Christ as the Savior of the world.

3. I come now to the consideration of another distinction suggested by the text.

It is difficult to resist the feeling that there was in Paul's mind the contrast between the rigid fixity of the letter on the one hand and the plastic spontaneity of the spirit on the other. *Litera scripta manet.* The written word does not change. But the living organism is constantly adjusting itself to new conditions, and changing to suit them. We have then the fixed and the variable, unbending law and changing life. The history of the world, of society, of religious opinion, is to a large extent the history of these two factors in their relations to each other. The legal code becomes too narrow to suit the exigencies of an expanding life, and it changes in fact but not in form. The needed work is done, but the forms of law are saved by legal fiction. *Ubi jus ibi remedium*; but there is no remedy at common law, and equity finds one through the edict of the praetor or the decisions of the Chancellor. We have a written constitution as the basis of government, and the powers of the coordinate branches of government are defined. But time develops the old conflict between the unyielding law and the living organism, with the odds, as Professor Wilson shows, in favor of the organism. We formulate our faith in creed statements and after a century or two find that the church and the creed are not in exact accord. There is nothing to wonder at. It is the old question of the letter and the spirit. The letter has controlled the life. It has given the law to its variations. Political development in this land will follow the lines of the Constitution. Theological development will follow the lines of the creed that controls it. Unless the letter goes into the life of the organism, it will become a dead letter; and if it goes into it, it will be modified and colored by circumstances of time and place. Now this question of the fixed and the variable is a much larger one than that of creed revision. It is at the root of nearly all the great questions of today. Men are realizing as never before the solidarity of mankind. The old Pelagian conception of individualism is abandoned, and there is a tendency to go to the opposite extreme. Individual opinion is hushed in the presence of advancing waves and irresistible movements, as they are called, and we are warned against the folly of trying to stop the rising tide. In the case of very advanced thinkers, this worship of the *Zeitgeist* is associated with the denial of all *a priori* ideas. Standards of measurement there are none. The movement is recognized, but there is no criterion by which to judge it, and the ideas that limit it and give it shape are ignored. Men say one must study the facts in a historical spirit and gather our induction out of what we see. The science of ethics becomes the science of what is, rather than of what ought to be, and if a doctrine of right survives at all, it is the doctrine that whatever is, is right. In the name of reason, I protest against this tendency of thought. As a sovereign thinker within the realm of my own activities, I refuse to abdicate under the terrorism of popular sentiment. I refuse to say that because the avalanche is irresistible, therefore it is right. I refuse to drown my reason in a tidal wave. And when any idea in philosophy, politics, or theology is "in the air," I claim the right to examine its credentials and scrutinize its claims before I give it my acceptance. Historic movements, as well as the actions of individual men, must be judged by fixed principles. It is easy then for me to define my position in regard to what is called progressive theology. Will you tie the church to the letter or give her the free life of the spirit? How will you adjust the relations between the letter and the spirit; the church and the creed; the organism and the law of its development? According to Schleiermacher, the New Testament is only the recorded religious experience of the apostolic age, genetically related to the ages follow-ing, but giving no rubric and imposing no law. It follows, then, that there is no standard of faith, that truth is relative, and that the Christian organism is a law unto itself. The Roman Catholic, again, says that the organism is infallible and can speak in the present tense. It is not necessary, therefore, to believe that all divine revelation is con-tained in the Bible. Transubstantiation came by way of doctrinal evo-lution with the second council of Nice and papal infallibility within the present generation. The doctrine of evolution applied to theolo-gy by Cardinal Newman helps Rome to adjust the relation between the fixed and the variable. Protestants, however, have the written word as their only rule of faith. Changing taste cannot obliterate its doctrines. Organic drifts cannot vacate words of their historic sense. We cannot eliminate doctrines because we do not like them, or insert new ones because popular sentiment calls for them. What is written is written. The Christian consciousness can no more change the meaning of a Greek word than it can upset the multiplication table. There is no legal fiction that can modify or change the Word of God. When men say, as in effect they do, that the old conception of a Sovereign God does not suit our republican ideas, they only blas-pheme. And when by and by they will seek to dethrone him and plainly say that each generation must elect its own ruler and dictate his administrative policy, they will only carry to their logical conse-quences some of the prevalent ideas of today. I do not deny, howev-er, that important truth is hinted at in the doctrine known as the Christian Consciousness. I am no advocate of ecclesiastical immo-bility. The Christian church is not an exact copy in mode of worship, methods of administration, and form of government of the church of the New Testament. We have discontinued the holy kiss, and feet washing is no part of Christian hospitality. We have salaried minis-ters and surpliced choirs, neither being known to the apostolic church. We have tried to foster the apostolic spirit and perpetuate apostolic ideas, but the church has altered her mode of life and work to suit altered conditions of society. Paul said that under certain circumstances, he would refuse the meat offered in sacrifice to idols, and would not drink wine that had any idolatrous associations. Interpret him literally, and his words have no application to modern life, for the conditions that controlled his decision no longer exist. Change his decision into a mandate of abstinence, and at once you tyrannize over the conscience and rob the act of abstinence of all ethical significance. Generalize the statement, however, and you have the great law of altruistic morality which, after all abatements for selfishness have been made, is the most potent factor in our practical lives. And so with doctrine. The dogmas of Christianity are fixed. The Bible does not change, and we have no extra-biblical revelation. But a dogma that is only read in the Bible or stated and subscribed to in a creed is only a dead letter. It must go into our lives and be part of our intellectual and moral experiences. But going into our individual and our organic lives, it adjusts itself to changing conditions, although unchanged itself. It will be read with a different emphasis in different periods; it will be interpreted in the light of the burning questions of those periods; it will be brought into relation with science and philosophy and acquire fresh interest from generation to generation from the new polemic conditions that are constantly emerging. Paul's vocabulary was affected by his contact with philosophy. Ours will be. The attempt to eliminate philosophy from theology is a vain attempt. The two departments deal largely with the same subjects and cover common ground. All the material, whatever be its source, whatever be its authority, that goes to make our theory of the universe, must pass into old life and bear the impress of our thought; and as we think in philosophy so we shall be compelled to think in theology. We handle the same questions regarding God, freedom,

and immortality that Paul did, that Augustine did, that Thomas
Aquinas did, that Calvin did, and though the Scriptures have not
changed, and our reading of them, so far as these topics are concerned, is not materially different from that of the men that have
been named, we see the same truth under different conditions. Our
heretics are not Cerinthus and Celsus, but Spencer and Kuenen. Our
foe is not credulity, but agnosticism. And as conditions change, our
mode of presenting the unchangeable truth must also change.
Remember, however, that if the letter without the life is dead, the life
needs the letter to give law to its movement. Do not be deceived by
the cry that the voice of the people is the voice of God. Do not hastily assume that every great movement is an inspired movement. We
have no personal infallibility. We believe in no corporate infallibility.
We have no faith in the inspiration of large masses of men. When,
therefore, under the influence of those who would have us put our
faith in the organism rather than tie it to the written word, and we
begin to lose faith in the authority of Scripture, we give up our only
basis of Christian certitude.

4. The letter killeth, the spirit giveth life. Outward rule and inward
principle are the two great agencies that operate on human conduct
and they seem contrasted in the text. There is the inner principle in
bent of inclination and dominant purpose seeking expression in our
spontaneities; and here is the objective code by which we seek to
guide our lives and which is put before us as an instructive and
restraining influence. The world, says Mr. Lecky, is governed by its
ideals. It is what we love to do that we do well. By help of rule alone,
men write no books and paint no pictures that wear the stamp of
genius. They perform no acts of heroism in grudging compliance
with law; they shine in none of the beauties of high and holy character when they have simply schooled themselves to follow another's
will. Work done in conformity with rule is drudgery and a weariness

of the flesh. There is the morality of principle and the morality of outward conformity. That there is a place for the morality of externalism and precept, of law and obedience to command, I do not doubt, yet I sometimes think that life is made more burdensome than it need be, and that we hinder rather than help the higher interests of morality by the excessive multiplication of rules. The state goes as far as it ought in encroaching upon the freedom of the individual, the church is taking liberties with the rights of conscience in saying that its members shall do this and shall not do that. We go to college, and a code of instructions is the first lesson we are required to learn. We enter business, and we find ourselves girt about by rule. We are more unwilling every day to assume that men will act right from principle and more disposed to think that they love to do wrong. Wholesale suspicion is the law of society. We are multiplying the machinery of detection. We cry, "Who will keep the keepers?" We are insuring ourselves at increasing cost against the dishonesty of those whom we have trusted. We watch the clerk at his desk, and the student in his examination. We put a bellpunch in the hands of the conductor and set traps for the night watchman. In forms more or less visible and in ways more or less irritating to the feelings, we proclaim our inability to trust men and our conviction that all men are liars. Necessary all this may be for protection, though I still believe that we owe more to conscience than to all our complicated machinery of police. But the trouble is that men suppose that all this is moral education. There is an impression that you make men moral when you make them fear to do wrong and that by repressing wrongdoing you are elevating character. Make wrongdoing so difficult that right-doing will be easier, and it is thought you will make men moral. And undoubtedly a great deal of the world's morality is of this sort. A man obeys the law because he fears the penalty. He will lose his place, incur the odium of society, be visited with social ostracism, or miss his diploma, and therefore he will do as he is told. And there are good men who fail to see that there is no morality in this. Not only do they fail to see it, but the opinion seems to be gaining ground that we can build up character by this system of externalisms. Men not only obey laws imposed by society for its own protection, but they take pledges, make promises, multiply vows for their own edification, and in place of the freedom of the spirit, they are going back to the legalism of an older dispensation, are rejoicing in the bondage of the letter. They should know, however, that enforced obedience is not moral education. Character is an endogenous plant and grows from within. Military training teaches men to obey law, but it does not teach them to love it. Deserters are shot, so the soldier does not desert. That is all. Kant is right. The law that comes from without is not ethical. There is no morality in doing right through calculation of consequences. Hence only self-legislated law is moral. Though it be God's law, it must be autonomous before it is ethical. It must address the conscience and be approved as good. It must become a maxim of reason and not a mere comment. "For the letter killeth, but the Spirit giveth life" (2 Cor. 3:6). The state, of course, must protect itself, and its main end is therefore not moral education. This must be left to the church. But what is to be our aim in the administration of a college? Shall we consider the good order of the organization, or the moral improvement of the student? It might be easy to do either; it may be hard to combine the two; but we must combine them. There must be rules, but they should be few, and the application of them should address the conscience. We must prepare men for the franchises which they are so soon to inherit by respecting their manhood and avoiding all petty legislation. We must protect the organism and at the same time labor for the good of the individual. We must hold law subservient to the end for which it is enacted and bend the rule if it be necessary in order to save the man. We must consider, it is true, the welfare of the mass, but we must sometimes, if need be, leave the ninety-nine, and care for the one who has gone astray.

The college student is ingenuous, as a rule. He makes mistakes and falls into mischief or sin. But the case is rare when you do not find something in him that draws you to him. He is frank. He will admit that he has abused kindness, trifled with good natur,e and acted meanly. He is sorry that he did so, and his climax of regret is generally the thought of his mother's anguish and his father's sorrow. I have a large place in my heart for the man who is capable of this filial love. But, my brother, you must stand on higher ground than this. You are going out to face the temptations of the world. You will be confronted with the lust of the flesh, the lust of the eye, and the pride of life. It is not enough that you recognize the authority of the outward law. You should make it an inner principle. It is not enough that wrong conduct be avoided because it is dishonorable and will bring disgrace. Learn to avoid it because it is wrong. Learn to do right because it is right. Learn to feel the sanctions of a higher morality and when your evil-doing fills you with regret, let it be because you have sinned against God and put a stain upon your soul.

5. And now, gentlemen of the graduating class, let me say a single closing word. This week marks an important era in the calendar of your lives. It means the severance of old ties; the full assumption of personal responsibility, and the facing of the future. We have tried hard to fit you for the work of life. We have not done what we might have done, partly perhaps through our neglect, partly also through your neglect. But to some extent in all of you, I trust, and to a large extent in most of you, I know, our aim has been realized. In sending you out into the world we are making a contribution to its working force of which we have no reason to be ashamed. We have tried to make the education we have given you a commentary upon the words that I have chosen for my text. We have tried to foster in you

high ideals in literature and high aims in science. We have tried to discipline your powers so that you will see the parts of truth in their proper relations to each other and in just proportion. We have tried to show that the unchanging word of God is not a fossil to be laid upon the shelf, but the directing principle of the life, the inspiration of its movement, and the law of its variation. We have tried to teach you also that the essence of all morality is a self-enunciated law of obligation, commanding without condition and despising calculation. And we have not forgotten in the services of this sanctuary that the contrast between the letter and the spirit bears witness also to another contrast between Law and gospel, to which reference was made in the beginning of this discourse. The apostle did not mean to disparage the Law when he contrasted it with the gospel. The gospel did not supersede the Law, it only supplemented it. The Law is holy, just and good. It came from God and is the expression of his will. It is perfect but unrelenting. It tells us what we ought to do. It sets before us an ideal that excites our admiration and provokes despair. You accept it as just, but you cannot comply with it. You resolve and fail. You promise and break your vow. You make an effort and fall short. But the Law accepts no excuse and makes no allowance. There is no pity in its tones. It meets your contrition with no encouraging word. Its face is rigid and its voice is hard. Your passing grade, it tells you, is a hundred, and you have failed. That is all it has to say. It measures; it does not pity. It tabulates results; it does not forgive. The Law is the embodiment of God's will, but there is also another embodiment of that will. And when conscious of your failure you go to Jesus and say, "Oh, Master, I know I ought to have done better, and I feel ashamed," then will come a look of such exquisite tenderness upon his face that will say before the words are spoken: "Thy sins are forgiven thee; go in peace." When after fruitless endeavor to learn the lessons of life and do its work, we go to him and say: "Oh, Divine Teacher, I want to learn, but I am very slow, and my poor powers are not equal to this high task," he will say to you again, "Have patience, child, and I will teach thee. I will put my Spirit within thee. I will perfect my strength in thy weakness." The Law came by Moses, but grace and truth came by Jesus Christ. Have fellowship with Christ. Walk with him. Turn ever to him for comfort, for strength, for guidance. Serve him while you live, and by and by you shall be like him, and you shall see him as he is.

George Campbell Morgan:
The Power of the Gospel

GEORGE CAMPBELL MORGAN WAS BORN at Tetbury, England, December 9, 1863. He was ordained to the ministry of the Congregational Church in 1889, and after various pastorates in England, became minister of Westminster Chapel, London, where he preached until 1917. From 1917 to 1929, he was engaged in conference preaching and special services in Great Britain and the United States. From 1929 until 1932, he was pastor at the Tabernacle Presbyterian Church in Philadelphia. Upon returning to London in 1933, he became pastor for a second term at Westminster Chapel, where he was joined by D. Martyn Lloyd-Jones in 1938. He continued at Westminster Chapel until his death in 1945. Dr. Morgan is the author of over sixty books, the best known of which is *The Crises of the Christ*. He was one of the best-known preachers of the English speaking world and commanded large congregations wherever he preached. His homiletic method was expository rather than topical, and he takes high rank as an expository preacher. Tall in stature and unique in manner and method, Dr. Morgan was one of the marked personalities of the contemporary pulpit.

The Power of the Gospel

"For I am not ashamed of the gospel of Christ: for it is the power of God unto salvation to every one that believeth; to the Jew first, and also to the Greek. For therein is the righteousness of God revealed from faith to faith: as it is written, The just shall live by faith" (Romans 1:16–17).

 HEN *Paul wrote this letter,* he had never visited Rome. He earnestly desired to do so and expected that his desire would be fulfilled. That desire was created by the fact of his Roman citizenship, and by his interest in the Christian Church in Rome; and especially because he desired that the church in that city should be an instrument for the evangelization of the Western world. Writing thus to the saints in the Imperial City, he declared that he was not ashamed of the gospel, and he gave his reasons.

The statement that he was not ashamed is in itself interesting. It is the only occasion on which we find Paul even suggesting the possibility of being ashamed of the gospel. I am perfectly well aware that this is a declaration that he was *not* ashamed; but why make the declaration? I think there can be but one answer, and it is suggested by the words immediately preceding the text: "So, as much as in me is, I am ready to preach the gospel to you that are in Rome also" (Rom. 1:15). The declaration that he was not ashamed of the gospel, with its implication of the possibility of being ashamed, was the result of his consciousness of Rome, of its imperial dignity, of its material magnificence, of its proud contempt for all aliens, of the vastness of its multitudes, of the profundity of its corruption. There was no question in his mind as to the power of his gospel, and yet we detect the undertone of inquiry as he wrote: "I am ready to preach the gospel to you that are in Rome also. For I am not ashamed of the gospel."

It is always easier to preach in a village than in a city, to the sweet, simple people of the countryside than to the satisfied metropolitans. It is not really so, but the feeling that it is so invariably assails the soul of the prophet of God. In answer to that consciousness of his soul, or perhaps in answer to his feeling that such a consciousness might exist in the minds of the Roman Christians, Paul affirmed his readiness to preach the gospel in Rome also, declaring that he was not ashamed of it, and giving as his reason that this gospel was "the power of God unto salvation." The only justification of a gospel is that it is powerful. A message that proclaims the need for and the possibility of spiritual and moral renewal must be tested by the results it produces. A word devoid of power is no word of the Lord. A gospel that fails to produce the results it announces as necessary and as possible is no gospel. Is our gospel the power of God?

Let me at once say that the particular burden of my message this evening has come to me as the result of a long letter which I now hold in my hand, four closely written pages which I am not going to read to you in full, but which I have read again and again for my own soul's profit and examination as a preacher of the gospel, and from which I propose to read a few sentences. The letter was written September 23, and referred to meetings which had been held in preparation for the winter's work:

"You were saying on Tuesday evening that men were everywhere inquiring after reality, and I quite agree. We often hear about the dynamic of Christianity. There are youths and young men—I speak only of those about whose temptations I know something—who have to face temptations, and even this week have cried to the Lord Jesus for help and have tried the best they knew how to overcome, yet have failed. When a young man comes to me and asks where he can get the power to overcome, what am I to say? One did remark to me, 'Is it not a lack in our religion that it supplies no real power to overcome such-and-such temptations, temptations that cannot be avoided, and that have to be faced?' Men don't want a merely theoretic idea or ideas about the dynamic of Christianity. They want to realize how they can practically appropriate that dynamic. Careful Christian workers want to know how far, and in what way, they may safely encourage those spiritually sick and blind to hope for spiritual help after they have believed for the forgiveness of their sins. Experience shows it must not be a matter of mere inference, for inference would be likely to promise more than what seems to be generally realized. To hold out hopes that experience must disappoint is disastrous. Yes, it is reality men are longing for."

I believe that letter expresses the inquiry and the feeling of many souls. I think that my friend has fastened upon a word that he knows I am peculiarly fond of, the word *dynamic*. I plead guilty; I love the word, and I use it a great deal, and I do so because it is a New Testament word. It is the very word of my text, The gospel is the power (*dunamis*) of God unto salvation. The letter of my friend is practically a challenge of the declaration of my text. The text says that "The gospel is the power of God unto salvation." My friend suggests that there are men who have heard the call of Jesus, who have been obedient to it, and yet have not experienced that power. I am not going to argue the points of the letter, but rather to consider the statement of Paul, hoping and believing that in that consideration and in an attempt to understand the meaning of the great apostle at this point, there may be help for honest souls whose difficulty is voiced by the writer of the letter.

Let me, however, say to the writer of the letter, and to all such, that I agree that there is nothing more important today than that the Christian preacher and teacher should be real in the use of terms. But all who are making that demand must recognize the extreme difficulty of reality in terminology when dealing with spiritual forces that can never be perfectly apprehended. Whenever we have to deal with great forces, we find ourselves in a similar difficulty. I am not an electrician, but I suggest a question as to whether the phrase, "to develop electricity," is an accurate phrase. I do not say that it is not, but I ask, Can you *develop* electricity? Is it not, after all, a word that we hazard until we come to fuller knowledge? Is there any man in this house, in London, or in the world, who is prepared to tell us the last thing about electricity, not only as to what can be done by it, but also as to what it is? The moment we get into the realm of great forces which are intangible, imponderable, demonstrated by what they do, we are at least in danger of seeming to be unreal in our terms. We are dealing now with the most wonderful of all forces. At the close of our meditation, undoubtedly there will be a sense in which some of the terms made use of seem to lack reality. It is not that the force dealt with is unreal, but that it is so beyond our final explanation that terms cannot be discovered which cover the facts of the case, while excluding everything that should be excluded.

Confining ourselves now to the words selected, let us consider: first, the affirmation, "The gospel . . . is the power of God unto salvation;" secondly, the condition upon which the power is appropriated, "to every one that believeth;" and finally, the exposition of the operation which the apostle added, "for therein is the righteousness of God revealed from faith to faith."

First, then, as to the affirmation. Here many sentences are not necessary. The apostle declares that "the gospel . . . is the power of God unto salvation to every one that believeth." The power; that is something which produces results, something which is more than a theory, something which is mightier than a law, an actual, spiritual force producing spiritual results, an actual power accomplishing things. What it is in itself may be a mystery; how it does its work may not be known; but the apostle declares that it accomplishes certain things, and we may know that the gospel is more than a theory, more than a law, that it is a power, by the results that it produces. He, moreover, makes the superlative declaration that it is "the power of God." This is the superlative way of declaring its sufficiency for the doing of certain things. In quality it is irresistible, in quantity it is inexhaustible. Yet, further, he declares that it is "the power of God unto salvation." This at once defines and limits the power of the gospel. The gospel is the power that operates to this end alone. The gospel is the power which operates to this end perfectly.

The word *salvation* immediately suggests the inquiry as to the danger that is referred to, for to know the danger is to know the scope of the salvation. Here, briefly to summarize, the danger is twofold: pollution of the nature and paralysis of the will. Men in the presence of temptation find their nature is so weakened that they yield; and their will is so paralyzed that even when they have willed not to yield, they still yield. That is the whole story of the danger. The apostle declares that the gospel is "the power of God unto salvation;" that is, for the cleansing of the nature from its pollution, and for the enabling of the will, so that henceforth a man shall not only will to do right, but shall do it.

It is perfectly clear, however, that the gospel only operates in human lives upon the fulfillment of conditions. The gospel is not the power of God to every man. "The gospel . . . is the power of God to every one that believeth." The apostle here recognized the human possibility; that is, a possibility common to all human nature, irrespective of race or privilege. "To the Jew first; and also to the Greek" and to the Greek, nonetheless and none the later. The conditions can be fulfilled by men as men, apart from the question of race, privilege, or temperament. The gospel can be believed by the metropolitan or the provincial, the dweller in Rome as surely as the dwellers in the hamlets through which he had passed, the learned or the illiterate. Belief is the capacity and possibility of human life everywhere.

What, then, is this capacity? We must interpret the use of the word *believe* here, by its constant and consistent use in the revelation of the New Testament. There must be conviction before there can be belief. Belief is always founded upon reason. How can they believe who have not heard? The conviction is not necessarily that of the truth of the claim; it is not necessarily conviction that the gospel will work. There can be faith before I am sure that this gospel is going to work. Indeed, thousands of people have a profound conviction that the gospel will work, who yet have never believed. The conviction necessary is that in view of the need experienced, and of the claim which the gospel makes, it ought to be put to the test. Jesus said to his critics upon one occasion, "If any man will do his will, he shall know of the doctrine, whether it be of God" (John 7:17). Surely that was a perfectly fair test. He that puts the gospel to the test of obeying it shall find out whether its claim of power be accurate. When a man is convinced, that in the presence of his need and of the claim which the gospel makes, he ought to put it to the test, he has come to the true attitude of mind in which it is possible for him to exercise faith. Faith, then, is volitional. That is the central responsibility of the soul. Faith is not a feeling that comes stealing across the soul. Faith is not an inclination toward the Lord Jesus Christ. Faith is not an intellectual conviction that this thing is so. Faith is that volitional act which decides in the presence of the great need, and in the presence of the great claim, to put that claim to the test by obedience thereto. Conduct is the resulting expression; conduct which is conformity to the claims made by the gospel, immediately and progressively. Whatever the proclamation of the gospel shall say to the soul, the soul is to put the gospel to the test by obeying. Invariably in the actual coming of a soul to Christ under conviction of sin, everything is focused at some one point; and when that is obeyed there will be other calls made upon the soul by this gospel, which is one of purity

and righteousness as well as of mercy and of love. Faith is that volitional act which puts the gospel to the test by obedience to its claims.
That is the condition of appropriation.

The whole situation is illuminated for the inquiring soul by the
explanatory word: "For therein is the righteousness of God revealed
from faith to faith." That is the exposition of what he has already
written concerning the gospel, both as to the nature of the power that
is resident within it, and as to the law by which that power is appropriated in individual lives. The declaration that in the gospel there is
a revelation of the righteousness of God does not mean that the
gospel has revealed the fact that God is righteous. That revelation
antedated the gospel; it was found in the Law; it was found in human
history; it was found everywhere in the human heart. Out of that
knowledge comes the agony of soul that seeks after a gospel. The
declaration clearly means that the Gospel reveals the fact that God
places righteousness at the disposal of men who in themselves are
unrighteous; that he makes it possible for the unrighteous man to
become a righteous man. That is the exposition of salvation.
Salvation is righteousness made possible. If you tell me that salvation
is deliverance from hell, I tell you that you have an utterly inadequate
understanding of what salvation is. If you tell me that salvation is forgiveness of sins, I shall affirm that you have a very partial understanding of what salvation is. Unless there be more in salvation than
deliverance from penalty and forgiveness of transgressions committed, then I solemnly say that salvation cannot satisfy my own heart
and conscience. That is the meaning of the letter I received: mere forgiveness of sins and deliverance from some penalty cannot satisfy
the profoundest in human consciousness. Deep down in the common
human consciousness there is a wonderful response to that which is
of God. Man may not obey it, but there in the deeps of human consciousness there is a response to righteousness, an admission of its

call, its beauty, its necessity. Salvation, then, is the making possible of that righteousness. Salvation is the power to do right. However enfeebled the will may be, however polluted the nature, the gospel comes bringing to men the message of power enabling them to do right. In the gospel there is revealed a righteousness of God; and as the apostle argues and makes quite plain as he goes on with his great letter, it is a righteousness which is placed at the disposal of the unrighteous man so that the unrighteous man may become righteous in heart, thought, will, and deed. Unless that be the gospel, there is no gospel. Paul affirms that was the gospel which he was going to Rome to preach.

Then we come to a phrase which is full of light. He tells us that this righteousness therein revealed, revealed in the gospel, is "from faith to faith;" and in that phrase he tells us exactly how men receive this power. He has already told us that it is to everyone that believes, then he gives us an exposition of that phrase. As he has given us an exposition of "salvation" as the revelation of righteousness of God at the disposal of men, so now he gives us an exposition of the phrase "every one that believeth" in the phrase "from faith to faith."

The phrase is at once simple and difficult. There can be no question as to its structure. Taking the phrase as it stands, and looking at it grammatically as apart from its context, it is evident that the second "faith" is resultant faith. The faith secondly referred to grows out of the faith first referred to. "From faith to faith." It is an almost surprising thing how successfully almost all expositors have hurriedly passed over this phrase. What did the apostle mean? Did he mean that is an initial faith on the part of man, which results in a yet firmer faith? That is possible; but there is another explanation. I believe the apostle meant that in the gospel, there is revealed a righteousness which is at the disposal of sinning men, by the faith of God unto the faith of man. The faith of God produces faith in man. The faith of

God. Ought such a phrase to be used of him? Verily, if faith be certainty, confidence, and activity based upon confidence. The faith of God is faith in himself, in his Son, and in man. Upon the basis of God's faith in himself, and upon the basis of his faith in his Son, and upon the basis of his faith in man, he places through his Son a righteousness at the disposal of man in spite of his sin. That faith of God becomes, when once it is apprehended, the inspiration of an answering faith in man. Inspired by God's faith, I trust him. I act in consonance with the faith that he has demonstrated in human history, by the sending of his Son, and by all the provision of infinite grace.

I take my way back from this epistle and observe once more the Lord Jesus as he revealed God to me; and that is what he always did in dealing with sinning souls. He always reposed confidence in them, in order to inspire their confidence in himself. "If thou can do anything," said one man to him; If thou can! "All things are possible to him that believeth" (Mark 9:23), was his answer. That was the Lord's declaration of his confidence in the possibility of the man who was face to face with the sense of his own appalling weakness. There are many yet more remarkable and outstanding illustrations in the New Testament. He ever dealt with men upon the basis of his confidence in them; in their possibility in spite of failure; always on condition that they would repose an answering confidence in himself. A supreme illustration of this was afforded in the upper room on that last night when he was dealing with the disciples in the sight of his approaching departure. Mark most carefully his conversation with Peter. Peter, demanding to understand him, in agony in the presence of the gathering clouds, said: "Lord, whither goest thou? Jesus answered him, Whither I go, thou canst not follow me now; but thou shalt follow me afterwards. Peter said unto him, Lord, why cannot I follow thee now? I will lay down my life for thy sake. Jesus answered him, . . . I say unto thee, The cock shall not crow, till thou hast denied me thrice. Let not your heart be troubled: ye believe in God, believe also in me. . . . I go to prepare a place for you. And if I go, . . . I will come again, and receive you unto myself" (John 13:36–14:3). Take out of that conversation its central value. It is that of Christ's confidence. He said to Peter in effect: "I know the worst that is in you, the forces that you have not yet discovered that will make you within four-and-twenty hours a denier, cursing and swearing; I know the worst; but if you will trust me, I will realize the best in you. I know the best in you. I have perfect confidence in you, providing you will have confidence in me."

Let me make a superlative declaration. Whatever we think about humanity, Christ thought it worth dying for! He believed in it, in spite of its sin, in spite of its unutterable failure. In all these Bible stories, when he confronted sinning souls, he believed in them. He knew their incapacity. He knew that of themselves they could do nothing; but he also knew that in them was the very stuff out of which he could make saints who should flash and shine in light forever. In spite of the spoiling of sin, there was that in them with which he could deal. If I may borrow an awkward word from the old theologians, God believes in the salvability of all men. God puts righteousness at the disposal of man by faith in himself, in his Son, and in the man at whose disposal he places it. If that once be seen, men respond to that faith of God, by faith in him.

Let us come away from the realm of argument, into the realm of experience. All true Christian workers, men and women who know what it is really to get into close touch with sinning souls, and into grip with the spiritual life of men, have learned that the way to lift men back out of the Slough of Despond is to let them see that they believe in them. The way to lift any woman back again out of the degradation into which she has come is to show her you know she is capable of the higher and the nobler in the power of the gospel of Jesus Christ. "From faith to faith." By faith a righteousness of God is revealed in the gospel.

By the confidence which God reposes in himself, and the confidence he has in the possibility of every human life, he has placed righteousness at man's disposal through Christ. No man will ever avail himself of that except by faith. No man can appropriate the great provision, save as he responds in faith to faith. As this faith of God in man is answered by the faith of man in God, then contact is made between the dynamic that is resident within himself, and placed at the disposal of men by the mystery of his passion, and the weakness and incapacity of the human soul.

Such was the gospel of which Paul was not ashamed. Such is the gospel. The accuracy of the theory can only be demonstrated by results. That is the whole theme. I am here this evening to affirm once more, and I do it no longer as theory, I do it as an experience, I speak from this moment not merely as advocate, but as witness, as I declare that "the gospel . . . is the power of God unto salvation." However hard and severe the affirmation may seem at the moment, I am nevertheless constrained and compelled to affirm that if the gospel does not work, the failure is in the man, and not in the gospel. If that be not true, the whole Christian history is a lie. If that be true, then all the thousands and tens of thousands of human beings who for two millennia have declared that the gospel has wrought in them, have been woefully deceived, or have been most mysteriously perpetrating fraud throughout the centuries and millennia. If it does not work, then that man who says that he has been delivered from besetting sin is a liar, and he is sinning in secret. Either this declaration is true, or the gospel is an awful deception, enabling men to hide secret sin. I pray you think again. If you have imagined that there is no dynamic in the gospel, think again, examine your own life again, and find out whether or not you have fallen into line with the claims of the gospel and fulfilled its conditions. I assert that it is not enough that man shall hate his sin and cry out for help; he must put himself into line with the power that operates; he must fulfill the conditions laid down. It is not enough to submit to the Lord; a man must also resist the devil. It is not enough to resist the devil; a man must also submit to the Lord. There are men who submit and cry for help, but they put up no fight against temptations. They will never appropriate the power. There are men who put up a strenuous fight against these temptations, but they never submit, never pray, never seek help. They will never find deliverance. "The gospel . . . is the power of God unto salvation to every one that believeth." The gospel is that wherein the fact is revealed that righteousness as a power is at the disposal of sinning men by God's faith in that man, inspiring man's faith in God. If man would discover the power of this gospel, they will do so as they submit to its claim immediately and thoroughly.

If this were the time and place, which it is not, I could call witnesses. They are in this house; men who have known these very temptations delicately referred to in this letter, subtle, insidious temptations; but who also know that the gospel has meant to them power enabling them to do the things they wanted to do, but could not until they believed in this gospel.

I would like my last note in this address to be an appeal to any man who is face-to-face with this problem. My brother, God believes in you, and that in spite of all the worst there is in you. God knows the worst in you, better than you know it yourself. Yet he believes in you; and because he believes in your possibility, he has provided righteousness in and through the Son of his love, and by the mystery of his passion. I want you to respond to God's faith in you by putting your faith in him and demonstrating your faith by beginning with the next thing in obedience. You also will find that the gospel is the power of God; not theory, not inference, but a power, that coming into the life, realizes within the life and experience all the things of holiness and of righteousness and of high and eternal beauty.